GLOSSARY OF UNITED STATES PATENT PRACTICE

ENGLISH—FRENCH—GERMAN

Applebaum, Riess & Lieberman

CLARK BOARDMAN CO. LTD.
New York, New York

SAGE HILL PUBLISHERS, INC.
Albany, New York

SWEET & MAXWELL LIMITED
London, England

Printed in United States of America

Library of Congress Catalog Card No. 70-103702
SBN No. 87632-037-X

DEDICATION

To the Patent fraternity, in the service of communicating the frontiers of technology. And to my daughters Phyllis and Ann, and to Ruth Bierman, for their translation and editorial assistance.

Louis B. Applebaum

THE AUTHORS

LOUIS B. APPLEBAUM (B. S., Columbia University; J. D., Columbia Law School) is Patent Counsel of the New York Regional Office, Office of Naval Research. He has been a member of the Navy Patent Organization since its inception in 1946. He is the author of "The One Line Picture Claim"; "The Art of Describing Structures in Patent Drawings"; "Claim Drafting"; "Outline for the Preparation of Patent Applications"; "Laboratory Notebook Guide"; "Restatement of the Patent Office Rules of Practice" and other articles and training material on patent law and rights in technical data. Dr. Applebaum has been a lecturer on United States patent and data matters in schools and other fora in the United States and abroad.

PAUL H. RIESS (B. A., College of the City of New York; J. D., Fordham University Law School; University of Munich) is in the practice of law in New York, New York. Dr. Riess was German Technical Documents Specialist with the office of Field Information Technical Agency of the United States Government, and established a technical documents library for the allied governments at Hoechst, Germany.

ARTHUR M. LIEBERMAN (B. S. E. E., New York University; J. D., Brooklyn Law School) is a member of the firm of Sandoe, Hopgood & Calimafde of New York, New York. He has specialized in patent, trade-mark, copyright and trade secrets practice, and has lectured on United States patent and data matters.

GLOSSARY OF UNITED STATES PATENT PRACTICE

INTRODUCTION

This glossary defines the principal words and phrases that have special meanings when used in United States patent law and practice. The French and German translations are presented to facilitate communication on United States patent matters, and do not purport to take into account a different meaning the words and phrases may have in countries other than the United States.

The glossary is intended to be used only as a guide; primary authorities should be referred to, where appropriate.

ABBREVIATIONS

Sec. ____ The indicated section of Title 35, U.S. Code

R. ____ The indicated rule of the U.S. Patent Office Rules of Practice

MPEP ____ The indicated section of the U.S. Patent Office Manual of Patent Examining Procedure, 3d ed.

GLOSSAIRE DE LA PRATIQUE DE BREVETS AMERICAINE

INTRODUCTION

Ce glossaire définit les phrases et les mots principaux qui ont des significations spéciales quand on les emploie dans la loi et la pratique américaine de brevets. Les traductions françaises et allemandes sont présentées pour faciliter la communication au sujet des questions de brevets des Etats-Unis, et ne prétendent pas à tenir compte d'une signification différente que les mots et les phrases peuvent avoir dans des pays hors des Etats-Unis.

Le but du glossaire est de servir seulement de guide; on devrait remonter aux sources primaires, où il y'en a besoin.

ABREVIATIONS

Sec. ——— La section indiquée de Titre 35, Code des Etats-Unis

R. ——— La règle indiquée des Règles de Pratique de l'Office des Brevets des Etats-Unis

MPEP ——— La section indiquée du Etats-Unis 'Patent Office Manual of Patent Examining Procedure, 3rd ed.' (Le manuel de l'Office des Brevets de la Procedure d'Examiner les Brevets, 3e edition)

SPEZIALWOERTERBUCH UEBER DIE HANDHABUNG VON PATENTEN IN DEN VEREINIGTEN STAATEN

EINLEITUNG

Dieses Glossar definiert die hauptsaechlichen Worte und Redewendungen, die bei der Anwendung im Patentrecht und in der Patentpraxis in den Vereinigten Staaten eine besondere Bedeutung haben. Die franzoesische und deutsche Ubersetzung werden zur Erleichterung der Verstaendigung in Patentangelegenheiten der Vereinigten Staaten vorgelegt; eine andere Bedeutung, die die Worte und Redewendungen in andern Laendern als den Vereinigten Staaten haben moegen, soll hier nicht in Betracht gezogen werden.

Das Glossar ist nur zum Gebrauch als Leitfaden gedacht; im Bedarfsfall muessen die einschlaegigen Autoritaeten zu Rat gezogen werden.

ABKUERZUNGEN

Sec.	——	Der angegebene Paragraph von Title 35, U.S. Code
R.	——	Die angegebene Vorschrift des U. S. Patent Office Rules of Practice
MPEP	——	Der angegebene Abschnitt des U. S. Patentamt Handbuchs zu Patentenpruefungsverfahren, 3. Ausgabe
vgl.	——	vergleiche

CONTENTS

SECTION I

ENGLISH

FRENCH

GERMAN

GLOSSARY OF UNITED STATES PATENT PRACTICE

ABBREVIATIONS

Sec. ____ The indicated section of Title 35, U.S. Code

R. ____ The indicated rule of the U.S. Patent Office Rules of Practice

MPEP ____ The indicated section of the U.S. Patent Office Manual of Patent Examining Procedure, 3d ed.

A

a—in claim interpretation, "a" is read to mean "at least a"

un—dans l'interprétation des revendications, "un" veut dire "au moins un"

ein (e)—bei der Auslegung eines Patentanspruchs ist "ein(e)" als mindestens "ein(e)" aufzufassen

abandoned application—a case that applicant has failed to prosecute within the time fixed, or a case that applicant has declared expressly will not be further prosecuted (R. 135)

demande abandonnée—une plainte que le demandeur n'a pas poursuivie pendant le temps détérminé, ou une plainte que le demandeur a declarée, d'une manière expressive, ne sera pas revendiquée (R. 135)

Fallengelassene Anmeldung—ein Fall, den der Anmelder innerhalb der festgesetzten Frist zu verfolgen versaeumt hat; oder ein Fall, der nach ausdruecklicher Erklaerung pas revendiquée (R. 135)

abandonment of contest—concession of priority or abandonment of the invention by a party in an interference. The written consent of the assignee is required when an assignment was made

abandon de contestation—la concession de la priorité ou l'abandon de l'invention par une partie de la "interférence". On a besoin de l'accord écrit du cessionnaire de propriété

Aufgabe des Wettstreits—Zugestaendnis der Prioritaet oder Fallenlassen der Erfindung durch eine Partei in einer Interferenz. Hat eine Patent uebertragung stattgefunden, so ist die schriftliche Zustimmung des Rechtsnachfolgers erforderlich

abandonment of invention—express or implied declaration by applicant that he will not assert a property right in the invention (Sec. 102)

abandon d'invention—une déclaration explicite ou tacite du demandeur qu'il ne prétendra pas un droit de propriété industrielle dans l'invention (Sec. 102)

Fallenlassen der Erfindung—ausdrueckliche oder stillschweigend verstandene Erklaerung des Patentanmelders, dass er kein Eigentumsrecht auf die Erfindung geltend machen wird (Sec. 102)

abstract of the disclosure—a concise, non-legal technical statement of the contents of the disclosure, included in the specification as a searching-scanning tool immediately after the title; a statement limited to about 100 words, omitting extensive mechanical and design details but including the organization and operation of a machine or apparatus, or the method of making an article, or the identity and use of a chemical compound, or the ingredients of a mixture, or the steps of a process (R. 72(b))

abstraction de la divulgation—une déclaration technique, qui est concise et non-légal, du contenu de la divulgation, incluse dans la spécification comme un instrument "cherchant-scrutant" immédiatement après le titre; une déclaration limitèe à environs cent mots, omettant de vastes détails mécaniques et désignatifs, mais comprenant l'organisation et l'opération d'une machine ou d'un appareil, ou la méthode de fabriquer une chose, ou l'identité et l'utilisation d'un composé chimique, ou les ingrédients d'une mixture, ou bien les démarches d'un procédé (R. 72(b))

Auszug aus der Offenbarung—eine knappe nichtjuristische technische Darstellung des Inhalts der Offenbarung, unmittelbar nach dem Titel in der Beschreibung (specification) als Untersuchungs und Pruefwerkzeug enthalten; eine auf ungefaehr hundert Worte begrenzte Darlegung, die ausfuehrliche mechanische und Muster Einzelheiten auslaesst, aber die Organisation und den Betrieb einer Maschine oder eines Apparates, oder die Methode zur Herstellung eines Artikels, oder die Identitaet und den Gebrauch einer chemischen Verbindung, oder die Bestandteile einer Mischung, oder die Stufen eines Vorgangs einschliesst (R. 72(b))

abstract of title—Patent Office record of ownership of a patent

abstraction de titre—les archives de l'Office des Brevets qui indiquent le propriétaire d'un brevet

Auszug aus dem Titel—Patentamt-Eintragung ueber das Eigentumsrecht an einem Patent

action—see Office action

action—voir action d'Office

Behandlung—vgl. Behandlung durch das (Patent)amt

actual abandonment of invention—see abandonment of invention

abandon actuel de l'invention—voir abandon de l'invention

tatsaechliches Fallenlassen der Erfindung—vgl. Fallenlassen der Erfindung

actual reduction to practice—construction of the device or carrying out the process of the invention

réduction actuelle à la pratique—la construction de l'invention ou du mécanisme, ou travaillant de procédé de l'invention

Tatsaechliche Umsetzung in die Praxis—Konstruktion des Geraetes oder Ausfuehrung des Erfindungsvorgangs

administrator—the representative of a legally incapacitated inventor

administrateur—le représentant d'un inventeur légalement incapacité

Sachwalter—der Vertreter eines Erfinders, der sich vor dem Gesetz nicht selbst vertreten kann

advancement of application—examination of an application in advance of its chronological turn, made on a showing of age or infirmity of applicant or jeopardy of commercial rights of the applicant

avancement d'une demande—l'examen d'une demande avant son tour chronologique, fait à preuve de l'âge ou de l'infirmité du demandeur, ou de l'hasard aux droits commerciaux du demandeur

Bevorzugung einer Anmeldung—die vorzeitige Pruefung einer Anmeldung, ausserhalb der zeitlichen Reihenfolge, aus Alters-oder Gesundheitsgruenden des Anmelders, oder wegen Gefaehrdung der kommerziellen Ansprueche des Anmelders

affidavit—statement of facts under oath to overcome a cited patent or publication (R. 131), to traverse a ground of rejection (R. 132), in support of an application for reissue (R. 175), before a declaration of interference (R. 202, 204), or after appeal (R. 195)

déclaration sour serment—la declaration des faits sous serment pour surmonter un brevet cité ou une publication (R. 131), pour nier une raison de rejet (R. 132), pour soutenir une demande pour "reissue" (R. 175), avant une déclaration de "interférence" (R. 202, 204), ou après un appel (R. 195)

beschworene schriftliche Erklaerung—Darlegung von Tatsachen unter Eid um ein angefuehrtes Patent oder eine Veroeffentlichung ausser Kraft zu setzen (R. 131), einen Grund zur Ablehnung zu ueberbruecken (R. 132), zur Unterstuetzung einer Anmeldung zur Wiedererteilung (R. 175), vor einer Interferenz Erklaerung (R. 202, 204), oder nach einer Berufung (R. 195)

agent—see patent agent

agent—voir agent de brevets

Vertreter—vgl. Patent-Vertreter

aggregation—the absence of a cooperative relation between an element of a claim and at least one other element of the claim. (MPEP 706.03(i))

"aggregation"—l'absence d'une relation coopérative entre un élément d'une revendication et au moins un autre élément de la revendication (MPEP 706.03(i))

Aneinanderreihung—die Abwesenheit einer zusammenwirkenden Beziehung zwischen einem Element eines Patentanspruches und mindestens einem zweiten (MPEP 706.03 (i))

allowability—see notice of allowability

"allowability"—voir la notification de "allowability"

Zulaessigkeit—vgl· Zulaessigkeits-Benach richtigung

allowable—see notice of allowability

acceptable—voir la notification de "allowability"

zulaessig—vgl. Zulaessigkeits-Benachrichtigung

allowance—see notice of allowance

acceptation—voir la notification d'acceptation

Zulassung—vgl. Zulassungsbenachrichtigung

alternative expression—definition of one element, in a claim, by more than one word or phrase (MPEP 706.03(d))

expression alternative—la définition d'un élément dans une revendication par plusieurs mots ou par une phrase (MPEP 706.03(d))

alternative Ausdrucksweise—Definition eines Elements in einem Patentanspruch durch mehr als ein Wort oder einen Ausdruck (MPEP 706.03 (d))

amendment—instruction to the Patent Office to add and/or delete matter from the application (R. 21(k), 33, 67, 85, 111, 115-119, 121-127, 135, 173, 174, 196, 203-206, 212, 222, 231, 312)

amendement—directive à l'Office des Brevets d'ajouter et/ou de rayer quelque chose de la demande (R. 21(k), 33, 67, 85, 111, 115-119, 121-127, 135, 173, 174, 196, 203-206, 212, 222, 231, 312)

Berichtigung—Anweisung an das Patentamt dem Antrag etwas zuzufuegen oder von dem Antrag etwas zu streichen (R. 21(k), 33, 67, 85, 111, 115-119, 121-127, 135, 173, 174, 196, 203-206, 212, 222, 231, 312)

an—in claim interpretation, "an" is read to mean "at least an"

un—dans l'interprétation des revendications, "un" veut dire "au moins un"

eine(e)—bei der Auswertung eines Patentanspruchs ist "ein(e)" als "mindestens ein(e)" aufzufassen

analogous art—a reference disclosing the same function or the same utility, in a technologically related field

technique analogue—un renvoi divulguant la même fonction ou la même utilité dans un domaine technologiquement relatif

analoge Technik—ein Hinweis, welcher dieselbe Funktion oder den gleichen Gebrauch auf einem technisch verwandten Gebiet enthuellt

antecedent—a positive recital of a word or phrase to permit abbreviated identification of such word or phrase at a later point in the sentence or paper

antécédent—le récit positif d'un mot ou d'une phrase pour permettre l'identification abrégée de tel mot ou telle phrase plus tard dans la phrase ou dans la composition

Vorhergehendes—bestimmte Anfuehrung eines Wortes oder eines Ausdrucks um die abgekuerzte Identifizierung eines solchen Wortes oder Ausdrucks im weiteren Verlauf des Satzes oder Schriftstuecks zu gestatten

anticipate—to establish that an alleged invention is not novel

antérioriser—établir qu'une invention alléguée n'est pas nouvelle

vorwegnehmen—Feststellung, dasse eine angebliche Erfindung nicht neu ist

anticipation—see anticipate

antériorité—voir antérioriser

Vorwegnahme—vgl· vorwegnehmen

appeal to Board of Appeals—see Board of Appeals

Appel à la Commission d'Appel—voir la Commission d'Appel

Berufung an den Board of Appeals (Berufungsinstanz)—vgl. Board of Appeals

appeal to Court of Appeals—see Court of Appeals

appel à la Cour de Cassation—voir Cour de Cassation

Berufung an den Court of Appeals (Berufungsgericht)—vgl. Court of Appeals

appeal to Court of Claims—see Court of Claims

appel à la Cour de Réclamation—voir la Cour de Réclamation

Berufung an den Court of Claims—vgl. Court of Claims

appeal to Court of Customs and Patent Appeals—see Court of Customs and Patent Appeals

appel à la "Court of Customs and Patent Appeals"—voir Court of Customs and Patent Appeals

Berufung an den Court of Customs and Patent Appeals—vgl. Court of Customs and Patent Appeals

applicant—the inventor or the joint inventors who have applied for a patent; or the legal representative (R. 42, 43) or joint inventor (R. 47(a)) or proprietary interest (R. 47(b)) who has applied for a patent in place of the inventor

demandeur—l'inventeur ou les co-inventeurs qui ont demandé un brevet; ou le représentant légal (R. 42, 43) ou le co-inventeur (R. 47 (a)) ou l'intérêt propriétaire (R. 47(b)) qui a demandé un brevet au lieu de l'inventeur

Anmelder—der Erfinder oder die Erfindergemeinschaft, die ein Patent eingereicht haben; oder der gesetzliche Vertreter (R. 42, 43), oder der Miterfinder (R. 47(a)), oder der rechtliche Eigentuemer (R. 47(b)) der an Stelle des Erfinders ein Patent zur Anmeldung eingereicht hat

application date—see filing date

date de demande—voir date de dépôt

Anmeldedatum—vgl. Einreichungsdatum

application for patent—a petition or request for a patent (R. 61), specification and claims (R. 71-77), oath or declaration (R. 65), necessary drawings (R. 81-88) and prescribed filing fee R. 21)

demande d'un brevet—un pétition ou une requête pour un brevet (R. 61), la spécification et les revendications (R. 71-77), le serment ou la déclaration (R. 65), les dessins nécessaires (R. 81-88) et la taxe de dépôt nécessaire (R. 21)

Patentanmeldung—ein Antrag oder Gesuch um Erteilung eines Patents (R. 61), Beschreibung (specification) und Ansprueche (R. 71-77), Eid oder eidesstattliche Erklaerung (R. 65), notwendige Zeichnungen (R. 81-88) und die vorgeschriebene Anmeldegebuehr (R. 21)

art—technical data of any form

technique—les données techniques de n'importe quelle forme

Technik—technische Daten aller Art

article of manufacture—see manufacture

produit industriel—voir fabrication

Gegenstand, der hergestellt wird—vgl. herstellen

assignee—the transferee of property rights in an invention

cessionnaire—le cessionnaire des droits de propriété dans une invention

Rechtsnachfolger(Gesamt)—die Person, auf die alle Eigentumsrechte an einer Erfindung uebertragen wurden (auch Zessionaer genannt)

assignment—instrument transferring property rights in an invention

cession—le document qui transfère les droits de propriété dans une invention

Rechtnachsfolge—das gesetzliche Instrument zur Uebertragung der Eigentumsrechte an einer Erfindung (auch Zession genannt)

assignor–the transferor of property rights in an invention

cédant–celui qui transfère les droits de propriété dans une invention

Zedent–die Person, die die Eigentumsrechte an einer Erfindung uebertraegt

attorney–see patent attorney

avocat–voir avocat de brevets

Anwalt–vgl. Patentanwalt

attorney of record–the patent agent or patent attorney appointed by applicant to transact his business before the Patent Office. The attorney's power to act must be recorded in the filed application.

avocat "of record"–l'agent de brevets ou l'avocat de brevets nommé par le demandeur pour fairs ses affaires avec l'Office des Brevets. Le pouvoir d'agir de l'avocat doit être enregistré dans la demande déposée.

Zustaendiger Anwalt–der Patentvertreter oder Patentanwalt, der vom Anmelder bestellt ist seine Interessen vor dem Patentamt zu vertreten. Die Handlungsvollmacht des Anwalts muss in der eingereichten Anmeldung beurkundet sein.

B

background of the invention—a general statement of the art in which the invention lies, of the specific branch of that art with a characterization of the invention, a brief description of the prior art, and the specific disadvantages of the prior art, included in the specification immediately after a cross-reference to any related application

fond de l'invention—une déclaration générale de la technique dans laquelle se trouve l'invention, de la branche (partie) spécifique de cette technique avec une caractérisation de l'invention, une brève description de la technique antérieure, et les désavantages spécifiques de la technique antérieure, incluse dans la spécification immédiatement après un renvoi à aucune demande relative

Hintergrund der Erfindung—eine allgemeine Darstellung der Technik, auf deren Gebiet die Erfindung liegt, des bestimmten Zweiges dieser Technik mit einer Charakterisierung der Erfindung, einer kurzen Beschreibung der bisherigen Technik und der besonderen Nachteile derselben; diese Darstellung ist in der Beschreibung (specification) eingeschlossen und folgt unmittelbar einem Hinweis auf alle verwandten Anmeldungen

bar to patent grant—a condition that prohibits the grant of a patent; a condition set forth in Sec. 102 (novelty and loss of right to patent) or in Sec. 103 (non-obvious subject matter)

interdiction à la délivrance d'un brevet—une condition qui défend la délivrance d'un brevet; une condition établie dans la Sec. 102 (nouveauté et perte du droit d'un brevet) ou dans la Sec. 103 (de la matière non-évidente)

Hinderungsgrund zur Patentverleihung—ein die Patentverleihung verbietender Umstand; Umstaende, die in Sec. 102 (Neuheit und Verlust des Rechts auf ein Patent) oder in S. 103 (nicht-selbstverstaendlicher Erfindungsgegenstand) dargelegt sind

basic patent—a patent that dominates many later patents, so that use of the later patents would constitute infringement of the basic patent. See pioneer patent.

brevet de base—un brevet qui domine plusieurs brevets postérieurs, de sorte que l'emploi des brevets postérieurs constituent la contrefaçon du brevet de base. Voir brevet de pionnier.

Grund-Patent—ein Patent, das ueber viele spaetere Patente vorherrscht, so dass die Benutzung der spaeteren Patente eine Verletzun des Grund-Patentes ausmachen wuerded. Vgl. Pionier-Patent.

Board of Appeals—the court in the Patent Office having jurisdiction to review the decision of an examiner on appeal by an applicant. The court consists of three members selected from the group of Commissioner, Assistant Commissioners and Examiners-in-Chief.

Commission d'Appel—le tribunal dans l'Office des Brevets qui a la juridiction de revoir la décision d'un examinateur sur l'appel d'un demandeur. Le tribunal consiste de trois membres choisis du groupe du Commissaire, des Commissaires Adjoints, et des Examinateurs-en-chef.

Board of Appeals—die Instanz innerhalb des Patentamts, welche bei einer Berufung des Anmelders zustaendig ist, die Entscheidung eines Pruefers nachzupruefen. Diese Instanz besteht aus drei aus der Gruppe des Commissioner, der Assistant Commissioners, und der Hauptpruefer ausgewaehlten Mitgliedern.

Board of Patent Interferences—the court in the Patent Office having jurisdiction to decide interference issues

Commission des "Interférences" des Brevets—le tribunal dans l'Office des Brevets qui a la juridiction de décider les questions de "interférence"

Board of Patent Interferences—die Instanz im Patentamt, der die Rechtsprechung in Interferenz Faellen obliegt

brackets—the symbols [ ] placed around a word or words in a claim as a direction to the examiner to delete such word or words from the claim (R. 121)

parentheses—les symboles [ ] mis autour d'un mot ou des mots dans une revendication comme une directive à l'examinateur de rayer tel mot ou tels mots de la revendication (R. 121)

(eckige) Klammern—wenn dieses Zeichen [ ] ein Wort oder Worte in einem Anspruch einklammert, so ist dies als eine Anweisung an den Pruefer solch ein Wort oder Worte von dem Anspruch zu streichen, zu verstehen (R. 121)

breadth of claim—the extent to which a claim dominates an art

largeur de la revendication—l'étendue à laquelle une revendication domine une technique

Ausmass des Anspruchs—der Umfang in welchem ein Anspruch ueber eine Technik vorherrscht

brief—statement of the facts, reasons and authorities relied upon to support a motion, petition, appeal, interference action or court proceeding (R. 181, 192, 243, 244)

dossier—une déclaration des faits, des raisons et des sources sur lesquels on a comptés pour soutenir une procédure, un pétition, un appel, une action de "interférence" ou les procédés d'un tribunal (R. 181, 192, 243, 244)

Schriftsatz—Darlegung der Tatsachen, Gruende und Autoritaeten zur Unterstuetzung eines Antrags, Gesuchs, einer Berufung, eines Interferenz-oder Gerichtsverfahrens (R. 181, 192, 243, 244)

Bristol board—the commercial name of the two-ply or three-ply drawing board, having a pure white, calendered and smooth erasable surface, that is required for use for drawings

planche de Bristol—le nom commercial d'une planche à dessin à deux ou trois laminae, ayant une surface d'une blanche pure, calendrée, effaçable et égale, dont on a besoin pour de tels dessins

Bristol Board—handelsueblicher Name der zwei-oder dreifachen Zeichenpappe mit reinweisser, glaenzender und glatt-radierbarer Oberflaeche, die fuer den Gebrauch von Zeichnungen verlangt wird

broader than the invention—claim of a scope that exceeds the limits of the invention defined in the application or patent

plus large que l'invention—des revendications d'une portée qui dépasse les bornes de l'invention définies dans la demande ou dans le brevet

Umfassender als die Erfindung—Anspruch auf einen die Grenzen der Erfindung—wie sie im Patentantrag festgelegt sind—uebersteigenden Umfang

burden of proof—the obligation to introduce evidence to sustain a position taken on an issue. In interferences, the burden of proof is on the junior party; in infringement suits, the burden of proof of infringement is on the plaintiff; where validity is an issue, the burden of proof of invalidity is on the defendant.

charge de la preuve—le devoir d'introduire de la preuve pour soutenir une position prise au sujet d'une question. Dans les "interférences", la charge de la preuve reste avec le "junior party"; dans le litigies de contrefaçon, la charge de la preuve de contrefaçon reste avec le plaignant; où il s'agit de la validité d'une question, la charge de la preuve d'invalidité reste avec le défendeur.

Last der Beweisfuehrung—die Verpflichtung Beweise zur Aufrechterhaltung eines eingenommenen Standpunkts zu erbringen. In Interferenz Faellen faellt die Last der Beweisfuehrung der Juniorpartei (mit dem spaeteren Anmeldetermin) zu; bei Patentverletzungsklagen muss der Klaeger den Beweis der Patentverletzung erbringen; wo die Gueltigkeit in Frage steht, muss der Angeklagte die Ungueltigkeit beweisen

C

cancellation of claims—deleting of claims from an application

annulation des revendications—la rayure des revendications d'une demande

Streichung von Anspruechen—Loeschen von Anspruechen einer Patentanmeldung

certificate of correction—statement by the Patent Office correcting a material error in an issued patent where the error is due to the fault of the Patent Office or is due to the excusable fault of the applicant

certificat de correction—la déclaration de l'Office des Brevets qui corrige une erreur matérielle dans un brevet délivré où l'erreur est par suite de la faute de l'Office des Brevets ou est par suite d'une faute pardonnable du demandeur

Korrektur-Beschernigung—Erklärung des Patentamts zwecks Korrektur eines sachlichen Irrtums in einem verliehenen Patent, wenn die Schuld an dem unterlaufenen Fehler beim Patentamt liegt, oder ein entschuldbarer Fehler des Patentanmelders vorliegt

certified copy—a copy bearing the attestation of the Patent Office that it is a true copy, as may be required in priority cases (Sec. 119) or for other purposes

copie certifiée—une copie portant l'attestation de l'Office des Brevets qu'elle est une vraie copie, qu'on peut exiger dans des affaires de priorité (Sec. 119) ou pour des autres intentions

beglaubigte Abschrift—eine Abschrift mit der Bestaetigung des Patentamts, dass es sich um eine wortgetreue Kopie handelt, wie sie in Prioritaetsfaellen (Sec. 119) oder zu anderen Zwecken verlangt wird

c. i. p.—see continuation-in-part

c. i. p.—voir continuation-en-partie

c. i· p.—vgl. Teilfortfuehrung

citation—prior art listed by the examiner as anticipatory or pertinent

citation—état de la technique enregistré par l'examinateur comme antériorisé ou pertinent

Entgegenhaltung—fruehere Technik, die vom Pruefer als vorwegnehmend oder einschlaegig angefuehrt wird

citation of authorities—laws, court cases or publications referred to in an action to support a position taken

citation des sources—les lois, les affaires de tribunal, ou les publications auxquelles on fait allusion dans une action pour soutenir une position prise

Anfuehrung von Autoritaeten—Hinweis auf Gesetze, Gerichtsfaelle order Veroeffentlichungen um eine im Klagefall eingenommene Position zu stuetzen

civil suit—action in the District Court for the District of Columbia to review a decision of the Board of Appeals (Sec. 145) or to review a decision of the Board of Patent Interferences (Sec. 146)

proces civil—action dans le District Court of the District of Columbia pour revoir une décision de la Commission d'Appel (Sec. 145) ou pour revoir une décision de la Commission des "Interférences" des Brevets (Sec. 146)

Zivilklage—Klage beim Distriktgericht fuer den Distrikt von Columbia (Washington, D. C.) um einen Entscheid des Board of Appeals (Sec. 145) oder des Board of Patent Interferences (Sec· 146) nachzupruefen

claims—the concluding part of a specification particularly pointing out and distinctly setting forth the subject matter of the invention (Sec. 112; R. 71, 75)

revendications—la partie finale d'une spécification signalant et nettement proposant la matière de l'invention (Sec. 112; R. 71, 75)

Ansprueche—der abschliessende Teil einer Beschreibung (specification), welcher den Gegenstand der Erfindung besonders hervorhebt und eindeutig darlegt (Sec. 112, R. 71, 75)

classification—the Patent Office numerical designation of the subject matter division of a patent or publication in the various arts. Classification is published in the Manual of Classification and in Classification Bulletins.

classification—la désignation numérique de l'Office des Brevets de la catégorie de la matière d'un brevet ou d'une publication das les diverses techniques. La classification est publiée dans le Manuel de Classification et dans les Bulletins de Classification.

Klassifizierung—die vom Patentamt bestimmte zahlenmaessige Einordnung eines Patentgegenstands oder einer Veroeffentlichung in die verschiedenen Sparten der Technik. Die Klassifizierung wird in einem Klassifizierungshandbuch und in Klassifizierungsbekanntmachungen veroeffentlicht.

co-inventors—two or more persons who jointly made an invention

co-inventeurs—plusieurs qui ont créé ensemble une invention

Miterfinder—zwei oder mehr Personen, die gemeinsam eine Erfindung gemacht haben

combination—two or more interacting elements

combinaison—plusieurs éléments dont l'action est réciproque

Verbindung—zwei oder mehr aufeinander einwirkende Elemente

combination of references—citation of two or more references that, considered together, show all of the significant features of the claimed combination and teach the association of such features of the claimed combination

combinaison de renvois—la citation de plusieurs renvois qui, considérés ensemble, montrent tous les traits significatifs de la combinaison revendiquée et enseignent l'association de tels traits de la combinaison revendiquée

Verbindung von Hinweisen—Anfuehrung von zwei oder mehr Hinweisen, die zusammen betrachtet, alle kennzeichnenden Eigenschaften der beanspruchten Verbindung tragen und die Assoziation solcher Eigenschaften der beanspruchten Verbindung lehren

commercial success—significant consumer acceptance of a product or process, tending to support the argument that the product or process is a notable advance in the art

succès commercial—acceptation significative des consommateurs d'un produit ou d'un procès tendant à soutenir l'argument que le produit ou le procès est un avancement remarquable dans la technique

geschaeftlicher Erfolg—bedeutende Verbraucherannahme eines Produktes oder Herstellungsverfahrens, welche die Auffassung, das Produkt oder Verfahren sei ein beachtenswerter Fortschritt in der Technik, unterstuetzt

Commissioner of Patents—the head of the Patent Office, designated by the President with the consent of the Senate, to serve for an indefinite term as administrator of the Patent Office

Commissaire des Brevets—le chef de l'Office des Brevets, désigné par le Président avec l'accord du Sénat, pour servir pendant un nombre d'années indéfinies comme administrateur de l'Office des Brevets

Commissioner of Patents—der Chef des Patentamts, vom Praesidenten mit der Zustimmung des Senats auf unbefristete Zeit als Verwaltungsbeamter ernannt

compensation—restitution for a loss

compensation—la restitution d'une perte

Abfindung—Rueckerstattung fuer einen Verlust

composition of matter—a class of patentable subject matter that involves the mixture of two or more ingredients to provide a solid, liquid or gas possessing properties different from or in addition to the properties possessed by the several ingredients, individually or in common

composition—une classe de matière brevetable qui comprend la mixture de plusieurs ingrédients pour produire un solide, un liquide, ou un gaz possédant les qualités différentes des, ou en addition aux qualités possédées par les plusieurs ingrédients, individuellement ou en commun

Stoffverbindung—eine Klase patentfaehiger Gegenstaende, welche die Mischung von zwei oder mehr Bestandteilen umfasst um eine feste Masse, eine Fluessigkeit oder ein Gas zu schaffen, mit Eigenschaften verschieden von, oder zusaetzlich zu den Eigenschaften, welche die individuellen Bestandteile im einzelnen oder gemeinsam aufweisen

comprising—a qualification that leaves a claim open for the inclusion of unspecified ingredients, even in major amounts. "Comprising essentially" has the same meaning.

"comprising"—une qualification qui laisse ouverte une revendication pour y inclure des ingrédients non-spécifiés, même dans des quantités majeures. "Comprising essentially" a la même signification.

inbegriffen—eine Qualifikation, welche einen Anspruch auf Einschluss sicht-spezifizierter Bestandteile selbst in groesseren Mengen offen laesst. "Im wesentlichen inbegriffen" bedeutet dasselbe.

concealment—keeping an invention secret

dissimulation—garder secrète une invention

Verheimlichung—eine Erfindung geheimhalten

conception—the mental part of the inventive act, which is completed when an operative embodiment of the invention is recognized. Conception must be capable of proof, such as by drawings or disclosure to another person, if it is to be relied upon. (MPEP 715.07)

conception—la partie mentale de l'acte inventif, qui est accompli quand on reconnaît une incarnation active de l'invention. On doit pouvoir prouver la conception, au moyen des dessins ou de la communication faite à une autre personne, si on peut y compter. (MPEP 715.07)

gedankliche Erfassung—der geistige Teil des Erfindungsprozesses der vollendet ist, wenn eine wirksame Ausfuehrungsform der Erfindung anerkannt ist. Die gedankliche Erfassung muss z. B. durch Zeichnungen oder Offenbarung einem anderen gegenueber beweisfaehig sein um sich darauf stuezen zu koennen. (MPEP 715.07)

conditional assignment—an assignment provided to be effective on the performance of an act or event; if recorded, such assignments are regarded as absolute assignments for Patent Office purposes. (R. 333)

cession conditionelle—une cession qui deviendra effective après l'accomplissement d'un acte ou événement; si elles sont enregistrées, de telles cessions sont regardées comme des cessions absolues selon les intentions de l'Office des Brevets. (R. 333)

bedingte Uebertragung—eine Uebertragung, welche auf Grund der Ausfuehrung einer Handlung oder eines Ereignisses in Kraft tritt; falls schriftlich niedergelegt, werden solche Uebertragungen fuer die Zwecke des Patentamts als definitive Uebertragungen betrachtet. (R. 333)

consisting of—a qualification that closes a claim to the inclusion of materials other than those recited, except for impurities ordinarily associated with the recited materials. Adding "essentially" to "consisting of" opens the claim to ingredients that do not materially affect the basic and novel characteristics of the composition.

"consisting of"—une qualification qui ferme une revendication à l'inclusion des substances ou des matériels hors de ceux qui sont énumérés, sauf les impuretés associées ordinairement avec les substances ou matériels énumérés. En ajoutant "essentiellement" à "consisting of" on ouvre la revendication aux ingrédients, qui n'influencent pas matériellement les caractéristiques fondamentales et nouvelles de la composition.

bestehend aus—eine Einschraenkung, welche einen Anspruch vom Einschluss von Materialien ausser den genannten ausschliesst, mit Ausnahme von Unreinheiten, welche im Allgemeinen mit den genannten Materielien verbunden sind. Wird "wesentlich" zu "bestehend aus" hinzugefuegt, so wird damit der Anspruch Bestandteilen geoeffnet, die die grundlegenden und neuartigen Eigentuemlichkeiten der Zusammensetzung nicht wesentlich beeintrachtigen.

constructive reduction to practice—the equivalent of actual reduction to practice, effected by filling an application for patent (MPEP 715.07)

réduction constructive à la pratique—déposant une demande pour un brevet (MPEP 715.07)

konstruktive Umsetzen in die Praxis—gleichbedeutend mit dem tatsaechlichen Umsetzen in die Praxis, zur Ausfuehrung gebracht durch das Einreichen einer Patentenanmeldung (MPEP 715.07)

continuation—a second application for the same invention claimed or disclosed in a prior application, where the second application is filed, before the original application is abandoned, by the same applicant, and no new matter is introduced. A continuation may be used to introduce a new set of claims after final rejection for further examination by the Primary Examiner (MPEP 201.07) and is entitled to the benefit of the filing date of the original application. (MPEP 201.11)

continuation—une deuxième demande pour la même invention revendiquée ou divulguée dans une demande antérieure, où la deuxiéme demande est déposée avant que la demande originale soit abandonnée, par le même demandeur, et il n'y introduit aucune matière nouvelle. On peut employer une continuation pour introduire un nouvel ensemble de revendications après le rejet final pour un autre examen par l'examinateur Primaire (MPEP 201.07) at a droit à la date de dépôt de la demande originale. (MPEP 201.11)

Fortfuehrung—eine zweite Anmeldung fuer die gleiche, in einer frueheren Anmeldung beanspruchte und offenbarte Erfindung, bei der die zweite Anmeldung von demselben Anmelder eingereicht wurde, ehe die Erst-Anmeldung aufgegeben war, und kein neues Material eingefuehrt wird. Eine Fortfuehrung kann dazu benutzt werden, eine neue Serie von Anspruechen—nach der endgueltigen Ablehnung des Vorpruefers—zur weiteren Pruefung einzureichen (MPEP 201.07); die Fortfuehrung berechtigt von dem Einreichungstermin der Erst-Anmeldung zu profitieren. (MPEP 201.11)

continuation-in-part application—an application filed during the lifetime of an earlier application by the same applicant, repeating some substantial portion of the earlier application and adding matter not disclosed in the earlier case (MPEP 201.8) or deleting matter disclosed in the earlier case

une demande de continuation—en-partie—une demande déposée pendant la vie d'une demande antérieure par le même demandeur, répétant quelque partie significative de la demande antérieure et ajoutant quelque chose qui n'était pas inclus dans l'affaire antérieure (MPEP 201.8) ou rayant quelque chose divulgé dans l'affaire antérieure

Teilfortfuehrungs-Anmeldung—eine Anmeldung, die weahrend der Laufzeit einer frueheren Anmeldung von demselben Anmelder eingereicht wurde, unter Wiederholung eines betraechtlichen Teils der frueheren Anmeldung und unter Hinzufuegung von in dem vorhergehenden Fall nicht offenbartem Material (MPEP 201.8), oder unter Streichung von in dem vorhergehenden Fall offenbartem Material

contributory infringement—inducing the practice of a claimed invention by an unauthorized person, or selling a component of a patented invention or a material or apparatus used in practising a patented process while knowing it was specially made and adapted for use in an infringement of such patent, unless the component is a staple article suitable for substantial non-infringing use (Sec. 271)

contribuant à la contrefaçon—encourageant l'utilisation d'une invention revendiquée par une personne sans autorisation, ou vendant une partie constituante d'une invention brevetée ou d'un matériel ou d'un appareil employé dans la partique d'un procédé breveté, tout en sachant qu'il était fabriqué et adapté spécialement pour l'employer dans un contrefaçon d'un tel brevet, à moins que la partie constituante soit un article régulaire ou établi à un grand emploi non-contrefaisant (Sec. 271)

Beihilfe zur Patentverletzung—die Veranlassung zur Ausfuehrung einer beanspruchten Erfindung durch Unbefugte; oder der Verkauf eines Teiles einer patentierten Erfindung, oder eines Stoffes, oder Apparates, die der Ausuebung eines patentierten Verfahrens dienen, wohlwissend, dass sie eigens zur Benutzung bei der Verletzung eines solchen Patents hergestellt oder dazu besonders angepasst wurden, sofern der Teil keine zu wesentlicher nicht-patent-verletzender Benutzung geeignete Stapelware ist (Sec. 271)

convention countries—member countries of the Union Convention of Paris, 1883, for the protection of industrial property

pays de pacte (unioniste)—les pays appartenant à l'union instituée par la Convention de Paris, 1883, pour la protection de la propriété industrielle

Verbandslaender—Mitgliedstaaten der Pariser Union Verbandsuebereinkunft zum Schutze Industriellen Eigentums von 1883

convention date—priority date of an application, and of the patent thereon, filed under the provisions of the Union Convention of Paris

date de priorité conventionnelle ou unioniste—la date de priorité d'une demande, et du brevet y inclus, déposée sous le bénéfice de la Convention d'Union de Paris

Datum der Verbands-Prioritaet—Prioritaetsdatum einer Anmeldung und des darauffolgenden Patents, eingereicht gemaess den Bestimmungen der Pariser Union Verbandsuebereinkunft

convention period—one year period (six months for designs) during which the date of an earlier convention application can be claimed for an application filed under the benefits of the Union Convention

période conventionnelle ou unioniste—période d'une année (six mois pour les modèles ou dessins) pendant laquelle on peut revendiquer la date d'une demande antérieure conventionnelle pour une demande déposée sous le bénéfice de la "Union Convention"

Uebereinkunfts-Frist—Frist eines Jahres (sechs Monate fuer Geschmacksmuster), waehrend welcher Zeit der Stichtag einer Anmeldung unter einem frueheren Abkommen fuer eine Anmeldung, welche unter den Vorrechten der Unionsuebereinkunft eingereicht wurde, beansprucht werden kann

convention rights—see convention period

droit conventionnel ou unioniste—voir période conventionnelle ou unioniste

Uebereinkunfts-Recht—vgl. Uebereinkunfts-Frist

copending—applications that are on file and active in the Patent Office at the same time

co-pendant—des demandes viables qui sont simultanément à l'Office des Brevets

gleichzeitig anhaengig—Anmeldungen, die zur gleichen Zeit in den Akten vorhanden und aktiv sind

copying a claim—amending an application to include a claim of another for the purpose of the declaring of an interference, to determine who is the first inventor of what the copied claim describes

copiant une revendication—faisant des amendements à une demande pour y inclure une revendication faite à un autre, dans le but de décider ce lui qui est le premier inventeur de ce que décrit la revendication copiée

Abschrift eines Anspruchs—eine Anmeldung dahingehend zu berichtigen, dass der Anspruch eines anderen zum Zwecke einer Interferenz Erklaerung eingeschlossen wird, um festzustellen, wer der erste Erfinder dessen ist, was in der Abschrift des Anspruchs beschrieben wird

copyright—a reservation to the originator, or to his successor in interest, of the right to reproduce a literary or artistic work, such reservation being protected by compliance with the provisions of the copyright statutes and supporting administrative regulations

copyright (droit d'auteur)—une restriction à l'initiateur ou à son successeur en intérêt, du droit de reproduire une oeuvre littéraire ou artistique, telle restriction étant protégée par conformité des stipulations des statuts des droits d'auteur et soutenant les règlements administratifs

Copyright (Urheberrecht)—ein Reservatsrecht des Urhebers oder seines Interessen-Nachfolgers ein literarisches oder kuenstlerisches Werk zu reproduzieren; dieses Reservatsrecht ist durch Erfuellung der Bestimmungen der Copyright Statuten und der Ausfuehrungsbestimmungen geschuetzt

copyright infringement—reproduction, performance or distribution of a copyrighted work without the permission of the author

violation de droits d'auteur—reproduction, représentation ou diffusion d'une oeuvre protégée au titre des droits d'auteur sans autorisation de l'auteur

Copyright Verletzung—Reproduktion, Auffuehrung, oder Verteilung eines unter copyright-Schutz stehenden Werkes ohne Erlaubnis des Urhebers

corroboration of an inventor—evidence to prove statements made by an inventor

corroboration d'un inventeur—la preuve des déclarations faites du part d'un inventeur

Bestaetigung—Beweismaterial zur Bezeugung der Darlegung eines Erfinders

count—in interference practice, an interfering claim (a claim made by the parties to an interference)

"count"—dans la practique d'interférence une revendication qui intervient (une réclamation faite des parties d'une "interference")

Klagepunkt—in Interferenz Praxis, ein kollidierender Anspruch (ein von den Parteien in einer Interferenz gemachter Anspruch)

coupon—a voucher sold by the Patent Office individually or in books in denominations of twenty cents and fifty cents for use in purchasing copies of patents, design and plant patents, and trademark registrations (R.24)

coupon—an garant vendu, par l'Office des Brevets, individuellement ou dans les livrets en dénominations de vingt ou cinquante cents, emploé pour l'achat des copies de brevets, des brevets de dessein et de plante, et des dépôts de marque de fabrique (R. 24)

Kupon—ein vom Patentamt einzeln oder in Heften mit Werten von 20 und 50 cents verkaufter Bezugschein zur Benutzung beim Erwerb von Patentabschriften, Geschmacksmuster und Pflanzen Patenten, sowie Registrierung von Warenzeichen (R. 24)

Court of Appeals—a court having jurisdiction in its area over appeals from final decisions of U. S. District Courts

Court of Appeals (cour de cassation—un tribunal qui a la jurisdiction dans son domaine sur des appels des décisions finales des United States District Courts

Berufungsgericht (Court of Appeals)—ein Gericht, welches in seinem Gebiet fuer die Einlegung von Berufung gegen endgueltige Entscheidungen des U. S. District Courts zustaendig ist

Court of Claims—a court that hears cases against the Government of the United States; in patent matters, such a case could be a claim for compensation for unauthorized use of a patent by the Government of the United States

Court of Claims (cour des réclamation)—un tribunal qui entend des plaintes contre le Gouvernement des Etats-Unis; en matières des brevets, une telle plainte pourrait être une réclamation pour restitution, à cause d'un emploi sans autorisation d'un brevet par le Gouvernement des Etats-Unis

Court of Claim—ein Gerichtshof, in dem Klagen gegen die Regierung der Vereinigten Staaten zur Verhandlung kommen; in Patentangelegenheiten koennte dies eine Schadenersatzklage wegen unbefugter Benutzung eines Patents durch die Regierung der Vereinigten Staaten sein

Court of Customs and Patent Appeals—a court in Washington, D. C. that hears appeals from decisions of the Board of Appeals and the Board of Interference Examiners, on the evidence produced before the Patent Office (Sec. 141)

Court of Customs and Patent Appeals—un tribunal à Washington, D. C. qui entend des appels des décisions de la Commission d'Appel et de la Commission des Examineteurs d'Interférence par le témoignage produit devant l'Office des Brevets (Sec. 141)

Court of Customs and Patent Appeals—ein Gerichtshof in Washington, D. C., in dem Berufungen gegen die Entscheidungen des Board of Appeals und des Board of Interference Examiners zur Verhandlung kommen, auf Grund von Beweismaterial, das vor dem Patentamt erbracht wurde (Sec. 141)

cross-license—the reciprocal grant of patent rights to each other by two or more owners of such rights

licences-réciproques—l'accord réciproque des droits de brevet l'un à l'autre par plusieurs proprietaires de tels droits

wechselseitige Lizenz—gegenseitige Bewilligung von Patentrechten, die zwei oder mehr Eigentuemer solcher Rechte einander zugestehen

cross-reference to a related application—the statement in a specification, immediately after the abstract of the disclosure, identifying an earlier filed co-pending application of the same applicant for the same invention by serial number, filing date and relationship, for the purpose of getting the benefit of the filing date of the prior application

cross-reference—renvoi à une demande relative—la déclaration dans une spécification, suivant immédiatement l'abstraction de la divulgation, identifiant une demande copendante, antérieurement déposée par le même demandeur pour la même invention par nombre successif, le date de dépôt et relation, dans le but d'obtenir l'avantage de la date de dépôt de la demande antérieure

Hinweis auf eine verwandte Anmeldung—die Angabe in einer Beschreibung (specification) sofort nach dem Auszug aus der Offenbarung, welche eine frueher eingerichte, gleichzeitig schwebende Anmeldung des gleichen Anmelders fuer die gleiche Erfindung mit laufender Nummer, Einreichungsdatum und Beziehung identifiziert, um in die Nutzniessung des Einreichungsdatums der frueheren Anmeldung zu gelangen

crowded art—a technology in which there have been numerous advances over a relatively short period of time

technique serrée—une technologie dans la quelle il y avait des progrès nombreux pendant une période de temps relativement courte

Ueberfuelltes Fach (gebiet)—ein technisches Gebiet, auf dem in verhaeltnismaessig kurzer Zeit zahlreiche Fortschritte gemacht wurden

D

damages for infringement—an award in dollars to compensate for unauthorized use of patent rights. Compensatory award includes a sum that is not less than a reasonable royalty for use, with interest and court costs. (Sec. 284)

dommages pour la contrefaçon—de l'argent pour restituer l'emploi sans autorisation des droits de brevet. La décision compensatrice comprend une somme qui n'est pas moins que les redevenances raisonnables pour l'emploi, avec l'intérêt et les frais du tribunal (les frais ne comprennent pas les frais d'un avocat). (Sec. 284)

Schadenersatz fuer Patentverletzung—eine Dollarpraemie als Entschaedigung fuer die unbefugte Benutzung von Patentrechten. Die zuerkannte Verguetung umfasst eine Summe, die nicht geringer als eine angemessene Gebuehr fuer die Benutzung inklusive Zinsen und Gerichtskosten ist. (Sec. 284)

date of grant—date of issue of a patent

date de délivrance—la date de la délivrance d'un brevet

Erteilungsdatum—Datum der Patentverleihung

declaration—statement of the applicant that he has complied with the provisions of Sec. 101 and Sec. 102, accepted in lieu of oath if it includes the averments that statements made of his own knowledge are true, that statements made on information and belief are believed to be true, and there is included the notice that willful false statements are punishable by fine and/or imprisonment (18 USC 1001) and may jeopardize the validity of the application or any patent issuing on such declaration. Declaration can also be used when presenting a claim for matter not claimed originally (R. 67), when applying for a reissue patent (R. 171, 172), when applying for a design patent (R. 151, 153), when applying for a plant patent (R. 161, 162) and when filing a statement required by 42 USC 2182 or 2457(c) (as to inventions under Atomic Energy Commission or National Space Program regulations).

déclaration—déclaration du demandeur qu'il a accédé aux stipulations de Sec. 101 et Sec. 102, acceptée au lieu d'un serment si elle comprend les affirmations que les déclarations faites de sa propre connaissance sont vraies, que les déclarations faites des renseignements et de la croyance sont crues d'être vraies, et qu'on punira les déclarations fausses faites volontairement par amende et/ou incarcération (18 USC 1001) et que telles déclarations peuvent nasarder la validité de la déclaration ou d'aucun brevet qui est délivré d'une telle déclaration. On peut aussi employer la déclaration quand on présente une revendication pour la matière qui n'était pas originalement revendiquée (R. 67), quand on demande un brevet "reissue" (R. 171, 172), quand on demande un brevet de dessein (R. 151, 153), quand on demande un brevet de plante (R. 161, 162), et quand on dépose une déclaration exigée de 42 USC 2182 ou 2457 (c) (comme les inventions sous les règlements de la Commission d'Energie Atomique ou le Programme de l'Espace Nationale).

eidesstattliche Erklaerung—Mitteilung des Anmelders, dass er die Vorschriften unter Sec. 101 und Sec. 102 erfuellt hat angenommen an Eides statt, sofern diese die Versicherung enthaelt, dass die aus eigener Kenntnis gemachten Behauptungen wahr sind und, dass Behauptungen begruendet auf Auskuenften und Glauben fuer wahr gehalten werden. Auch ist die Benachrichtigung, dass absichtlich gemachte falsche Aussagen mit Geldstrafe und/oder Gefangenschaft strafbar sind enthalten (18 USC 1001) und die Gueltigkeit der Anmeldung oder eines auf der Erklaerung begruendeten Patents gefaehrden. Eine eidesstattliche Erklaerung kann auch dann benuetzt werden, wenn ein Anspruch auf urspruenglich nicht beanspruchte Materie geltend gemacht wird (R. 67), beim Anmelden eines Wiedererteilungs-Patents (R. 171, -172), beim Anmelden eines Geschmacksmusters (R. 151, 153), beim Anmelden eines Pflanzenpatents (R. 161, 162), und beim Einreichen einer vom 42 USC 2182 oder 2457 (c) verlangten Aufstellung (mit Hinsicht auf Erfindungen, die unter die Vorschriften der Atomic Energy Commission oder des National Space Program fallen.

declaratory judgment—a decision by a court, in an action started by a party threatened with infringement suit, as to whether the patent is valid and/or infringed

jugement déclaratif—une décision par un tribunal, dans une action commencée par une partie menacée d'un procès de contrefaçon, au sujet de la validité ou de la contrefaçon d'un brevet

Feststellungs-Urteil—ein Gerichtsentscheid ueber Patentgueltigkeit oder Patentverletzung in einer Klage, die von einer mit Patentverletzung bedrohten Partei angestrengt wurde

dedication—making an invention available for free use. Accomplished by direct statement, or by disclosing and not claiming an invention in such a manner that a statutory or other bar to patenting takes effect.

dédicace—rendant disponible une invention pour l'utilisation libre. Accompli par une déclaration directe, ou en divulguant et ne revendiquant pas une invention d'une telle manière qu'il opère une interdiction statutaire de breveter.

Verzicht zu Gunsten der Allgemeinheit—eine Erfindung zum freien Gebrauch zur Verfuegung stellen. Ausfuehrbar entweder durch deutliche Erklaerung oder durch Offenbarung und Nicht-Beanspruchung der Erfindung in einer Weise, die einen gesetzlichen oder anderen Hinderungsgrund zur Patentierung in Kraft treten laesst.

defensive publication—conditional waiver of right to a patent by filing an application, a waiver of patent rights, consent to a publication by the Patent Office of an abstract of the disclosure, an authorization to open the application to public inspection, and a declaration of abandonment. Applicant retains rights to an interference for five years from the earliest effective United States filing date, and is entitled to the benefit of the filing date of the defensively published application by filing a continuing application within thirty months of the earliest effective United States filing date. (R. 139)

publication défensive—abandon du droit à un brevet en déposant une demande, un abandon des droits de brevet, le consentement à une publication de l'Office des Brevets d'un abstraction de la divulgation, une autorisation d'ouvrir la démande à l'examen public, et une déclaration d'abandon. Le demandeur retient les droits à une "interférence" pendant cinq années de la date d'effet de dépô la plus ancienne des Etats-Unis. (R. 139)

Einspruchs-Bekanntmachung—bedingter Verzicht auf das Recht zu einem Patent durch Einreichung einer Anmeldung, eines Verzichts auf Patentenrechte, Zustimmung zu einer Veroeffentlichung des Auszugs aus der Offenbarung durch das Patentamt, einer Ermaechtigung zur oeffentlichen Einsichtnahme der Anmeldung und einer Aufgaberklaerung. Der Anmelder behaelt fuenf Jahre vom fruehest wirksamen United States Einreichungsdatum das Recht zu einer Interferenz; er ist durch Einreichung einer Fortfuehrungs-Anmeldung innerhalb von dreissig Monaten vom fruehest wirksamen United States Einreichungsdatum zu dem aus dem Einreichungsdatum der Bekanntmachung der Einspruchsanmeldung erwachsenden Vorteil berechtigt. (R. 139)

dependent claim—a claim that refers back to and restricts a single preceding claim. Several series of dependent claims may appear in a single application, but all claims in each series must be in immediate consecutive order or as close to such order as physically possible. (R. 75)

revendication subordonnée—une revendication qui fait allusion à, et limite, une revendication précédante. Plusieurs séries de revendications subordonnées peuvent paraître dans une demande unique, mais toutes les revendications dans chaque série doivent être en ordre exact et consécutif, ou aussi près qu'il soit physiquement possible à un tel ordre. (R. 75)

Unteranspruch—ein Anspruch, der auf einen einzelnen vorhergegangenen Anspruch zurueckverweist und diesen begrenzt. Mehrere Serien von Unteranspruechen koennen in einer einzigen Anmeldung erscheinen, aber alle Ansprueche in jeded Serie muessen in unmittelbar aufeinanderfolgender Ordnung oder so dicht wie moeglich zusammenstehen. (R. 75)

deposit account—a sum, maintained at a minimum of $50.00, kept on deposit with the Patent Office by an attorney or agent to be charged to cover filing, final, appeal and petition fees, and cost of Patent Office services such as requests for copies of records, file histories, and correction of drawings (R. 25)

compte de dépôt—une somme, maintenue à un minimum de $50.00, gardée sur dépôt avec l'Office des Brevets par un avocat ou un agent, chargée pour couvrir les taxes de délivrance, les taxes finales, les taxes d'appel et de pétition, et la coûte des services de l'Office des Brevets, tel que des requêtes des copies des archives, des histoires du brevet, et la correction des dessins (R. 25)

Hinterlegungs-Konto—eine Summe von mindestens $50., die ein Anwalt oder gesetzlicher Vertreter zur Deckung von Anmelde—und Schluss—gebuehren, Berufungs—und Eingebegebuehren, sowie Kosten fuer Dienstleistungen des Patentamts, wie Gesuche um Abschriften einer Akte und Zeichnungs-Korrekturen, beim Patentamt unterhaelt (R. 25)

deposition—the record of the oral examination of a witness in an interference under the provisions of R. 272 et seq.

dépôt—la transcription des épreuves orales d'un temoin dans une "interférence sous les conditions de R. 272 et seq.

eidliche Aussage—Protokoll des muendlichen Verhoers eines Zeugen in einer Interferenz unter den Bestimmungen von R. 272 et seq.

design patent—patent on a new, original and ornamental design for an article of manufacture, granted for a period of three and one-half, seven or fourteen years, the term being at the option of applicant (R. 151-155)

dessin ou modèle déposé—un brevet sur un dessin nouveau, original et ornémental, conçu pour un produit industriel, délivré pour une période de trois et demie, sept ou quatorze ans, la durée est au choix du demandeur (R. 151-155)

Geschmacksmusterpatent—Patent fuer ein neues, eigenartiges und ornamentales Muster fuer einen gewerblichen Artikel, das fuer eine Zeitspanne von dreieinhalb, sieben oder vierzehn Jahren erteilt wird; die Dauer der Laufzeit liegt beim Anmelder (R. 151-155)

design patent series—the separate series of numbers for design patents preceded by the letter D (MPEP 901.04)

serie de dessin ou modèle déposé—la distincte série de numéros pour des dessin ou modèles déposés, précédée par la lettre D (MPEP 901.04)

Geschmacksmuster–Patentserie—die besondere Serie von Nummern fuer Geschmacksmusterpatente, der der Buchstabe D voransteht (MPEP 901.04)

diligence—continuous activity at a reasonable rate in reducing an invention to practice or in acting to correct an error in an issued patent

diligence—activité continue d'un progrès raisonnable en réduisant à la pratique une invention, ou en agissant pour corriger une erreur dans un brevet octroyé

Sorgfalt—in angemessenem Grad andauernde Taetigkeit die Erfindung in die Praxis umzusetzen, oder einen Irrtum in einem schon erteilten Patent zu korrigieren

disclaimer—written statement of abandonment of an invalid claim that had been filed without deceptive intent. The disclaimer must be recorded in the Patent Office. (Sec. 253, R. 321)

renonciation—une déclaration écrite de l'abandon d'une revendication invalide qu'on a déposée sans intention déceptive. La renonciation doit être enregistrée dans l'Office des Brevets. (Sec. 253, R. 231)

Widerruf—schriftliche Erklaerung, durch die ein ungueltiger Patentanspruch, der ohne Taeuschungsabsicht gemacht war, aufgegeben wird. Der Widerruf muss beim Patentamt aktenmaessig beurkundet sein. (Sec. 253, R. 321)

disclosure—statement of the invention as set forth in any evidence, i.e. as set forth in the specification, drawings or claims

divulgation—la déclaration d'une invention présentée, i.e. présentée dans la spécification, les dessin ou les revendications

Offenbarung—Darlegung der Erfindung durch jede Art von Beweismaterial, wie durch Beschreibung (specification), Zeischnungen oder Ansprueche

disclosure document—an invention disclosure signed by the inventor and forwarded to the Patent Office by the inventor or his assignee, with the $10. fee, a stamped self-addressed envelope and the inventor's separate signed request that the invention disclosure be accepted and preserved for two years under the Patent Office Disclosure Document Program as proof of conception

divulgation document—la déclaration d'une invention avec signature de l'inventeur, dépôt dans l'Office des Brevets par l'inventeur ou son cessionnaire avec la taxe de $10., une enveloppe timbrée addressé à l'inventeur, et une lettre signé par l'inventeur demandant dépôt et maintenance de la déclaration pendant deux ans dans l'Office de Brevets Programme de Divulgation des Documents en evidence de conception

Offenbarungs-Urkunde—eine Erfindungs-Offenbarung, vom Erfinder unterzeichnet und vom Erfinder oder seinem Rechtnachsfolger dem Patentamt mit der Gebuehr von $10. zugesandt, einem an den Absender zurueckadressierten Freiumschlag—und getrennt davon—das unterzeichnete Ersuchen des Erfinders die Erfindungs-Offenbarung anzunehmen und sie zwei Jahre unter dem Patentamt Offenbarungs-Urkunden-Programm als Beweis fuer die geistige Erfassung aufzubewahren

District Court—a Federal court having jurisdiction of an action relating to patents. Infringement suit can be brought in the district where the defendant resides, or has committed acts of infringement and has an established business. (28 USC 1338, 1400)

District Court—un tribunal Fédéral qui a la juridiction d'une action relative aux brevets. On peut présenter les procès de contrefaçon dans le district où demeure le défendeur, ou dans le district, où il a commis des actes de contrefaçon et où il a établi ses affaires. (28 USC 1338, 1400)

District Court—ein Bundesgerichtshof (Federal Court), der die Gerichtsbarkeit in Zivilklagen mit Bezug auf Patente hat. Patentverletzungsklagen koennen im Wohnbezirk des Angeklagten angestrengt werden oder dort, wo er das Patent verletzt hat oder ein eingefuehrtes Geschaeft besitzt. (28 USC 1338, 1400)

District Court for District of Columbia—a Federal court having jurisdiction of appeals from decisions of the Board of Appeals and the Board of Patent Interferences, when adverse parties reside in different judicial districts not within one state or in a foreign country, and when the appeal is not filed with the Court of Customs and Patent Appeals (Sec. 145, 146)

District Court for District of Columbia—un tribunal Fédéral qui a la juridiction des appel d'une décision de la Commision d'Appel et de la Commission des "Interférences" des Brevets, quant des parties opposées habitent des districts judiciaux différents, pas dedans un état ou habitent un pays étranger, et quand l'appel n'est pas déposé avec la Court of Customs and Patent Appeals (Sec. 145, 146)

District Court for District of Columbia—ein Bundesgerichtshof (Federal Court), der die Gerichtsbarkeit in Berufungen gegen Entscheidungen des Board of Appeals und des Board of Patent Interferences hat, wenn die Gegenparteien in verschiedenen Gerichtsbezirken, nicht innerhalb desselben Bundesstaates, oder im Ausland wohnhaft sind und, wenn beim Court of Customs and Patent Appeals keine Berufung eingelegt wurde (Sec. 145, 146)

division—see divisional application

division—voir demande divisionnaire

Ausscheidung—vgl. ausgeschiedene Anmeldung

divisional application—an application setting forth an independent and distinct invention that had been included in an application setting forth another independent and distinct invention

demande divisionnaire—une demande présentant une invention indépendante et distincte qu'on a incluse dans une demande présentant une autre invention indépendante et distincte

Ausgeschiedene Anmeldung—eine Anmeldung, die eine von einer andern unabhaengige und verschiedene Erfindung darlegt, die in einer Anmeldung eingeschlossen war, welche eine andere unabhaengige und verschiedene Erfindung darlegt

dominate—having a claim scope that includes another development

dominer—avoir une étendue de revendication qui comprend un autre développement

vorherrschen—einen Anspruchsbereich haben, der eine andere Entwicklung einschliesst

dominating patent—see basic patent

brevet dominant—voir brevet de base

vorherrschendes Patent—vgl. Grundpatent

double patenting—where two or more applications and/or patents have the same inventive entity and an invention claimed in one case is the same as, or not patentably distinct from, an invention in the other case (MPEP 804)

breveter double—où plusieurs demandes et/ou brevets ont la même entité inventive et une invention revendiquée dans un cas est la même que, ou n'est pas brevetablement distincte de, une invention dans l'autre cas (MPEP 804)

Doppelpatentierung—zwei oder mehr Anmeldung und/oder Patente haben diesselbe erfinderische Einheit und eine beanspruchte Erfindung ist diesselbe, oder patentmaessig nicht verschieden, von der Erfindung im andern Fall (MPEP 804)

drawing—a showing of every feature of the invention specified in the claims, prepared in accordance with Rules 81-88 of the Rules of Practice

dessin—une représentation de chaque trait de l'invention spécifiée dans les revendications, préparée en accord avec les R. 81-88 des Règles de la Preatique

Zeichnung—das Aufzeigen eines jeden Merkmals der im Patentanspruch beschriebenen Erfindung, angefertigt in Uebereinstimmung mit den Vorschriften 81-88 der Rules of Practice

due date—the last day of the time period in which applicant must answer an action by the Patent Office

date due—le dernier jour de la période de temps dans laquelle le demandeur doit répondre à une action de l'Office des Brevets

Faelligkeitstermin—der letzte Tag der Frist, innerhalb welcher der Anmelder auf eine Klage des Patentamts antworten muss

E

effective date of application—the date of filing of a parent application, or of an application filed by the same person for the same invention in a foreign convention country and complying with the provisions of Sec. 119

date d'effet de demande—la date de dépôt d'une "parent" demande, ou d'une demande déposée de la même personne pour la même invention dans un pays étranger unioniste et accédant aux conditions de Sec. 119

Datum des Inkrafttretens einer Anmeldung—das Einreichungsdatum einer Stamm-Anmeldung oder einer Anmeldung, die von derselben Person fuer diesselbe Erfindung in einem auslaendischen Verbandsstaat eingereicht wurde und die Vorschriften unter Sec. 119 erfuellt

election of species—selection by applicant, in response to an action holding that no generic claim presented is allowable, of the species of his invention to which his claims shall be restricted if no generic claim is finally held allowable (R. 146)

choix de variantes—choix d'un demandeur, en réponse à une action avançant qu'aucune revendication générique ne soit acceptable, de la variante de son invention à laquelle seront restreintes ses revendications, si on ne tient finalement aucune revendication générique comme acceptable (R. 146)

Wahl der Gattung—Auswahl der Gattung seiner Erfindung durch den Anmelder in Erwiderung auf eine Klage, dass kein vorgebrachter umfassender Anspruch zulaessig ist. Durch Auswahl der Gattung soll der Anspruch auf diese Gattung beschraenkt bleiben, sofern kein umfassender Anspruch als endgueltig zulaessig anerkannt wird. (R. 146)

enjoin—to require a litigant, by court order, to desist from performing specified acts

enjoindre—imposer à un litigant, par ordonnance d'un tribunal, de cesser d'exécuter des actes détérminés

verwarnen—einen Prozessfuehrnden durch Gerichtsbescheid dazu auffordern von der Ausfuehrung bestimmter Handlungen Abstand zu nehmen

entered—made a permanent part of the file wrapper (MPEP 717)

entré—fait une partie permanente de l'histoire du brevet (MPEP 717)

eingetragen—zu einem permanenten Teil der Akte gemacht (MPEP 717)

equivalent—functionally duplicate technology taught by the pertinent prior art

équivalent—technologie enseignée par la technique antérieure et pertinente

gleichwertig—durch den zutreffenden Stand der Technig gelehrtes technisches Koennen

essential material—see incorporation by reference

matière essentielle—voir incorporation par renvoi

wesentliches Material—vgl. Eingliederung durch Hinweis

estop—see estoppel

estop—voir estoppel

Ausschliessung—vgl. Untersagung

estoppel—a prohibition against alleging or denying a fact, the prohibition having been created by some previous action or statement by the person estopped; a prior act that bars certain subsequent actions. For example, publication of an invention for more than one year acts as a bar or estoppel to obtaining a patent for such invention.

estoppel—une interdiction d'alléguer ou de nier un fait, l'interdiction ayant été créée par une déclaration ou une action antérieure de la personne "estopped"; un acte antérieure qui défend certaines actions postérieures. Par exemple, la publication d'une invention pendant plus d'une année agit comme une interdiction ou "estoppel" d'obtenir un brevet pour telle invention.

Untersagung—ein Verbot gegen die Behauptung oder Verneinung einer Tatsache. Das Verbot wurde durch eine vorhergehende Handlung oder Aussage der mit der Untersagung belegten Person hervorgerufen; ein frueheres Handeln, das gewisse folgende Handlungen ausschliesst. Die Veroeffentlichung einer Erfindung seit mehr als einem Jahr stellt, zum Beispiel, einen Hinderungsgrund oder eine Untersagung zur Erlangung eines Patents fuer eine solche Erfindung dar.

ex parte proceeding—a proceeding between an applicant and the Patent Office, with no third and opposing party

procédé ex parte—un procédé entre un demandeur et l'Office des Brevets, sans aucune troisième partie opposante

einseitiges Verfahren—Verfahren zwischen einem Anmelder und dem Patentamt ohne eine dritte und Gegenpartei

examination—see examiner

examen—voir examinateur

Pruefung—vgl. Pruefer

examiner—a Patent Office employee who reviews patent applications to determine the patentability and the scope of inventions and, with other examiners, the question of priority between rival applicants claiming the same subject matter

examinateur—un employé de l'Office des Brevets qui revoit les demandes de brevets pour déterminer la brevetabilité et l'étendue d'une invention et, avec des autres examinateurs, la question de la priorité entre des demandeurs rivaux revendiquant la même matière

Pruefer—ein Beamter der Patentamts, der Patentanmeldungen nachprueft um die Patentfaehigkeit und den Umfang von Erfindungen zu bestimmen und, mit andern Pruefern, die Frage der Prioritaet zwischen konkurrierenden Anmeldern, die den gleichen Gegenstand beanspruchen, zu entscheiden

examiner's amendment—an amendment to an application made by the examiner, with notice to applicant, to correct "obvious errors and omissions" (MPEP 1302.04)

amendement de l'examinateur—un amendement à une demande, fait par l'examinateur, avec une notification au demandeur, pour corriger des "erreurs évidentes et des omissions" (MPEP 1302.04)

Pruefers Berichtigung—eine Berichtigung zu einer Anmeldung die von einem Pruefer unter Benachrichtigung des Anmelders gemacht wird, um "augenfaellige Irrtuemer und Auslassungen" zu korrigieren (MPEP 1302.04)

examiner's answer—response by primary examiner to brief of appellant to Board of Appeals, such answer including any necessary explanation of the invention claimed and of the references and grounds of rejection (R. 193)

réponse de l'examinateur—réponse d'un examinateur primaire au dossier du demandeur à la Commission d'Appel, une telle réponse comprenante aucune explication nécessaire de l'invention revendiquée et des raisons de rejet (R. 193)

Pruefers Antwort—Erwiderung des Vorpruefers auf den Schriftsatz des Berufungsklaegers beim Board of Appeals, mit einem Bescheid, der alle notwendigen Erklaerungen fuer die beanspruchte Erfindung und die Belege und Gruende der Ablehnung enthaelt (R. 193)

examiners-in-chief—senior patent examiners who, with the Commissioner of Patents and the Assistant Commissioners, constitute the Board of Appeals

examinateurs-en-chef—"senior" examinateurs des brevets qui, avec le Commissaire des Brevets et les Commissaires Auxiliaires, constituent la Commission d'Appel

Haupt-Pruefer—"Oberpatentpruefer" (dienstaeltere Pruefer), die zusammen mit dem Commissioner of Patents und den Assistant Commissioners den Board of Appeals bilden

exclusive license—see license

licence exclusive—voir licence

ausschliessliche Lizenz—vgl. Lizenz

execution of application—signature of an application before a notary or other authorized person in the United States. An application executed abroad before a notary or other authorized person must be legalized by a United States consular or diplomatic officer. Alternatively, a declaration (R. 68) may be made instead of signature before a notary or other authorized person

exécution de demande—signature d'une demande devant un notaire, ou une autre personne autorisée aux Etats-Unis. Une demande exécutée à l'étranger devant un notaire ou une autre personne autorisée doit être légalisée par un consulat ou par un officier diplomatique des Etats-Unis. Alternativement, on peut faire une déclaration (R. 68) au lieu d'une signature devant un notaire ou une autre personne autorisée

Ausfertigung der Anmeldung—Leistung der Anmeldungsunterschrift vor einem Notar oder einer andern dazu befugten Person in den Vereinigten Staaten. Eine Anmeldung, die im Ausland vor einem Notar oder einer andern dazu befugten Person ausgefertigt wurde, muss durch einen Konsulats-oder Botschaftsbeamten der Vereinigten Staaten beglaubigt werden. Andern Falls kann auch eine eidesstattliche Erklaerung (R. 68) an Stelle der Unterschrift vor einem Notar oder einer anderen dazu befugten Person abgegeben werden

executor—the representative of a legally incapacitated inventor

exécuteur—le représentant d'un inventeur légalement incapacité

Treuhaender—der Vertreter eines vor dem Gestz unfaehigen Erfinders

exhausted combination—a combination of elements shown by the prior art to be anticipated

"exhausted combination"—une combinaison d'éléments démontrée d'être antériorisée par la technique antérieure

ausgeschoepfte Verbindung—eine Verbindung von Elementen, die sich durch den Stand der Technik als vorweggenommen erweist

experimental use—use of an invention by an inventor to test its operability

utilisation à titre expérimental—l'utilisation d'une invention par un inventeur pour essayer son "operability"

experimentelle Benutzung—von einem Erfinder zur Pruefung ihrer Wirksamkeit benutzte Erfindung

expired patent—the denotation of a patent after the end of the term for which it was granted

brevet expiré—la désignation d'un brevet après la fin de la durée pour laquelle il a été délivré

abgelaufenes Patent—die Bezeichnung eines Patents nach Beendigung der Laufzeit, fuer die as erteilt war

exploded view—a drawing in which the separated parts of a figure, embraced by a bracket, are illustrated to show the relationship or order of assembly of various parts (R. 84(i))

vue éclatée—un dessin où les parties distinctes d'une figure, renfermées des parenthèses, sont illustrées pour montrer le rapport ou l'ordre d'assemblage des parties diverses (R. 84(i))

Aufriss—eine Zeichnung, auf der die einzelnen Teile einer Abbildung dargestellt sind, von einer Klammer zusammengehalten, um die Beziehung zueinander oder die Reihenfolge der Zusammensetzung der verschiedenen Teile zu zeigen (R. 84(i))

F

false marking—imitating the name of the patentee, the patent number or the word "patent" or the like to deceive the public into believing that the article was made or sold with the consent of the patentee; marking an unpatented article to deceive the public into believing the article was patented; or marking an article "patent applied for", or "patent pending" or the like to deceive the public into believing a patent application is pending (Sec. 292)

marquage faux—imitant le nom due breveté, le numéro du brevet ou le mot "brevet", etc., pour faire croire le public que le produit ait été fabriqué ou vendu avec l'accord du breveté; en marquant un produit non-breveté pour faire croire le public que le produit ait été breveté; ou en marquant un produit "brevet demandé", ou "brevet pendant", etc. pour faire croire le public que le brevet soit pendant (Sec. 292)

falsche Bezeichnung—Nachahmung des Namens des Patentinhabers, der Patentnummer, des Wortes "Patent" oder dergleichen um das Publikum zu taeuschen und glauben zu lassen, dass der Artikel mit Zustimmung des Patentinhabers hergestellt oder verkauft wurde; Bezeichnung eines unpatentierten Gegenstandes um das Publikum zu taeuschen und glauben zu lassen der Artikel sei patentiert; oder die Bezeichnung eines Gegenstandes mit "Patent angemeldet" oder "Patentanmeldung anhaengig" oder dergleichen, um das Publikum zu taeuschen und glauben zu lassen, dass eine Patentanmeldung anhaengig ist (Sec. 292)

fee—the statutory or administrative charges for Patent Office services (R. 21-26)

taxe—les frais statutaires ou administratifs pour les services de l'Office des Brevets (R. 21-26)

Gebuehr—die gesetzlichen oder Verwaltungskosten fuer Dienstleistungen des Patentamts (R. 21-26)

field of the invention—see background of the invention

domaine de l'invention—voir fond de l'invention

Gebiet der Erfindung—vgl. Hintergrund der Erfindung

file wrapper—the total written record in the Patent Office file of an application

histoire du brevet—tous les archives écrits dans le dépôt d'une demande à l'Office des Brevets

Akte—die gesamten schriftlichen Aufzeichnungen ueber eine Anmeldung im Archiv des Patentamts

file wrapper estoppel—the prohibition established by a concession made by an applicant in the course of prosecution of an application. For example, when the scope of a claim is narrowed in response to the examiner's rejection of that claim, there is a file wrapper estoppel prohibiting the reassertion of a claim that is broader than the narrowed claim.

histoire du brevet "estoppel"—l'interdiction établie par une concession faite du demandeur dans le cours de la poursuite d'une demande. Par example, quand l'étendue d'une revendication est limitée en réponse au rejet de la revendication par l'examinateur, il y a un hisoire du brevet "estoppel" (file wrapper estoppel) défendant la nouvelle assertion d'une revendication qui est plus large que la revendication limitée.

Untersagung in der Akte—ein Verbot begruendet auf einem Zugestaendnis, das von einem Anmelder im Verlauf der Verfolgung einer Anmeldung gemacht wurde. Wenn, zum Beispiel, der Umfang eines Anspruches in Erwinderung auf die Ablehnung des Pruefers dieses Anspruchs enger gehalten wird, dann befindet sich eine Untersagung in der Akte, welche die Wiedergeltendmachung eines Anspruchs, der umfassender als der verengte Anspruch ist, verbietet.

filing date—the date on which the complete or the last part of an application, in form acceptable for examination, is received in the Patent Office (R. 55)

date de dépôt—la date où la demande entière ou la dernière partie d'une demande, dans une forme acceptable pour l'examen, est reçue dans l'Office des Brevets (R. 55)

(offizielles) Einreichungsdatum—das Datum, an dem die vollstaendige Anmeldung oder der letzte Teil derselben, in zur Pruefung annehmbarer Form, im Patentamt empfangen wird (R. 55)

filing fee—the fee for filing an application; the filing fee for an original patent is $65. plus $10. for each independent claim in excess of one plus $2. for each claim in excess of ten; the filing fee for a design patent is $20.; the filing fee for a reissue patent is $65. plus $10. for each independent claim in excess of the number of independent claims in the original patent plus $2. for each claim in excess of ten and also in excess of the number of claims in the original patent (Sec. 41)

taxe de dépôt—la taxe pour la déposition d'une demande; la taxe de dépôt pour un brevet original est $65., $10. de plus pour chaque revendication indépendante en excès d'une, $2. de plus pour chaque revendication en excès de dix; la taxe de dépôt pour un brevet de dessin est $20.; la taxe de dépôt pour un brevet "reissue" est $65. plus $10. pour chaque revendication en excès du nombre de revendications indépendantes dans le brevet original plus $2. pour chaque revendication en excès de dix et aussi en excès du nombre de revendications dans le brevet original (Sec. 41)

Anmeldegebuehr—die Gebuehr fuer die Anmeldung eines Patents; die Gebuehr fuer ein Hauptpatent ist $65., plus $10. fuer jeden weiteren Anspruch ausser einem, und $2. fuer jeden Anspruch nach den ersten zehn; die Anmeldegebuehr fuer ein Geschmacksmuster ist $20.; die Gebuehr fuer Wiedererteilung eines Patents ist $65., plus $10. fuer jeden unabhaengigen Anspruch, der ueber die Anzahl der unabhaengigen Ansprueche im Hauptpatent hinausgeht, plus $2. fuer jeden weiteren Anspruch nach den ersten zehn, und der auch ueber die Anzahl der Ansprueche im Hauptpatent hinausgeht (Sec. 41)

final fee—the fee for issue of an original or reissue patent, $100. plus $10. for each page of printed specification plus $2. for each sheet of drawing; in design cases, the final fee is $10. for a term of three and one half years, $20. for seven years and $30. for fourteen years (Sec. 41)

taxe finale—la taxe pour la délivrance d'un brevet original ou "reissue", $100. plus $10. pour chaque page de spécification imprimée plus $2. pour chaque feuille de dessin; en cas des dessins, la taxe finale est $10. pour une durée de trois ans et demi, $20. pour une durée de sept ans et $30. pour une durée de quatorze ans (Sec. 41)

Schlussgebuehr—die Gebuehr fuer die Erteilung eines Hauptpatents oder die Wiederausgabe eines Patents, $100., plus $10. fuer jede Seite mit gedruckter Beschreibung, plus $2. fuer jeden Bogen mit Zeichnungen; im Falle von Geschmacksmustern ist die Schlussgebuehr $10. fuer eine Frist von dreieinhalb Jahren, $20. fuer sieben Jahre und $30. fuer vierzehn Jahre (Sec. 41)

final rejection—an action by the examiner that concludes prosecution before the examiner, limiting applicant to appeal to the Board of Appeals, petition to the Commissioner from objections or requirements not involved in the rejection of a claim, amendment placing the application in condition for allowance or, at the discretion of the examiner, amendment placing the application in better form for appeal (R. 116)

rejet final—une action de l'examinateur qui termine le procédé devant l'examinateur, limitant le demandeur à un appel devant la Commission d'Appel, un pétition au Commissaire des objections ou des exigences qui n'entrent pas dans le rejet d'une revendication, un amendement rendant la demande recevable ou, à la discrétion de l'examinateur, un amendement rendant la demande d'une meilleure forme un appel (R. 116)

endgueltige Zurueckweisung—eine Handlung des Pruefers, die die Verfolgung (der Patentanmeldung) vor dem Pruefer beendet, den Anmelder darauf beschraenkend beim Board of Appeals Beschwerde einzulegen, den Commissioner mit Entgegenhaltungen und Anforderungen, welche nicht in die Ablehnung eines Anspruchs einbezogen waren zu ersuchen, eine Verbesserung, die die Zulassung der Anmeldung ermoeglicht, oder, im Ermessen des Pruefers, eine Verbesserung, welche die Anmeldung in eine bessere Form fuer Berufung bringt (R. 116)

foreign filing authorization—permission by the Commissioner of Patents to file an application in a foreign country in less than six months after the filing of such application in the United States. License to file abroad will not be granted for an application under a secrecy order, but may be granted retroactively in other cases where an application has been filed abroad inadvertently without such license. (Sec. 184)

autorisation étrangere de dépôt—permission du Commissaire des Brevets déposêr une demande dans un pays étranger dans moins de six mois après avoir déposé la même demande aux Etats-Unis. On ne concédera pas une licence pour déposer a l'étranger une demande frappée d'une decision de mise au secret, mais on peut la concéder rétroactivement dans les autres instances où on a déposé par inadvertance une demande à l'ètranger sans une telle licence. (Sec. 184)

Genehmigung ein Patent im Ausland anzumelden—Erlaubnis vom Commissioner of Patents ein Patent weniger als sechs Monate nach seiner Anmeldung in den Vereinigten Staaten im Ausland anzumelden. Die Genehmigung eine unter Geheimhaltungs-Befehl stehende Anmeldung im Ausland einzureichen wird nicht erteilt werden, wenn eine Anmeldung im Ausland versehentlich ohne Genehmigung eingereicht worden war. (Sec. 184)

forfeited application—an application on which the patent did not issue because applicant failed to pay the final fee (R. 316). If the final fee is not accepted within one year after the six months period for payment has passed, the application stands abandoned as of the date of forfeiture.

forfeited application (demande)—une demande sur laquelle on n'a pas délivré le brevet parce que le demandeur a manqué de payer la taxe finale (R 316). Si la taxe finale n'est pas acceptée dans le delai imparti d'une année après que la periode de paiement de six mois est passée, on considère la demande comme abandonnée de la date de "forfeiture."

verfallene Anmeldung—eine Anmeldung, zu der das Patent nicht verliehen wurde, da der Anmelder versaeumte die Schlussgebuehr zu bezahlen (R. 116). Falls die Schlussgebuehr innedhalb eines Jahres and Ablauf der sechs Monatsfrist nicht angenommen wird, gilt die Anmeldung vom Verfallsdatum an als fallengelassen.

functional claim—a claim that fails to comply with S. 112 because at least one element or step is defined in whole or in part in terms of its behavior or in terms of the results that follow from its behavior, and such definition makes the claim too broad or indefinite

revendication functionnelle—une revendication qui ne conforme pas à S. 112 parce qu'au moins un élément ou procédé est défini entièrement ou partiellement en termes de sa conduite ou en termes des résultats qui proviennent de sa conduite, et une telle définition rend la revendication trop large ou indéfinie

funktioneller Anspruch—ein Anspruch, welcher nicht Sec. 112 entspricht, da mindestens ein Element oder eine Stufe im Ganzen oder teilweise in der Terminologie seines Verhaltens definiert ist, oder in der Terminologie der Resultate, die aus seinem Verhalten hervorgehen; und diese Definition macht den Anspruch zu breit oder unbestimmt

G

generic claim—a claim that includes within its scope two or more disclosed embodiments (species) of the invention

revendication générique—une revendication qui comprend dans son étendue plusieurs variantes de l'invention

Gattungen umfassender Anspruch—ein Anspruch, der in seinen Bereich zwei oder mehr offenbarte Ausfuehrungsformen (Gattungen) der Erfindung einschliesst

genus—a class that is broader than or includes more than one species

genre—une classe qui est plus large que, ou comprend plus d'une variante

Art (genus)—ein Klasse, die umfangreicher ist und mehr als eine Gattung umfasst

grant date—see date of grant

date de délivrance—voir date de délivrance

Datum der Patenterteilung—vgl. Erteilungsdatum

H

hearing—presentation by appellant of oral argument before the Board of Appeals; the examiner has the option of also presenting oral argument (R. 194)

audience—la présentation d'un argument, oral par le demandeur devant la Commission d'Appel; l'examinateur peut aussi choisir de présenter un argument oral (R. 194)

muendliche Verhandlung—Vorbringung muendlicher Beweisgruende vor dem Board of Appeals durch den Beschwerde-Fuehrenden (Berufungsklaeger); es steht dem Pruefer frei auch seinerseits muendliche Beweisgrunde vorzubringen (R. 194)

hatching—illustration of a cut section in a drawing by oblique parallel lines not less than about one-twentieth of an inch apart (R. 84(d))

hachure—illustration d'une section coupée d'un dessin par lignes obliques et parallèles qui ne se séparent pas de moins d'une vingtième d'une pouce (R. 84 (d))

Schraffierung—Illustration eines Schnitts in einer Zeichnung durch schraege Parallellinien, die nicht weniger als ungefaehr einen zwanzigstel Zoll (inch) auseinander sind (R. 84 (d))

holiday—an official non-work day in the District of Columbia: New Year's Day, January 1; Washington's Birthday, February 22; Memorial Day, May 30; Independence Day, July 4; Labor Day, first Monday in September; Veterans Day, November 11; Thanksgiving Day, fourth Thursday in November; Christmas Day, December 25; and Inauguration Day, January 20 every four years; when the holiday falls on a Saturday, the preceding Friday is observed as a holiday

congé—un jour officiel où on ne travaille pas dans le District of Columbia: le Jour de l'An, le 1er janvier; l'anniversaire de Washington, le 22 février; le Jour Commémoratif, le 30 mai; le Jour d'Indépendance, le 4 juillet; le Jour de Travail, le premier lundi de septembre; le Jour des Anciens Combattants, de 11 novembre; le Jour des Actions de Grâce, le quatrième jeudi de novembre; le Jour de Noël, le 25 décembre; et le Jour de l'Inauguration, le 20 janvier, tous les quatre ans. Quand le congé est le samedi, on observe le vendredi précédant comme jour de congé.

Feiertag—ein amtlicher Nicht-Arbeitstag im District of Columbia: der Neujahrstag am 1. Januar; Washington's Geburtstag am 22. Februar; Memorial Day am 30. Mai; Unabhaengigkeitstag am 4. Juli; Labor Day am ersten Montag im September; Tag der Veteranen am 11. November; Weihnachten am 25. Dezember; und alle vier Jahre der 20. Januar, die Amtseinsetzung des Praesidenten; faellt der Feiertag auf einen Samstag, ist der vorhergehende Freitag ein Feiertag

I

improvement—an inventive advance of a degree less than a "pioneer invention"

perfectionnement—un avancement inventif d'un degré moins d'une "invention pionnière"

Verbesserung—ein erfinderischer Schritt vorwaerts von geringerem Rang als eine "bahnbrechende Erfindung"

incomplete—a claim or disclosure that omits an essential element, step, or structural cooperative relationship of elements

incomplet—une revendication ou une divulgation qui omet un élément, une démarche, ou une relation structurele coopérative essentielle des éléments

unvollstaendig—ein Anspruch oder eine Offenbarung, welche einen wesentlichen Bestandteil, eine Stufe, oder eine strukturell zusammenwirkende Beziehung von Elementen auslassen

incorporation by reference—including data in an application by means of a summary statement identifying the information in such detail that it can be retrieved; excluded from matter that can be incorporated by reference are secret or privileged materials such as some abandoned applications, and material not easily available to the public or the Patent Office such as unpublished papers, obscure foreign publications, and publications on which there are no available English translations. Essential material (subject matter that is necessary to support the claims or for adequate disclosure of the invention) may be incorporated by reference to a United States patent or an allowed United States application. Non-essential material may be incorporated by reference to United States or foreign patents, prior filed commonly owned United States applications and non-patent publications to indicate the background of the invention or the state of the art. (MPEP 608.01(p))

incorporation par renvoi—inclure dans une demande des données au moyen d'une déclaration sommaire identifiant les renseignements d'une facon si détaillée qu'on peut l'obtenir; exclues de la matière qu'on peut incorporer par renvoi sont les matières secrètes ou privilégiées, comme des demandes abandonnées, et de la matière qui n'est pas facilement disponible au public, tel que des études inédites, des publications étrangères et obscures, des publications auxquelles il n'y a pas de traductions disponibles en anglais. La matière essentielle (matière qui est nécessaire pour soutenir les revendications ou pour une divulgation suffisante de l'invention) peut être incorporée par renvoi à un brevet des Etats-Unis, ou une demande acceptée des Etats-Unis. La matière qui n'est pas essentielle peut être incorporée par renvoi aux brevets étrangers ou des Etats-Unis, des demandes des Etats-Unis antrieurement déposées, du même propriétaire, et des publications qui ne sont pas brevetées pour indiquer le fond de l'invention ou l'état de la technique. (MPEP 608.01))

Eingliederung durch Hinweis—Einschluss von Daten in einer Anmeldung mittels einer Zusammenfassung, welche die Information in genuegender Einzelheit identifiziert, um sie wieder auffinden zu koennen; ausgenommen von der Materie, die durch Hinweis eingegliedert werden kann, sind geheime oder privilegierte Materialien, wie einige fallengelassene Anmeldungen, und Material, das der Oeffentlichkeit oder dem Patentamt nicht ohne Weiteres zugaenglich ist, wie unveroeffentlichte Schriften, wenig bekannte auslaendische Veroeffentlichungen und Veroeffentlichungen, von denen keine englischen Uebersetzungen vorhanden sind. Wesentliches Material (Gegenstaende, die zur Unterstuetzung der Ansprueche oder ausreichender Offenbarung der Erfindung notwendig sind) duerfen durch Hinweis auf ein amerikanisches Patent oder eine angenommene amerikanische Anmeldung eingegliedert werden. Nicht-wesentliches Material darf durch Hinweis auf amerikanische oder auslaendische Patente, auf früher eingereichte amerikanische Anmeldungen in gemeinsamen Besitz und auf nicht-Patent-Veroeffentlichungen eingeordnet werden, um den Hintergrund der Erfindung oder den Stand der Technik anzudeuten. (MPEP 608.01 (p))

indefinite—see vague and indefinite

indefini—voir vague et indéfini

unbestimmt—vgl. verschwommen und unbestimmt

index of patents and patentees—an annual publication, sold by the Superintendent of Documents, U. S. Government Printing Office, Washington, D. C. 20402, that lists patentees (including reissue patentees), design patentees, plant patentees, disclaimers and dedications, and decisions published in the Official Gazette

index des brevets et de brevetés—une publication annuelle, vendue par le Directeur des Documents, l'Office d'Imprimerie du Gouvernement des Etats-Unis, Washington, D. C. 20402, qui enregistre les brevetés (y inclus les "reissue" brevetes), les brevetés de dessin, les brevetés de plante, les renonciations et les dédicaces, et les décisions publiées dans la Gazette Officielle

Verzeichnis von Patenten und Patentinhabern—eine jaehrliche Veroeffentlichung, die vom Superintendent of Documents, U. S. Government Printing Office, Washington, D. C. 20402, verkauft wird; darin sind die Patentinhaber (inklusive Inhaber von Wiedererteilungs-Patenten), Geschmacksmuster-und Pflanzenpatentinhaber, Widerrufe und Verzichte zu Gunsten der Allgemeinheit, und im oeffentlichen Amtsblatt (Official Gazette) veroeffentlichte Entscheidungen aufgezaehlt

informal drawing—a drawing that fails to comply with the requirements of R. 81-84, which may be admitted for purpose of examination but must be corrected or a new drawing furnished, as required

dessin casuel—un dessin qui ne conforme par aux exigences de R. 81–84, qu'on peut admettre pour l'examen mais on doit le corriger ou en présenter un nouveau dessin, comme exigé

nicht-formgerechte Zeichnung—eine Zeichnung, die mit den Anforderungen von R. 81–84 nicht uebereinstimmt, die zum Zweck der Pruefung zugelassen werden darf, aber korrigiert werden muss, oder—nach jeweiligem Verlangen —durch eine neue Zeichnung ersetzt werden muss

infringement—use or sale of a patented invention without authority, or active inducement of such use or sale (Sec. 271)

contrefaçon—l'utilisation ou la vente d'une invention brevetée sans autorisation, ou l'encouragement actif d'une telle utilisation ou vente (Sec. 271)

Verletzung—Benutzung oder Verkauf einer patentierten Erfindung ohne Berichtigung oder taetige Veranlassung zu solchem Gebrauch oder Verkauf (Sec. 271)

injunction—a court order directing that a party desist from further infringement of a patent

injonction—une ordonnance d'un tribunal imposant à une partie de cesser de contrfaire un brevet

Verfuegung—eine gerichtliche Verfuegung, die anordnet, dass eine Partei von weiterer Verletzung eines Patents Abstand zu nehmen hat

inspection—the right of the public to inspect and obtain copies of an issued patent and its specification, drawings and all papers of record relating to the case, and to inspect and obtain copies of the file of a terminated interference involving a patent or an application on which a patent issued (R. 11, 15)

inspection—le droit du public d'examiner et d'obtenir des copies d'un brevet délivré et ses dessin de spécification et tous les histoires du brevet de la demande, et d'examiner et d'obtenir des copies des archives d'une "interférence" terminée entraînant un brevet ou une demande sur laquelle on a délivrée un brevet (R. 11, 15)

Inspektion—das Recht der Oeffentlichkeit ein erteiltes Patent einzusehen, sowie Kopien desselben und seiner Beschreibungs- (specification) Zeichnungen und aller zu den Akten genommenen Schriftstuecke zu erhalten—soweit sie sich auf den Fall beziehen; die Akte einzusehen und Kopien zu erhalten von einer beendeten Interferenz, bei der es sich um ein Patent oder um eine Anmeldung, zu der ein Patent erteilt wurde, behandelt (R. 11, 15)

insufficient disclosure—a disclosure that fails to include data that would enable a person skilled in the art to which the invention relates to make and use the invention (MPEP 608.01(p))

divulgation insuffisante—une divulgation qui manque d'inclure les données qui permettraient à une personne habile dans la technique à laquelle rapporte l'invention, de fabriquer et d'employer l'invention (MPEP 608.01 (p))

ungenuegende Offenbarung—eine Offenbarung, welche versaeumt Daten einzuschliessen, die jemanden, der mit der Technik auf die sich die Erfindung bezieht vertraut ist, in den Stand setzen wuerde die Erfindung herzustellen und zu benutzen (MPEP 608.01 (p))

inter partes proceeding—a proceeding involving two or more opposing applicants or inventors

procédé inter partes—un procédé comprenant plusieurs demandeurs ou inventeurs opposés

inter partes Verfahren—ein Verfahren, bei dem es sich um zwei oder mehr "einsprechende" Anmelder oder Erfinder handelt

interference—a proceeding to determine which of two or more applicants for a patent is the first inventor. The interference may involve an application and a patent, provided the claim is made in the application prior to one year from the date on which the patent issued. (Sec. 135)

"interférence"—une procédure tendant à déterminer lequel des plusieurs demandeurs de brevet est le premier inventeur. "Interférence" peut s'agir d'une demande et d'un brevet, pourvu que la revendication soit faite dans la demande avant une année de la date sur laquelle le brevet a été délivré. (Sec. 135)

Interferenz—ein Verfahren, das dazu dient zu bestimmen, welcher von zwei oder mehr Patentanmeldern der Erst-Erfinder ist. Es kann sich bei der Interferenz um eine Anmeldung und ein Patent handeln, vorausgesetzt der Anspruch in der Anmeldung ist mehr als ein Jahr vor dem Datum der Patenterteilung gemacht. (Sec. 135)

International Convention for Protection of Industrial Property—an agreement respecting patents and trademarks giving an applicant in one member country the same effective filing date in other Convention Countries for an application filed within a year of the first filing date. The application must comply with the patent laws of the country in which filing is sought.

Convention Internationale pour la Protection de la Propriété Industrielle—un acord au sujet des brevets et des marques de fabrique, concédant à un demandeur d'un pays unioniste la même date d'effet de dépôt dans d'autres pays unionistes pour une demande déposée dans le délai d'une année de la première date de dépôt. La demande doit acceder aux lois des brevets du pays où on veut le déposer.

Internationale Uebereinkunft zum Schutz gewerblichen Eigentums—eine Vereinbarung ueber Patente und Warenzeichen, die Anmeldern in einem Mitgliedsland dasselbe Einreichungsdatum als Termin des Inkrafttretens, wie in anderen Uebereinkunftslaendern, fuer eine innerhalb eines Jahres vom ersten Einreichungsdatum eingereichte Anmeldung, zugesteht. Die Anmeldung muss den Patentgesetzen des Landes, in dem um die Einreichung nachgesucht wird, genuegen.

interview—oral discussion of objections and rejections with the examiner in the Patent Office, usually at the request of the examiner, to expedite resolution of issues (R. 133)

entrevue—discussion orale des objections et des rejets, avec l'examinateur à l'Office des Brevets, d'ordinaire à la requête de l'examinateur, pour expédier la résolution des questions (R. 133)

Interview—muendliche Eroerterung der Einwaende und Zurueckweisungen mit dem Pruefer im Patentamt—gewoehnlich auf Wunsch des Pruefers—um die Loesung von Streitfragen zu beschleunigen (R. 133)

invention–see patentable invention

invention–voir invention brevetable

Erfindung–vgl. patentfaehige Erfindung

issue–the grant of a patent

délivrance–l'octroi d'un brevet

Ausgabe–die Erteilung eines Patents

J

Jepson claim—a form of claim in which the known matter is recited in a preamble, thus setting forth the environment, and the improvement is set forth in the remaining portion of the claim

revendication Jepson—une espéce de revendication où la matière connue est récitée dans un préambule, ainsi présentant l'environnement, et le perfectionnement est présenté dans la portion restante de la revendication

Jepson Anspruch—eine Art von Anspruch, wobei die bekannte Materie in einer Einleitung vorgetragen—damit die Umwelt darlegend—und die Verbesserung im restlichen Teil des Anspruchs dargelegt wird

joint applicants—joint inventors who apply for a patent

co-demandeurs—des co-inventeurs qui demandent un brevet

Mitanmelder—Erfindergemeinschaft, die ein Patent anmeldet

joint inventor—one of two or more inventors who, together, make an invention

co-inventeur—un de plusieurs inventeurs qui, ensemble, créent une invention

Miterfinder—einer von zwei oder mehr Erfindern, die zusammen eine Erfindung machen

judicial notice—the recognition by a court of the truth of certain facts as common knowledge, and therefore not requiring the introduction of evidence to prove such facts

notification judicaire—la reconnaissance par un tribunal de la vérité de certains faits comme connaissance commune, at ainsi ne pas exigeant l'introduction d'évidence pour prouver de tels faits

gerichtliche Anerkennung—die Anerkennung bestimmter Tatsachen als allgemeine Kenntnis durch ein Gericht, das daher die Einfuehrung von Material zum Beweis dieser Tatsachen nicht verlangt

junior party—in an interference, the applicant having the later established effective filing date

"junior party"—dans une "interférence", le demandeur qui a la date d'effet de dépôt la plus postérieure

juengere Partei (Junior Partei)—in einer Interferenz der Ansmelder, der den spaeter festgesetzten Termin fuer das Inkrafttreten des Einreichungsdatums hat

K

know-how—practical information or knowledge permitting practice of a technology

savoir-faire—les renseignements ou les connaissances pratiques qui permettent la pratique d'une technologie

know-how (gewusst wie . .)—Informationen und Sachkenntnis, die die Ausuebung technischen Koennens in der Praxis erlauben

L

laches—neglect, failure or unreasonable delay in acting to enforce a right; enforcement of the right is barred to prevent inequitable treatment of the party asserting laches

laches—négligence, manque ou délai déraisonnable en agissant pour faire valoir un droit; le droit est défendu pour empêcher le traitement inéquitable de la partie qui présente des "laches"

Verzug—Vernachlaessigung, Versaeumnis oder unbillige Verzoegerung in der Durchsetzung eines Rechts; es ist untersagt Durchsetzung des Rechts zur Verhinderung ungerechter Behandlung der Partei, die Verzug geltend macht, anzuwenden

lapse of patent—termination of patent term by reason of failure to pay the balance of the issue fee due within three months of the date of the patent (860 OG 2)

déchéance du brevet—la terminaison de la durée du brevet parce qu'on a manqué de payer le solde de la taxe de délivrance dans le délai de trois mois de la date du brevet (860 OG 2)

Verfallen des Patents—Beendigung der Laufzeit des Patents durch Versaeumnis die Restsumme der Erteilungsgebuehr, die innerhalb von drei Monaten von Datum des Patents faellig ist, zu bezahlen (860 O. G. 2)

legal representative—an entity that has been designated to apply for a patent on behalf of a legally incapacitated (dead, incompetent, etc.) inventor

représentant légal—une entité qu'on a désignée pour demander un brevet au nom d'un inventeur légalement incapacité (mort, incompétent, etc.)

gesetzlicher Vertreter—eine juristische Person, die ernannt worden ist im Namen eines gesetzlich in der Verfuegung beschraenkten (tot, inkompetent, usw.) Erfinders ein Patent anzumelden

letters patent—the grant to an inventor of the right to exclude others, for a limited time, from using his invention. Also refers to the certificate of the patent grant

"letters patent"—accorder à un inventeur le droit d'exclure autrui, pendant un terme limité, d'utiliser son invention. Cela fait aussi référence au certificat de la délivrance du brevet.

Patenturkunde—einem Erfinder das Recht erteilen andere auf begrenzte Zeit vom Gebrauch seiner Erfindung auszuschliessen. Weist auch auf den Patenterteilungs-Schein (Patentverleihungs-Schein) hin.

license—the grant of a right to practice an invention on terms specified

licence—la cession d'un droit d'utiliser une invention aux conditions spécifiées

Lizenz—die Erteilung eines Rechts eine Erfindung zu bestimmten Bedingungen praktisch auszufuehren

license for foreign filing—see foreign filing authorization

licence de déposer à l'étranger—void autorisation de déposer à l'étranger

Lizenz zur Einreichung im Ausland—vgl. Genehmigung ein Patent im Ausland anzumelden

licensee—party to whom a license is granted

licencié—une partie à qui on a concédé une licence

Lizenztraeger—die Partei, der eine Lizenz erteilt wird

licensor—applicant or patentee who grants a license

concédant—un demandeur ou un breveté qui accorde la licence

Lizenzgeber—Anmelder oder Patentinhaber, der eine Lizenz erteilt

linking claim—a claim that is inseparable from claims to two or more properly divisible inventions, such as a genus claim linking species claims

revendication liante—une revendication qui est inséparable des revendications à plusieurs inventions convenablement divisibles, comme une revendication générique qui lie des revendications des variantes

verkettender Anspruch—ein Anspruch, der untrennbar von Anspruechen auf zwei oder mehr richtig teilbare Erfindungen ist, wie zum Beispiel ein Art-(genus) Anspruch, der Gattungs-Ansprueche zusammenkettet

litigation—see patent litigation

litigie—voir litigie des brevets

Prozess—vgl. Patentprozess

M

machine—a class of patentable subject matter covering a combination of elements that cooperate to perform a function

machine—une classe de matière brevetable qui couvre une combinaison d'éléments qui coopérent pour accomplir une fonction

Vorrichtung (Maschine)—eine Klasse von patentfaehigen Gegenstaenden, die eine Verbindung von Elementen umfassen, die zur Ausfuehrung einer Funktion zusammenarbeiten

Manual of Classification—a book listing all classes and subclasses in the United States patent classification system, a subject matter index, and related information

Manuel de Classification—un livre qui enregistre toutes les classes et toutes les sous-classes du système des Etats-Unis de classification des brevets, un index de matière, et des renseignements relatifs

Klassifizierungs-Handbuch—ein Buch, das alle Gruppen und Untergruppen im Patent-Klassifizierungssystem der Vereinigten Staaten aufzaehlt, ein Sachverzeichnis und verwandte Informationen

Manual of Patent Examining Procedure—a detailed reference work on patent examining practice and procedure, primarily for use by the Examining Corps of the Patent Office

Manuel de la Procédure d'Examiner les Brevets—un ouvrage à consulter détaillé, au sujet de la pratique et du procédé d'examiner les brevets, principalement employé par le Corps d'Examinateurs de l'Office des Brevets

Patentpruefverfahren-Handbuch—ein ausfuehrliches Nachschlagewerk ueber die Praxis und das Verfahren bei Patentpruefungen, hauptsaechlich zum Gebrauch des Prueferstabs des Patentamts

manufacture—a class of patentable subject matter providing a physical tangible thing

> **fabrication**—une classe de matière brevetable rendant une chose physìque et tangible

> **Herstellungsweise**—eine Klasse von patentfaehigen Gegenstaenden, die ein koerperlich greifbares Objekt liefern

marking—applying the patent number. To recover damages for infringement, the patentee must mark the patented article or its package with the word "Patent" (or "Pat.") and the number, or must prove that the infringer continued to infringe after being otherwise notified of the infringement.

> **marquer**—mettre le numéro du brevet. Pour réparer les dommages de la contrefaçon, le breveté doit marquer ou l'article ou son paquet du mot "Brevet" (ou "Pat.") et du numéro, ou doit prouver que le contrefacteur continuait à contrefaire après avoir été autrement notifié de la contrefaçon.

> **kennzeichnen**—mit einer Patentnummer versehen. Um Schadenersatz fuer Patentverletzung zu erlangen, muss der Patentinhaber den patentierten Artikel oder dessen Verpackung mit dem Wort "Patent" (oder "Pat.") und der Nummer kennzeichnen, oder er muss beweisen, dass der Patentverletzer die Verletzung fortsetzte nachdem er anderweitig von der Patentverletzung in Kenntnis gesetzt war.

Markush claim—a claim of the form ". . wherein ______ is a material selected from the group consisting of ______, ______ and ______" or ". . wherein ______ is ______, ______ or ______", used as a generic expression covering a group of two or more materials where there is no generic name for the group, permitted where the materials belong to a recognized physical, chemical or art-recognized class, or possess at least one property in common that is mainly responsible for their function in the claimed relationship

revendication Markush—une revendication de la forme ". . en quoi________est un matérial choisi du groupe qui consiste de________, ________et________", or ". . en quoi ________est________, ________ou________", employé comme une expression générique couvrant un groupe de plusieurs matériels où il n'y a pas de nom générique pour le groupe, permis où les matériels appartiennent à une classe physique, chimique, ou technique reconnue, ou possèdent en commun au moins une qualité qui est principalement responsible de leur fonction dans la relation revendiquée

Markush Anspruch—ein Anspruch in der Art ". . worin ________ist ein Stoff ausgewaehlt aus der Gruppe bestehen aus________, ________und________"oder ". . worin ________ist________, ________oder________", als Gattungen umfassender Ausdruck benutzt fuer eine Gruppe von zwei oder mehr Stoffen, fuer die es keinen Gattungen umfassenden Gruppenamen gibt; dies est erlaubt, sofern die Stoffe zu einer anerkannten physikalischen, chemischen, oder einer technisch anerkannten Klasse gehoeren, oder wenigstens eine gemeinsame Eigenschaft haben, die hauptsaechlich fuer ihre Funktion in dem mit Anspruch belegten Verhaeltnis verantwortlich ist

means—a force applied; a mode of operation; a specific treatment of specific objects; a part accomplishing a mechanical result

moyen—une force appliquée; une façon d'opérer; un traitement spécifique des objets spécifiques; une partie qui accomplit un résultat mécanique

Mittel—angewandte Kraft; eine Art der Betriebsmethode; besondere Behandlung besonderer Objekte; ein Teil, der ein mechanisches Ergebnis erzielt

mechanical skill—the skill of a technician in his own field. A negative test for invention, in the holding that the abilities of an ordinary mechanic are not at the level of invention.

habileté mécanique—l'habileté d'un technicien dans son propre domaine. Une épreuve négative d'invention, dans la croyance que les habiletés d'un technicien moyen ne soient pas au niveau d'invention.

technische Geschicklichkeit—die Geschicklichkeit eines Technikers auf seinem Fachgebiet. Eine negative Probe auf's Exempel—der Erfindung naemlich: die feste Annahme, dass die Fertigkeit eines Durchschnittsfachmanns nicht an das Niveau von Erfindungen heranreicht.

mental steps—steps in a process that can be performed in the human mind, such as calculating, comparing, determining, counting, observing, recording and computing

démarches mentales—les démarches dans un procédé qu'on peut exécuter dans l'esprit humain, tel que calculer, comparer, déterminer, compter, observer, enregistrer et supputer

geistige Schritte—Schritte in einem Vorgang, die im menschlichen Verstand geleistet werden koennen, wie zum Beispiel, rechnen, vergleichen, bestimmen, zaehlen, beobachten, registrieren und auswerten

method—see process

méthode—voir procédé

Methode—vgl. Verfahren

minimum issue fee—sum due from applicant, his assignee, attorney, or a party of record interest, payable within three months after the date of notice of allowance, consisting of $100. plus $10. for the first page of printed specification plus $2. for each sheet of drawing. Any balance of the issue fee due, in payment for any additional pages of printed specification, is billed by attachment to the patent grant, and must be paid within three months of the date of the patent to avoid lapse of the patent. (860 OG 2)

taxe minimale de délivrance—la somme dûe du demandeur, son concessionnaire, son avocat, ou une partie d'intérêt enregistrée, payable dans le délai de trois mois après la date de la notification d'acceptation, consistante de $100. plus $10 pou la première page de spécification imprimée plus $2. pour chaque feuille de dessin. Tout solde de la taxe de délivrance dûe, comme paiement pour des pages additionnelles de spécification imprimée, est attachée à l'octroi du brevet, et on doit le payer dans le délai de trois mois de la date du brevet pour éviter la déchéance du brevet. (860 OG 2)

Minimum-Erteilungsgebuehr—Summe, die vom Anmelder, seinem Rechtsnachfolger, Anwalt, oder einer Partei, deren Interesse aktenkundig ist, faellig ist; zahlbar innerhalb von drei Monaten vom Datum der Zulassungs-Benachrichtigung, bestehend aus $100. plus $10. fuer die erste Seite gedruckter Beschreibung (specification) plus $2. fuer jeden Bogen mit Zeichnungen. Jede faellige Restsumme der Erteilungsgebuehr—zur Bezahlung von zusaetzlichen Seiten gedruckter Beschreibung (specification)—wird auf einer Beilage zur Patenterteilung berechnet, und ist innerhalb von drei Monaten vom Datum des Patents zu zahlen, um Verfallen des Patents zu vermeiden. (860 O. G. 2)

misuse of patent—employment of a patent by a patent owner to control matters outside the scope of the rights in the patent, providing a defense against a claim of infringement of the patent

abus de brevet—l'utilisation d'un brevet par un titulaire de brevet pour contrôler des matières hors de l'étendue des droits dans le brevet, rendant une défense contre une revendication de contrefaçon du brevet

Missbrauch eines Patents—Verwendung eines Patents durch einen Patentinhaber um dinge ausserhalb des Bereichs der Rechte in dem Patent zu lenken und eine Verteidigung gegen einen Patentverletzungs-Anspruch zu schaffen

model—a structural embodiment of the invention; not received by the Patent Office unless specifically called for by the Commissioner (R. 91)

modèle—une incarnation structurale de l'invention; pas recu de l'Office des Brevets à moins que le Commissaire le demande spécifiquement (R. 91)

Modell—eine strukturelle Darstellung, die dem Patentamt—wenn vom Commissioner nicht besonders angefordert—nicht uebergeben wird (R. 91)

motion—an application to obtain an order directing a particular action. Motions may be made in interferences to dissolve, to amend, to add another application, and to shift the burden of proof. (R.231-237)

motion—une demande pour obtenir une ordonnance dirgeante une action spécifique. On peut faire des motions dans une "interférence" pour désoudre, pour amender, pour ajouter une autre demande, et pour transférer la charge de la preuve. (R. 231-237)

Antrag—ein Gesuch um Erhalt einer Verfuegung, die eine bestimmte Handlung anordnet. Solche Antraege koennen in Interferenz Faellen zur Aufloesung, zur Verbesserung, zur Hinzufuegung einer weiteren Anmeldung und zur Verschiebung der Beweislast gemacht werden. (R. 231-237)

multiple dependent claim—a claim that refers back to any of the preceding independent or dependent claims in the alternative. (MPEP Change Notice 17-2 of 4 June 1968) Discontinued—cf. 864 O. G. 323, 8 July 1969.

revendication multiple dépendante—une revendication qui fait référence à n'importe quelle revendication antérieure, indépendante ou dépendante, dans l'alternatif. (MPEP Change Notice 17-2 du 4 juin 1968) Discontinuer—cf. 864 O. G. 323, 8 July 1969.

mehrfacher Unteranspruch—ein Anspruch, der auf die vorhergehenden unabhaengigen oder abhaengigen Ansprueche in der Alternative zurueckverweist. (MPEP Change Notice 17-2 of 4 June 1968). Unterbrechen—864 O. G. 323, 8 July 1969.

multiplicity of claims—claims that are held to be unreasonable in number, in view of the nature and scope of the invention, because the number of claims presented tend to obscure the invention

multiplicité de revendications—des revendications qui sont jugées d'être d'un nombre extravagant, en vue de la nature et de l'étendue de l'invention, parce que le nombre de revendications présentées ont la tendance d'obscurcir l'invention

Vielheit von Anspruechen—Ansprueche, deren Anzahl im Hinblick auf die Natur und den Umfang der Erfindung fuer uebermaessig gehalten wird, da die Anzahl der vorgebrachten Ansprueche dazu fuehrt die Erfindung unklar erscheinen zu lassen

N

name used in trade—a nonproprietary name by which a product is known in an art; use of a name used in trade in a patent application to define a product is permitted if its meaning is established by an accompanying definition that is precise and definite, and the meaning is known and defined in the literature in the United States

nom employé dans la commerce—un nom qui n'est pas possédé, par lequel un produit industriel est connu dans une technique; on permet l'emploi d'un nom employé en commerce dans une demande de brevet pour définir un produit industriel si sa signification est établie par une définition accompagnante qui est précise et claire, et si la signification est connue et définie dans la littérature aux Etats-Unis

handelsueblicher Name—ein nicht gesetzlich—(patentlich) geschuetzter Name, unter welchem ein Erzeugnis auf einem Fachgebiet bekannt ist; es ist gestattet einen handelsueblichen Namen zur genauen Bezeichnung eines Erzeugnisses zu benutzen, wenn seine Bedeutung durch eine beiliegende, genaue und deutliche Definition festgelegt ist, und die Bedeutung in der Literatur in den Vereinigten Staaten bekannt und genau umrissen ist

negative limitation—a word or phrase in a claim that is vague and indefinite because it recites what is not present in the claim

limitation négative—un mot ou une phrase, dans une revendication, qui est vague et indéfinie parce qu'elle récite quelque chose qui n'est pas présent dans la revendication

negative Begrenzung—ein Wort oder Satz in einem Anspruch, der verschwommen und unbestimmt ist, da etwas ausgesagt wird, was in dem Anspruch nicht vorhanden ist

new matter—a disclosure not set forth in the specification, or drawings or claims of the original application. An addition to the original disclosure, and therefore not admissible by amendment or by reissue application. (R. 118, Sec. 132, 251)

nouvelle matière—une divulgation qui n'est pas présentée dans la spécification, ou dans les dessins, ou dans les revendications de la demande originale. Une addition à la divulgation originale, et ainsi pas admissible par amendement ou par "reissue" demande. (R. 118, Sec. 132, 251)

neue Materie—eine Offenbarung, die in der Beschreibung (specification) oder den Zeichnungen oder Anspruechen der urspruenglichen Anmeldung nicht gemacht wurde. Eine Hinzufuegung zu der urspruenglichen Offenbarung und daher durch Berichtigung oder Antrag auf erneute Erteilung nicht zulaessig. (R. 118, Sec. 132, 251)

new use—a class of patentable subject matter providing a process based on an inventive use of a known process, machine, manufacture, composition of matter or material Sec. 100)

application nouvelle—une classe de matière brevetable fournissant un procédé basé sur une utilisation inventive d'un procédé, sur une machine, sur une fabrication, et sur la composition connus de matière ou de matériel (Sec. 100)

neue Anwendung—eine Klasse patentfaehiger Gegenstaende, die ein auf dem erfinderischen Gebrauch eines bekannten Verfahrens, einer Vorrichtung, Herstellungsweise, Zusammensetzung von Gegenstaenden oder eines Stoffes, beruhendes Verfahren hervorbringen (Sec. 100)

non-essential material—see incorporation by reference

matière non-essentielle—voir incorporation par renvoi

nicht-wesentliches Material—vgl. Eingliederung durch Hinweis

non-exclusive license—a license under a patent that is limited as to duration or geographical or other scope, and thus does not prohibit the granting of rights to others under the patent

licence non-exclusive—une licence d'un brevet qui est limitée de la durée ou de l'étendue géographique ou autre, et ainsi ne défend pas la cession des droits à autrui sous le brevet

nicht-ausschliessliche Lizenz—Lizenz unter einem Patent, das in seiner Laufzeit in geographischem oder anderm Umfang begrenzt ist und daher die Erteilung von Rechten an andere unter dem Patent nicht verbietet

non-statutory subject matter—inventions or discoveries that are not patentable under Sec. 101, such as the mere arrangement of printed matter, a thing occurring in nature that is substantially unaltered, a method of doing business, or a scientific principle divorced from any tangible structure (MPEP 706.03(a))

matière non statutaire—des inventions ou des découvertes qui ne sont pas brevetables sous Sec. 101, tel que le simple arrangement de matière imprimée, une chose qui arrive dans la nature qui est vraiment sans changement, une méthode de faire les affaires, ou une principe scientifique qui est séparée d'aucune structure tangible (MPEP 706.03(a))

nicht-rechtsverbindliche Gegenstaende—Erfindungen oder Entdeckungen, die unter Sec. 101 nicht patentfaehig sind, wie zum Beispiel, die blosse Anordnung von Gedrucktem, etwas in der Natur Vorkommendes und im Wesentlichen unveraendert Bleibendes, eine Methode der Geschaeftsfuehrung, oder ein von jeder greifbaren Struktur entfernter wissenschaftlicher Grundbegriff (MPEP 706.03(a))

notice and reasons of appeal—notice to the Commissioner of the grounds of appeal to the Court of Customs and Patent Appeals, to be filed within sixty days from the date of the decision appealed from, or within thirty days after the date of a decision by the Board of Appeals or the Board of Patent Interferences on a petition for rehearing or reconsideration (R. 302, 304)

notification et raisons d'appel—la notification au Commissaire des raisons d'appel à la "Court of Customs and Patent Appeals", qui doit être déposée dans le délai de soixante jours de la date de la décision appelée, ou dans le délai de trente jours après la date d'une décision de la Commission d'Appel ou la Commission des "Interférences" des Brevets sur un pétition pour une nouvelle considération (R. 302, 304)

Beschwerdeschriftsatz und Berufungsbegruendung—Beschwerdeschrift an den Commissioner ueber die Gruende fuer eine Berufung an den Court of Customs and Patent Appeals, einzureichen innerhalb von sechzig Tagen vom Datum der angefochtenen Entscheidung des Board of Appeals oder des Board of Patent Interferences ueber ein Gesuch zur Wiederverhandlung oder Wiederwaegung (R. 302, 304)

notice of allowability—advice by the Patent Office that the applicant is entitled to a patent, but grant of a patent will be postponed because the application contains matter that will not be published to protect national security

notification de "allowability"—conseil de l'Office des Brevets que le demandeur a droit à un brevet, mais que l'octroi d'un brevet sera remis parce que la demande contient de la matière qu'on ne publiera pas pour protéger la sécurité nationale

Zulaessigkeits-Benachrichtigung—Mitteilung des Patentamts, dass der Anmelder zu einem Patent berechtigt ist, aber die Erteilung des Patents aufgeschoben wird, da die Anmeldung Material enthaelt, das zum Schutz der nationalen Sicherheit nicht veroeffentlicht wird

notice of allowance—advice by the Patent Office that the applicant is entitled to a patent, calling for the payment of the issue fee within three months from the date of the advice (R. 311)

notification d'acceptation—conseil de l'Office des Brevets que le demandeur a droit à un brevet, demandant le paiement de la taxe de délivrance dans le délai de trois mois de la date du conseil (R. 311)

Zulassungs-Benachrichtigung (Annahme-Nachricht) – Benachrichtigung durch das Patentamt, dass der Anmelder zu einem Patent berechtigt und die Erteilungsgebuehr innerhalb von drei Monaten vom Benachrichtigungsdatum zu entrichten ist (R. 311)

notice of infringement—written communication from a patent owner asserting that specified claims of a patent are being infringed, and demanding that such infringement cease

notification de contrefaçon—un communiqué écrit par le titulaire d'un brevet prétendant qu'on est en train de contrefaire des revendications spécifiees d'un brevet, et demandant qu'on cesse une telle contrefaçon

Beschwerdeschrift ueber Verletzung—schriftliche Mitteilung eines Patentinhabers mit der Behauptung, dass aufgefuehrte Ansprueche eines Patents verletzt werden und mit der Forderung auf Einstellung solcher Verletzung

novel—not present in the art

nouveau—pas présent dans la technique

neuartig—in dem Fachgebiet nicht vorhanden

novelty search—see search

recherche de la nouveauté—voir recherche

Untersuchung auf Neuheit—vgl. Untersuchung

O

oath—sworn or affirmed statement of the applicant that he has complied with the provisions of Sec. 101 and Sec. 102 (R. 65)

serment—une déclaration jurée ou affirmée du demandeur qu'il a accédé aux stipulations de Sec. 101 et Sec. 102 (R. 65)

Eid—beschworene oder bekraeftigte Erklaerung des Patentanmelders, dass er die Bedingungen unter Sec. 101 und Sec. 102 erfuellt hat (R. 65)

objection—criticism by examiner directed to matters of form, rather than substance, in the application (MPEP 706.01). To overrule the examiner, applicant may petition the Commissioner; an objection is not appealable.

objection—une critique par l'examinateur au sujet de la forme, plutôt que de l'essentiel, de la demande (MPEP 706.01). Pour maîtriser l'examinateur, le demandeur peut pétitionner le Commissaire; une objection n'est pas sujet à appel

Einwand—Kritik des Pruefers, die auf die Form und nicht den Inhalt der Anmeldung gerichtet ist (MPEP 706.01). Der Anmelder kann beim Commissioner einkommen die Meinung des Pruefers beiseitezusetzen; gegen einen Einwand kann keine Berufung eingelegt werden

obvious—see definition of unobviousness

évident—voir la définition de "unobviousness"

selbstverstaendlich—zur Erklaerung vgl. Nicht-Selbstversstaendlichkeit

office action—a paper from the examiner setting forth the Patent Office position on the application, enumerating rejections and/or objections

action d'office—un document de l'examinateur déclarant l'attitude de l'Office des Brevets au sujet de la demande, énumérant les rejets et/ou les objections

Behandlung durch das Amt—ein Schriftsatz des Pruefers mit der Stellungnahme des Patentamts zu der Anmeldung, unter Aufzaehlung von Zurueckweisungen und/oder Einwaenden

Official Gazette—the official weekly publication of the Patent Office that contains an abstract of the disclosure of each patent issued that day; information on patents, trademarks, designs and plant patents; and orders, notices, suits filed and selected court decisions in the patent and trademark fields

Gazette Officielle—la publication officielle hebdomadaire de l'Office des Brevets qui contient une abstraction de la divulgation de chaque brevet délivré ce jour-là; des renseignements au sujet des brevets, marques de fabrique, brevets de dessin et de plante; et des ordonnances, des notifications, des litigies déposées et des décisions choisies du tribunal dans le domaine des brevets et des marques de fabrique

Amtsblatt—woechentliche, amtliche Veroeffentlichung des Patentamts mit einem Auszug aus der Offenbarung jeden, an diesem Tag erteilten Patents; mit Information ueber Patente, Warenzeichen, Geschmacksmuster- und Pflanzenpatente; mit Verfuegungen, Amtsbescheiden, eingereichten Klagen und ausgewaehlten Gerichtsentscheiden auf dem Patent- und Warenzeichengebiet

one—in claim interpretation, "one" is read to mean "at least one"

un—dans l'interprétation des revendications, "un" veut dire "au moins un"

ein (eine, eins)—bei der Auslegung von Patentanspruechen ist "ein (eine, eins)" als "mindestens ein (eine, eins)" aufzufassen

or—see alternative expression; Markush claim

ou—voir expression alternative; revendication "Markush"

oder—vgl. alternative Ausdrucksweise; Markush Anspruch

ordinary skill in the art—see mechanical skill

habileté moyenne dans la technique—voir habileté mécanique

uebliche Fachkenntnis—vgl. technische Geschicklichkeit

P

paper patent—a patent whose teaching has not been practised commercially

"paper" brevet—un brevet dont on n'a pas pratiqué commercialement l'enseignement

Papier-Patent—ein Patent, dessen "lehren" nicht handelsmaessig ausgefuehrt worden sind

parent application—the original application on which a continuation or continuation-in-part application is based

"parent" demande—la demande originale sur laquelle on base une demande de continuation ou de continuation-en-partie

Stamm-Anmeldung—die urspruengliche Anmeldung eines Patents, worauf eine Fortfuehrungs- oder Teilfortfuehrungs-Anmeldung begruendet ist

Paris Convention—the International Convention for Protection of Industrial Property

Convention de Paris—la Convention Internationale pour la Protection de la Propriété Industrielle

Pariser Verbandsuebereinkunft—die internationale Verbandsuebereinkunft zum Schutz gewerblichen Eigentums

patent—a grant by the Government of the right to prevent others from making, using or selling the invention defined in the claims of the patent

brevet—octroi par le Gouvernement du droit d'empêcher à autrui de fabriquer, d'employer ou de vendre l'invention définie dans les revendications du brevet

Patent—ein von der Regierung erteiltes Recht andere zu verhindern die in den Patentanspruechen definierte Erfindung herzustellen, zu benutzen oder zu verkaufen

patent agent—a person, not an attorney at law, who has the qualifications required for and who has been admitted to practice before the Patent Office (R. 341)

agent de brevets—une personne, pas un avoué, qui a les qualifications exigées pour la pratique et qu'on a admise à la pratique aupres de l'Office des Brevets (R. 341)

Patent-Vertreter—eine Person—kein Rechtsanwalt—die die Bedingungen erfuellt und die zugelassen ist vor dem Patentamt zu praktizieren (R. 341)

patent applied for—notice by an applicant that an application for patent on an invention has been filed in the Patent Office

brevet demandé—notification par un demandeur qu'une demande de brevet pour une invention a été déposée à l'Office des Brevets

Patent angemeldet—Mitteilung eines Anmelders, dass eine Patentanmeldung an einer Erfindung beim Patentamt eingereicht worden ist

patent attorney—a member of a Federal or State bar who has the qualifications required for and who has been admitted to practice before the Patent Office (R. 341). Includes persons not a member of any bar who were admitted as "registered patent attorneys" before 1931.

avocat de brevets—un membre d'un barreau Fédéral ou d'état qui a les qualifications exigées pour la pratique et qu'on a admis à la pratique auprès de l'Office des Brevets (R. 341). Cela comprend des personnes qui n'appartiennent à aucun barreau, qui etaient admises comme "avocats enregistrés de brevets" avant 1931.

Patent-Anwalt—Mitglied einer Bundes- oder Landesanwaltskammer, der den Bedingungen entspricht und beim Patentamt zugelassen ist (R. 341). Dies schliesst Personen ein, die nicht Mitglieder einer Anwaltskammer sind, die vor 1931 als "eingetragene Patent-Anwaelte" zugelassen wurden.

patent law—the statutes covering patents (found principally in Title 35 of the US Code) and court and administrative agency interpretations of such statutes

loi de brevets—les statuts au sujet des brevets (trouvés principalement dans Titre 35 du Code des Etats-Unis) et les interprétations juridiques et administratives de tels statuts

Patent-Gesetz—die Statuten, die auf Patente Bezug nehmen (hauptsaechlich im Titel 35 des US Code) und die Auslegungen dieser Statuten durch Gerichte und Verwaltungsbehoerden

patent litigation—a civil legal action brought in a Federal court by a patent owner against an alleged infringer to enjoin further infringement of the patent and/or for compensation for the alleged infringement; an action brought to have a patent declared invalid and/or not infringed by the claimant

litigie de brevet—une action civile et légale, présentée dans un tribunal Fédéral par un titulaire de brevet contre un contrefacteur allégué pour enjoindre la contrefaçon continuée du brevet et/ou pour la restitution dûe à cause de la contrefaçon alléguée; une action présentée par le demandeur pour faire déclarer invalide et/ou pas contrefait un brevet

Patent-Prozess—eine zivilrechtliche Klage, die von einem Patentinhaber gegen einen angeblichen Verletzer bei einem Bundesgericht erhoben wird, um von weiterer Patentverletzung abzuhalten und/oder auf Entschaedigung fuer die angebliche Verletzung; eine Klage, die erhoben wird um ein Patent fuer ungueltig und/oder als durch den Klaeger nicht verletzt erklaeren zu lassen

patent pending—see patent applied for

brevet pendant—voir brevet demandé

Patent anhaengig—vgl. Patent angemeldet

patentability search—see search

recherche de brevetabilité—voir recherche

Patentfaehigkeits-Untersuchung—vgl. Untersuchung

patentable invention—a new, useful and unobvious process, machine, manufacture or composition of matter, or improvement thereof

invention brevetable—un procédé, une machine, la fabrication ou la composition de matière, ou le perfectionnement de cela, qui est nouveau, utile et non évident

patentfaehige Erfindung—ein neues, nuetzliches und nichtselbstverstaendliches Verfahren, Vorrichtung, Herstellungsweise oder Zusammensetzung von Gegenstaenden, oder eine Verbesserung davon

petition—the introductory paragraph of an application, requesting the grant of a patent by the Commissioner of Patents

pétition—le paragraphe introductif d'une demande, demandant la délivrance d'un brevet par le Commissaire des Brevets

Gesuch—der einleitende Abschnitt einer Anmeldung um die Erteilung eines Patents durch den Commissioner of Patents

petition to Commissioner—request for review of objections or requirements of an examiner as to matters of form or compliance with the Rules of Practice

pétition au Commissaire—la demande pour une revue des objections ou des exigences d'un examinateur au sujet de la forme ou de l'acquiescement aux Règles de la Pratique

Eingabe beim Commissioner—Ersuchen um Nachpruefung der Einwaende oder Forderungen eines Pruefers mit Hinsicht auf Form oder Uebereinstimmung mit den Rules of Practice (Ausfuehrungsbestimmungen)

pioneer patent—the first patent in a field, claiming means or a function never before disclosed. It is interpreted liberally and is entitled to a broad range of equivalents.

brevet pionnier—le premier brevet d'un domaine, revendiquant les moyensou une fonction qu'on n'a jamais encore divulgée. On l'interprète libéralement et a droit à une large étendue d'équivalents.

Pionier-Patent—das erste Patent auf einem Gebiet, das niemals vorher offenbarte Mittel oder eine Funktion mit Anspruch belegt. Es wird grosszuegig ausgelegt und ist zu einem weiten Bereich von Aequivalenzen berechtigt.

plant patent—patent for the invention or discovery and asexual reproduction of a distinct and new variety of plant (including cultivated sports, mutants, hybrids and newly found seedlings, other than a tuber propagated plant or a plant found in an uncultivated state). (Sec. 161–164, R. 161–167)

brevet de plantes—un brevet pour l'invention ou la découverte et pour la réproduction asexuelle d'une espèce de plante nouvelle et distincte (y inclus les variations des burgeons, les mutations, les hybrides cultivés, et les semis nouvellement trouvés, pas une plante tuberculeuse propagée ou une plante trouvée dans un état incultivé) (Sec. 161–164, R. 161–167)

Pflanzen-Patent—Patent fuer die Erfindung oder Entdeckung und Vermehrung ohne Befruchtung einer bestimmten und neuen Pflanzensorte (einschliesslich von Kulturabarten, Mutationen, Hybriden und neugefundenen Saemlingen, ausser einem Knollengewaechs oder einer in einem unkultivierten Stadium gefundenen Pflanze) (Sec. 161–164, R. 161–167)

plant patent series—the separate series of numbers for plant patents preceded by the letters "P.P." (MPEP 901.04)

série de brevets de plantes—la serie distincte de numéros pour les brevets de plantes précédée des lettres "P.P." (MPEP 901.04)

Pflanzen-Patentserie—die besondere Serie von Nummern fuer Pflanzen-Patente, der die Buchstaben "P.P." voranstehen (MPEP 901.04)

plurality—in a claim, "plurality" means two or more elements

pluralite—dans une revendication pluralité veut dire deux éléments ou plus que deux éléments

Vielheit—in einem Anspruch bedeutet "Vielheit" zwei oder mehr Elemente

positive inclusion of elements—recital in a claim, in a positive word or phrase, of every feature on which the claim depends for patentability

inclusion positive d'éléments—le récit dans une revendication, dans un mot ou une phrase positive, de chaque trait dont dépend la revendication pour être brevetable

ausdrueecklicher Einschluss von Elementen—Aufzaehlung mittels eines ausdruecklichen Wortes oder Satzes jeder Eigenschaft in einem Anspruch, von der die Patentfaehigkeit des Anspruche abhaengt

post office address—the address at which the applicant customarily receives his mail (MPEP 605.03)

adresse—l'adresse où le demandeur reçoit d'ordinaire son courrier (MPEP 605.03)

Postanschrift—die Adresse, unter welcher der Anmelder ueblicherweise seine Post empfaengt (MPEP 605.03)

power of attorney–the instrument authorizing one person to act for another person

pouvoir d'avocat–l'instrument qui autorise une personne d'agir pour une autre personne

Vollmacht–das Instrument, das eine Person ermaechtigt fuer eine andere Person zu handeln

practising an invention–making, using or selling an invention

mise en pratique d'une invention–la fabrication, l'utilisation ou la vente d'une invention

Erfindung praktisch ausfuehren–Herstellung, Benutzung oder Verkauf einer Erfindung

preferably–used to indicate that the word to which it relates is optional and not essential, or not necessarily effective in changing the result to a degree constituting a difference of kind

préférablement–employé pour indiquer que le mot auquel cela rapporte est facultatif et non essentiel, ou n'est pas nécessairement effectif à altérer le résultat à un degré constituant une différence de type

vorzugsweise–benutzt um anzuzeigen, dass das Wort, worauf es sich bezieht, beliebig gewaehlt und nicht wesentlich ist oder nicht notwendigerweise das Ergebnis in einem Mass, das einen Unterschied in der Art ausmachen wuerde, verandert

preliminary injunction—a restraining order issued by a court, requiring a litigant to desist from performing specified acts until the court can hear evidence and determine whether he has the right to perform such acts

injonction préliminaire—ordonnance conservatoire délivrée par un tribunal, exigeant qu'un litigant cesse d'exécuter des actes spécifiés jusqu'à ce que le tribunal puisse entendre les preuves et déterminer s'il a droit à exécuter de tels actes

einstweilige Verfuegung—eine gerichtliche Verhinderungs-Verfuegung, die von einer prozessierenden Partei verlangt von der Ausfuehrung bestimmter Handlungen Abstand zu nehmen, bis das Gericht Beweismaterial aufnehmen und bestimmen kann, ob die Partei das Recht hat solche Handlungen auszufuehren

preliminary search—an examination of patents, usually made in the Patent Office by a private searcher at the expense of the inventor, to determine whether the invention is anticipated by prior art

recherche préliminaire—un examen des brevets, fait d'ordinaire à l'Office des Brevets par un chercheur privé au dépens de l'inventeur, pour déterminer si l'invention est antériorisée par une technique antérieure

Voruntersuchung—eine Ueberpruefung von Patenten, gewoehnlich im Patentamt durch eine Privatperson auf Kosten des Erfinders vorgenommen, um festzustellen, ob die Erfindung durch den Stand der Technik vorweggenommen ist

preliminary statement—as to each count of an interference, on an invention made in the United States, a statement of the facts and acts that establish the date on which the first drawing of the invention was made (or a statement that no drawing was made prior to filing), the date on which the first written description of the invention was made (or a statement that no written description was made prior to filing), the date of first disclosure of the invention to another (or a statement that there was no disclosure prior to filing), the date and nature of the first provable acts that would establish conception of the invention (or a statement that there were no such acts), the date of actual reduction to practice of the invention (or a statement that there was no actual reduction to practice prior to filing), and the date when active exercise of reasonable diligence toward reducing the invention to practice began. If a party relies solely on a prior domestic or foreign application, the preliminary statement may so state, and need not be signed. (R. 216)

When the invention was made abroad, the preliminary statement should state when the invention was introduced into the United States, giving the circumstances and dates of activity in the United States. (R. 217)

déclaration préliminaire—pour chaque "count" d'une "interférence", au sujet d'une invention créée aux Etats-Unis, une déclaration des faits et des actes qui établissent la date où on a fait le premier dessin de l'invention (ou une déclaration qu'on n'a fait aucun dessin de l'invention avant de déposer), la date où on a fait la première description écrite de l'invention (ou une déclaration qu'on n'a fait aucune description écrite avant de déposer), la date de la première divulgation de l'invention à autrui (ou une déclaration qu'il n'y avait aucune divulgation faite avant de déposer), la date et la nature des premiers actes prouvables qui établiraient la conception de l'invention (ou une déclaration qu'il n'y avait pas de teks actes), la date de la réduction actuelle à la pratique de l'invention (ou une déclaration qu'il n'y avait pas de réduction à la pratique avant de déposer), et la date où il a commencé l'exercice actif pour réduire à la pratique l'invention. Si une partie dépend uniquement d'une demande antérieure des Etats-Unis, ou étrangère, la déclaration préliminaire peut le proclamer et ne doit pas être signée (R. 216).

Quand on a créé l'invention à l'étranger, la déclaration devrait proclamer l'heure où on a introduit l'invention aux Etats-Unis, énumérant les circonstances et les dates de l'activité aux Etats-Unis. (R. 217)

Vorerklaerung—in Bezug auf jeden Klagepunkt in einer Interferenz bei einer in den Vereinigten Staaten gemachten Erfindung: eine Darstellung des Sachverhalts und Verhaltens, die das Datum an dem die erste Zeichnung fuer die Erfindung gemacht wurde, festlegen (oder eine Erklaerung, dass keine Zeichnung vor dem Einreichen gemacht wurde), das Datum an dem die erste schriftliche Schilderung gemacht wurde (oder eine Erklaerung, dass keine schriftliche Schilderung vor dem Einreichen gemacht wurde), das Datum der ersten Offenbarung der Erfindung einem andern gegenueber (oder eine Erklaerung, dass vor dem Einreichen keine Offenbarung gemacht wurde); das Datum und die Beschaffenheit der ersten beweisfaehigen Handlungen, die die gedankliche Erfassung der Erfindung festlegen (oder eine Erklaerung, dass solche Handlungen nicht stattgefunden haben), das Datum des tatsaechlichen Umsetzens der Erfindung in die Praxis (oder eine Erklaerung, dass ein tatsaechliches Umsetzen in die Praxis vor dem Einreichen nicht stattgefunden hat), und das Datum an dem die taetige Aufwendung angemessener Sorgfalt um die Erfindung in die Praxis umzusetzen, began. Wenn eine Partei sich ausschliesslich auf eine fruehere in- oder auslaendische Anmeldung stuetzt, so kann dies in der Vorerklaerung angegeben und braucht nicht unterzeichnet zu werden (R. 216). Falls die Erfindung im Ausland gemacht wurde, sollte in der Vorerklaerung—unter Angabe der Umstaende und Betaetigungsdaten in den Vereinigten Staaten—angegeben werden wann die Erfindung in die Vereinigten Staaten eingefuehrt wurde (R. 217).

presumption of validity—the rebuttable assumption that an issued patent is valid

présomption de validité—la supposition refutable qu'un brevet délivré soit valide

mutmassliche Gueltigkeit—die wiederlegbare Annahme, dass ein erteiltes Patent gueltig ist

primary examiner–the chief of an examining group in the Patent Office

examinateur primaire–le chef d'un groupe d'examinateurs à l'Office des Brevets

Hauptpruefer–der Chef einer Pruefungsgruppe im Patentamt

principal examiner–see primary examiner

examinateur principal–voir examinateur primaire

erster Pruefer–vgl. Hauptpruefer

printed publication–a document that is printed and is made accessible to the public, raising a presumption that the public concerned with the art would know of it

publication imprimée–un document qui est imprimé et rendu disponible au public, présumant que les personnes intéressées à la technique en sachent

gedruckte Veroeffentlichung–ein Dokument, das gedruckt und der Allgemeinheit zugaenglich gemacht worden ist, und daher zu der Annahme berrechtigt, dass das fachlich interessierte Publikum davon weiss

prior art–all subject matter that is pertinent to the novelty of a claimed invention under Sec. 102

état de la technique–toute matière pertinente à la nouveauté de l'invention revendiquée sous Sec. 102

Stand der Technik–Alles aus dem Fachgebiet, das auf die Neuheit einer beanspruchten Erfindung Bezug hat

prior knowledge or use–see anticipation

connaissance ou usage antérieur–voir antériorité

fruehere Kenntnis oder Benutzung–vgl. Vorwegnahme

priority date—see priority right

date d'antériorité—voir droit de priorité

Prioritaetsdatum—vgl. Prioritaetsrecht

priority of invention—determination of the first to invent by determining the first to reduce to practice and, where appropriate, the date of commencement of continuing diligence by one who was first to conceive but last to reduce to practice

priorité d'invention—détermination du premier d'inventer en déterminant le premier de réduire à la pratique et, ou cela importe, la date du commencement de la diligence continuante par l'un qui était le premier de concevoir mais le dernier de réduire à la pratique

Erfindungsprioritaet—Bestimmung des Ersten, der eine Erfindung gemacht hat durch Bestimmung dessen, der sie als Erster in die Praxis umgesetzt hat und—wo es zutrifft—das Datum des Beginns der andauernden Sorgfalt dessen, der zwar die Erfindung als Erster gedanklich erfasst, aber sie als Letzter in die Praxis umgesetzt hat

priority right—the right to promote the effective date of filing an application to the filing date of the first corresponding foreign application, provided the foreign country is a "treaty" country and the filing date in that country is not more than one year prior to the date of filing in the United States

droit de priorité—le droit d'avancer la date d'effet de dépôt d'une demande à la date de dépôt de la première demande correspondante et étrangère, pourvu que le pays étrangèr soit un pays "unioniste" et que la date de dépôt dans ce pays—la ne soit plus qu'un an antérieur à la date de dépôt aux Etats-Unis

Prioritaetsrecht—das Recht den Termin des Inkrafttretens fuer das Einreichen einer Anmeldung auf das Einreichungsdatum der ersten entsprechenden auslaendischen Anmeldung vorzuverlegen, vorausgesetzt der auslaendische Staat ist ein "Vertragsland" und das Einreichungsdatum in diesem Land liegt nicht mehr als ein Jahr vor dem Einreichungsdatum in den Vereinigten Staaten

process—a class of patentable subject matter covering a connected series of steps or operations for accomplishing a physical result

procédé—une classe de matière brevetable au sujet d'une série cohérente de démarches ou d'opération pour accomplir un résultat physique

Verfahren—eine Klasse von patentfaehigen Gegenstaenden, die sich ueber eine zusammenhaengende Reihe von Stufen oder Vorgaengen erstreckt um ein greifbares Ergebnis zu erzielen

prolixity—reciting unimportant details in such a manner as to hide or obscure the invention (MPEP 706.03(g))

prolixité—réciter des détails insignifiants d'une telle façon qu'on cache ou obscurcit l'invention (MPEP 706.03 (g))

Weitschweifigkeit—unwichtige Einzelheiten so vortragen, dass dadurch die Erfindung verborgen oder unverstaendlich gemacht wird (MPEP 706.03 (g))

prosecution—the procedures followed to obtain the grant of a patent

poursuite—les procédés suivis pour obtenir la délivrance d'un brevet

Verfolgung—die Massnahmen, die getroffen werden um ein Patent erteilt zu bekommen

protest—opposition to the grant of a patent, submitted by a member of the public. The Patent Office merely acknowledges and files such papers after referral to the examiner for his information. (R.291)

protestation—l'opposition à la délivrance d'un brevet, soumise par un membre du public. L'Office des Brevets reconnaît simplement et dépose de tels documents après les avoir révélés à l'examinateur pour sa propre référence. (R. 291)

Protest—Widerspruch gegen die Erteilung eines Patents aus der Oeffentlichkeit. Nachdem die Pruefer zu seiner Information darauf hingewiesen wurde, bestaetigt das Patentamt nur den Eingang eines solchen Schriftstuecks und laesst es zu den Akten legen. (R. 291)

Public Search Room—a room in the Patent Office, open to the public, in which copies of all United States patents are filed according to the Patent Office classification. An adjunct Scientific Library, open to the public, contains scientific and technical books and periodicals in various languages, the official journals of foreign patent offices, and copies of foreign patents arranged in numerical order and according to the classification of the country of origin of the patent. An adjunct record room, open to the public, contains the records and files of issued patents, United States patents arranged in numerical order, and a set of the Official Gazette.

Salle Publique de Recherche—une salle à l'Office des Brevets, ouverte au public, où sont déposées selon la classification de l'Office des Brevets, des copies de tous les brevets des Etats-Unis. Une Bibliothèque Scientifique adjointe, ouverte au public, contient des livres et des périodiques scientifiques et techniques en langues diverses, les journaux officiels des offices étrangers des brevets, et des copies des brevets étrangers, organisées en ordre numérique et selon la classiffication du pays d'origine du brevet. Une salle d'archives adjointe, ouverte au public, contient les archives et les dossiers des brevets délivrés, les brevets des Etats-Unis organisés en ordre numérique, et un ensemble de la Gazette Officielle.

oeffentlicher Nachschlag-Saal—ein der Oeffentlichkeit zugaenglicher Raum im Patentamt, wo Kopien aller Patente der Vereinigten Staaten nach ihrer patentamtlichen Klassifizierung eingeordnet sind. Eine zusaetzliche auch der Allgemeinheit zugaengliche wissenschaftliche Bibliothek enthaelt wissenschaftliche und technische Buecher und Zeitschriften in verschiedenen Sprachen, die officiellen Veroeffentlichungen auslaendischer Patentamter und Kopien auslaendischer Patente in zahlenmaessiger Anordnung und gemaess den Klassifizierungen des Ursprungslandes des Patents. Ein zusaetzliches, ebenfalls der Oeffentlichkeit zugaengliches Aktenzimmer enthaelt die Protokolle und Akten von erteilten Patenten, mit den Patenten der Vereinigten Staaten in zahlenmaessiger Ordnung und eine Ausgabe des Amtsblatts.

public use proceedings—based upon a petition supported by affidavits, the hearing and the taking of testimony on the question of whether an invention had been in public use or on sale one year before the filing of the application, or before the date alleged in a preliminary statement or before the date of invention established by a party (R. 292)

procédés de l'utilisation publique—basé sur un pétition soutenu d'attestations, l'audience et l'enregistrement d'évidence concernant la question de savoir si l'invention avait été à l'utilisation publique ou en vente un an avant le dépôt de la demande, ou avant la date alléguée, dans une déclaration préliminaire ou avant la date d'invention établie par une partie (R. 292)

Verfahren ueber offenkundige Benutzung—diese Verfahren beruhen auf einem durch beschworene schriftliche Erklaerungen gestuetzten Gesuch; die Verhandlung und das Aufnehmen von Zeugenaussagen ueber die Frage, ob eine Erfindung ein Jahr vor dem Einreichungsdatum der Anmeldung, oder vor dem in einer Vorerklaerung angegebenen Datum, oder vor dem von einer Partei festgesetzten Erfindungsdatum in offenkundigem Gebrauch oder verkaeuflich war (R. 292)

publication—see printed publication

publication—voir publication imprimée

Veroeffentlichung—vgl. gedruckte Veroeffentlichung

R

record room—see Public Search Room

salle d'archives—voir Salle Publique de Recherche

Aktenzimmer—vgl. oeffentlicher Nachschlage-Saal

reduction to practice—a process is reduced to practice when it is successfully performed; a machine is reduced to practice when it is assembled and used; a manufacture is reduced to practice when it is completely manufactured; a composition is reduced to practice when it is completely composed

réduction à la pratique—un procédé est réduit à la pratique quand il est exécuté avec succès; une machine, est réduite à la pratique quand elle est assemblée et employée; une fabrication est réduite à la pratique quand elle est complètement fabriquée; une composition est réduite à la pratique quand elle est complètement composée

Umsetzen in die Praxis—ein Verfahren ist in die Praxis umgesetzt, wenn es erfolgreich ausgefuehrt wird; eine Vorrichtung ist in die Praxis umgesetzt, wenn sie zusammengesetzt und benutzt wird; ein Herstellungsverfahren ist in die Praxis umgesetzt, wenn es vollstaendig hergestellt ist; eine Zusammensetzung ist in die Praxis umgesetzt, wenn sie vollstaendig zusammengesetzt ist

reference—prior art relied upon by the examiner in rejecting a claim as unpatentable. The pertinence of the reference, if not obvious, must be clearly explained and each rejected claim must be specified.

renvoi—une technique entérieure dont dépend l'examinateur en rejetant une revendication comme non brevetable. La convenance du renvoi, si elle n'est pas évidente, doit être expliquée et chaque revendication rejetée doit être spécifiée.

Hinweis—Stand der Technik, worauf sich der Pruefer bei der Zurueckweisung eines Anspruchs als nicht patentfaehig beruft. Sofern der Hinweis nicht offensichtlich zutrifft, muss er deutlich erklaert und jeder zurueckgeweisene Anspruch einzeln beschrieben werden

rehearing—reconsideration of an appeal by the Board of Appeals, granted optionally on a request made within thirty days from the date of the original decision (R. 197(b))

nouvelle audience—la réconsideration d'un appel, accordée facultativement sur une demande faite dans le délai de trente jours de la date de la décision originale (R. 197 (b))

Wiederverhandlung—nochmalige Erwaegung einer Beschwerde durch den Board of Appeals; nach freiem Ermessen, auf ein Ersuchen innerhalb von dreissig Tagen vom Datum der urspruenglichen Entscheidung bewilligt (R. 197(b))

reissue—the grant of a substitute patent for the remainder of the term of the original patent, made when the patent granted originally, through error and without deceptive intent, is found to be wholly or partly inoperative (R.171–179)

"reissue"—la délivrance d'un brevet substitut pour le reste du terme du brevet original, faite quand le brevet originalement délivré, par erreur et sans intention déceptive, est découvert d'être entièrement ou partiellement inopératif (R. 171–179)

erneute Erteilung—die Erteilung eines Ersatzpatents fuer die verbleibende Laufzeit des Stammpatents; dies wird getan, wenn das urspruenglich erteilte Patent durch Irrtum und ohne Taeuschungsabsicht ganz oder teilweise unwirksam befunden wird (R. 171–179)

reissue patent series—the separate series of numbers for reissue patents preceded by "Re". (MPEP 901.04)

"reissue" série de brevets—la distincte série de numéros des brevets "reissue" précédée de "Re." (MPEP 901.04)

Serie fuer erneut erteilte Patente—die separate Reihenfolge von Nummern fuer erneut erteilte Patente mit dem Vorsatz "Re." (MPEP 901.04)

rejection—action of the Patent Office denying patentability, and including notice of the reasons for the action together with the information and references on which the rejection was based (Sec. 132)

rejet—action de l'office des Brevets niant la brevetabilité et y inclus la notification des causes de l'action accompagnée des renseignements et des renvois sur lesquels a été basés le rejet (Sec. 132)

Zurueckweisung—eine Handlung des Patentamts, welche die Patentfaehigkeit in Abrede stellt, einschliesslich einer Mitteilung ueber die Beweggruende der Handlung, zusammen mit Auskuenften und Hinweisen auf denen die Zurueckweisung begruendet war (Sec. 132)

reply brief—response to new points of argument raised by the examiner's answer, to be filed within twenty days from the date of such answer (R.193)

dossier de réplique—réponse aux nouveaux points d'argument posés par la réponse de l'examinateur, qui doit être déposée dans le délai de vingt jours de la date de telle réponse (R. 193)

Erwiderungs-Schriftsatz—Entgegnung auf neue Argumente, die durch die Antwort des Pruefers hervorgerufen wurden; sie ist innerhalb von zwanzig Tagen vom Datum dieser Antwort einzureichen (R. 193)

res adjudicata—a finding that the identical issue was previously decided finally against the same party (MPEP 706.03(w))

res adjudicata—un verdict que la question identique a été décidée antérieurement finalement contre la même partie (MPEP 706.03 (w))

res adjudicata—der Befund, dass dieselbe Streitfrage gegen die gleiche Partei schon frueher endgueltig entschieden wurde (MPEP 706.03 (w))

reservation clause—an effort to assert ownership of subject matter disclosed but not claimed in an application; has no legal effect in United States applications

clause de réserve—un effort d'affirmer ou de réserver la possession d'une matière divulguée mais pas revendiquée dans une demande; cela n'a pas d'effet légal dans les demandes des Etats-Unis

Vorbehalts-Klausel—das Bestreben Eingetumsrechte auf die in einer Anmeldung offenbarten aber nicht mit Anspruch belegten Gegenstaende geltend zu machen; hat keinerlei gesetzliche Wirkung in Anmeldung in den Vereinigten Staaten

residence—the city and state or country in which the applicant lives (MPEP 605.02)

demeure—la ville et l'état ou le pays où demeure le demandeur (MPEP 605.02)

Wohnort—die Stadt, oder der Staat, oder das Land in dem der Anmelder wohnhaft ist (MPEP 605.02)

response—reply to a rejection

réponse—réplique à un rejet

Erwiderung—Antwort auf eine Ablehnung

restriction—directing claims to a single invention. After a requirement for restriction (formerly called division) because two or more independent inventions are claimed in a single application, a restricted application may be directed solely to one of said inventions. If filed before the patenting, abandonment or termination of proceedings on the original application, the new case is entitled to the benefit of the filing date of the original application, and neither the original nor the restricted applications or patents can be used as references against each other. (Sec. 121, R.147)

restriction—limitant les revendications à une seule invention. Après une exigence de restriction (autrefois appelé division) parce qu'on revendique plusieurs inventions dans une seule demande, une demande restreinte peut se concerner seulement d'une des inventions mentionnées. Si on le dépose avant d'être breveté, l'abandon ou la terminaison des procédés sur la demande originale, le nouveau cas a droit au bénéfice de la date de dépôt de la demande originale, et on ne peut employer comme référence l'un contre l'autre ni le cas original ni le nouveau cas. (Sec. 121, R. 147)

Beschraenkung—Ansprueche auf nur eine Erfindung ausrichten. Nach einer Forderung zur Beschraenkung (frueher Ausscheidung genannt), da zwei oder mehr unabhaengige Erfindungen in einer einzigen Anmeldung beansprucht wurden, kann eine beschraenkte Anmeldung allein nur auf eine der beiden erwaehnten Erfindungen ausgerichtet werden. Wird der neue Fall vor der Patentierung, dem Fallenlassen, oder der Beendigung des Verfahrens gegen die Erstanmeldung eingereicht, so steht ihm das Einreichungsdatum der urspruenglichen Anmeldung zu; weder die urspruenglichen noch die beschraenkten Anmeldungen oder Patente koennen als Belege gegeneinander verwendet werden (Sec. 121, R. 147).

revival—restoring the pendency of an abandoned application by petition to the Commissioner with a verified showing of unavoidable delay in prosecuting the abandoned application, together with the proposed response and the petition fee of $15.00 (R.137)

renouvellement—rendre la viabilité d'une demande abandonnée par pétition au Commissaire avec une preuve vérifiée d'un délai inévitable en poursuivant la demande abandonnée, accompagné de la réponse offerte et la taxe de pétition de $15. (R. 137)

Wiederinkraftsetzung—Wiederherstellung der Anhaegigkeit einer fallengelassenen Anmeldung durch Gesuch beim Commissioner mit einem beglaubigten Nachweis unvermeidlichen Verzugs in der Verfolgung der fallengelassenen Anmeldung, zusammen mit der vorgeschlagenen Entgegnung und der Antragsgebuehr von $15. (R. 137)

revocation—ruling of a court cancelling the patent grant

révocation—décision d'un tribunal qui annule la délivrance du brevet

Widerrufung—Gerichtsentscheid, der eine Patenterteilung fuer nichtig erklaert

royalty—payment for use of an invention

redevances—paiement pour l'utilisation d'une invention

Lizenzgebuehr—Bezahlung fuer die Benutzung einer Erfindung

Rules of Practice—the regulations established by the Commissioner of Patents governing the conduct of proceedings in the Patent Office (Sec. 6, 11)

Règles de Pratique—les règlements établis du Commissaire des Brevets qui gouvernent la conduite des procédés à l'Office des Brevets (Sec. 6, 11)

Ausfuehrungsbestimmungen (Rules of Practice)—die vom Commissioner of Patents festgesetzten Vorschriften, die das Verhalten bei Verfahren im Patentamt bestimmen (Sec. 6, 11)

S

Scientific Library—see Public Search Room

Bibliothèque Scientifique—voir Salle Publique de Recherche

wissenschaftliche Bibliothek—vgl. oeffentlicher Nachschlage-Saal

scope of claim—see breadth of claim

portée de la revendication—voir largeur de la revendication

Umfang des Anspruchs—vgl. Ausmass des Anspruchs

search—a review of patents and other publications to determine what is known to the public in relation to an alleged invention, thus collecting the information to support an opinion on the patentability of the invention or on the validity of a patent on the invention, or on the state of the art

recherche—une revue des brevets et d'autres publications pour déterminer ce que sait le public au sujet d'une invention alléguée, ainsi ramassant les renseignements pour soutenir une opinion au sujet de la brevetabilité de l'invention, ou de la validité d'un brevet sur l'invention, ou de l'état de la technique

Untersuchung—Nachpruefung von Patenten und andern Veroeffentlichungen um festzustellen, was der Oeffentlichkeit in Bezug auf eine angebliche Erfindung bekannt ist; dadurch wird die Information zur Unterstuetzung eines Gutachtens ueber die Patentfaehigkeit der Erfindung, oder ueber die Gueltigkeit eines Patents an der Erfindung, oder am Stand der Technik gesammelt

secrecy—when the publication of data in a patent application might affect national security, the application is made available for inspection by an appropriate agency of the Government. If the agency finds that publication of the invention would be detrimental to the national security, the Commissioner shall order the invention kept secret; during this period, prosecution will proceed, but no appeal hearing will be set nor will the patent issue until the secrecy order is removed. (Sec. 181)

secret—quand la publication des données pourrait affecter la sécurité nationale, on rend la demande disponible pour l'inspection de l'agence convenable du Gouvernement. Si l'agence trouve que la publication de l'invention serait nuisible à la sécurité nationale, le Commissaire ordonnera qu'on garde secrète l'invention; pendant cette période, la poursuite continuera, mais on n'établira aucune audience d'appel et on ne délivrera pas le brevet jusqu'à ce que la décision de mise au secret soit ôtét. (Sec. 181)

Geheimhaltung—Koennte die Veroeffentlichung von Angaben in einer Patentanmeldung die nationale Sicherheit beeintraechtigen, so wird die Anmeldung einer zustaendigen Dienststelle zur Einsichtnahme zugaenglich gemacht. Befindet die Dienststelle, dass Veroeffentlichung der Erfindung von Nachteil fuer die nationale Sicherheit waere, dann soll der Commissioner die Geheimhaltung der Erfindung anordnen; waehrend dieser Zeitspanne wird die Weiterverfolgung aufrechterhalten, aber keine Berfungsverhandlung anberaumt, noch wird das Patent erteilt bis die Geheimhaltungsanordnung entfernt ist (Sec. 181)

senior party—in an interference, the party having the earlier established effective filing date

senior party—dans une "interférence", la partie qui a la date d'effet de dépôt plus ancienne

aeltere Partei (Senior Party)—die Partei in einer Interferenz, die der ersten festgesetzen Termin fuer das Inkrafttreten des Einreichungsdatums hat

shifting ground—changing position as to what the invention comprises, or as to what the differences are between the references and the invention

"shifting ground"—changer de position quant à ce que comprend l'invention, ou quant à ce que sont les différences entre les renvois et l'invention

Veraenderung des Standpunkts—Aenderung der Einstellung im Hinblick auf das, was die Erfindung in sich fasst oder was die Unterschiede zwischen den Hinweisen und der Erfindung sind

shop right—the right of an employer to use in his shop the invention made by an employee with the employer's equipment or time

"shop right"—le droit pour un employeur d'utiliser dans son entreprise l'invention d'un employé, lorsque celui-ci l'a faite avec l'équipement de l'employeur ou durant les heures de travail

shop right—Recht eines Arbeitgebers, die von einem Arbeitnehmer mit den Einrichtungen oder in der Zeit des Arbeitgebers gemachte Erfindung in seinem Betrieb zu benutzen

signature—the full first name without abbreviation, middle initial or name, if any, and full surname of the applicant, which must be endorsed on the application (R. 57)

signature—le complet prénom sans abréviation, l'initiale ou le nom intermédiaire, s'il y en a, et le complet surnom du demandeur, qu'on doit endosser sur la demande (R. 57)

Unterschrift—der vollstaendige, unabgekuerzte Vorname, der Anfangsbuchstabe oder volle Mittelname—wenn vorhanden—und der vollstaendige Nachname des Anmelders, der auf der Anmeldung gegengezeichnet sein muss (R. 57)

single signature form—a combined petition, oath or declaration, and power of attorney attached to the specification as the last page, for execution by the inventor

forme avec une signature—une pétition, serment ou déclaration, et le pouvoir d'avocat combinés attaché à la spécification comme la dernière page, pour la signature par l'inventeur

Alleinunterschrifts-Formblatt—eine Kombination von Gesuch, Eid oder eidesstattlicher Erklaerung und gesetzlicher Vollmacht, als letzte Seite der Beschreibung (specification) zur Ausfuehrung durch den Erfinder angehaftet

skilled in the art—the imaginary person assumed to be familiar with all the teachings in his technical field. To be patentable, the difference from the prior art must be such that the claimed subject matter, as a whole, would not have been obvious, at the time the invention was made, to a person having ordinary skill in the field of the invention (Sec. 103)

adroite dans la technique—la personne imaginaire qu'on assume est au courant de tous les enseignements de son domaine. Pour être brevetable, la différence de la technique antérieure doit être telle que la matière revendiquée, en tout, n'aurait pas été évidente, à l'heure où on a créé l'invention, à une personne qui a de l'habileté moyenne dans le domaine de l'invention. (Sec. 103)

"wahrer Fachmann"—die nur in der Vorstellung vorhandene Person, von der angenommen wird, dass sie mit allen Kenntnissen auf ihrem Fachgebiet vertraut ist. Um patentfaehig zu sein, muss der Unterschied zum Stand der Technik derart sein, dass die beanspruchten Gegenstaende als Ganzes, zur Zeit als die Erfindung gemacht wurde, einem auf dem Gebiet des Erfindungsgegenstandes Sachverstaendigen nicht selbstverstaendlich gewesen waeren (Sec. 103)

soft copy—a copy of the specification, claims and drawing of an issued utility or design patent

"soft copy"—une copie de la spécification des revendications et des dessins d'un brevet délivré d'utilité ou de dessin

inoffizielle Abschrift—eine Abschrift der Beschreibung (specification), Anspruechen und Zeichnungen eines Gebrauchs- oder Geschmacksmusterpatents

sole inventor—a person who singly made an invention

inventeur unique—une personne qui seule a créé une invention

alleiniger Erfinder—eine Person, die allein eine Erfindung gemacht hat

soliciting—the preparation and prosecution of patent applications

soliciter—la préparation et la poursuite des demandes de brevet

Bewerbung—die Vorbereitung und Verfolgung von Patentanmeldungen

special examining procedure—accelerated examination of a new application based upon a written petition to make special, agreement to keep the application limited to ten claims or less, and submission of a pre-examination search and differentiation of the claims from the references of that search. A complete first action will be made prior to all applications except those in condition for allowance or under a fixed time limit for action by the Examiner; applicant will be given three months to respond; after an optional interview, the response must be limited to the rejections, objections and requirements made; final disposition will be made by the Examiner within one month of the response. (R. 102, MPEP 708.01 and 708.02)

procédé spécial d'examiner—l'examen accélére d'une nouvelle demande basé sur une pétition écrit de rendre spéciale la demande, la concession de limiter la demande à dix revendications au moins, et la soumission d'une recherche faite avant l'examen et la différenciation des revendications des renvois de cette recherche. Une première action complète sera faite avant toutes les autres demandes sauf celles qui sont en condition pour action de l'examinateur; on donnera au demandeur trois mois pour y répondre; après une entrevue facultative, on doit limiter la réponse aux rejets, objections et exigences faits; le jugement final sera fait par l'examinateur dans le délai d'un mois de la réponse. (R. 102, MPEP 708.01 et 708.02)

Sonderpruefverfahren—beschleunigte Pruefung einer neuen Anmeldung auf einem schriftlichen Gesuch um Sonderbehandlung beruhend, Uebereinkommen die Anmeldung auf zehn oder weniger Ansprueche beschraenkt zu halten, und Vorlage einer Vorpruefungs-Untersuchung und Differenzierung der Ansprueche von dem Hinweisen in dieser Untersuchung. Eine vollstaendige erste Behandlung wird vor allen Anmeldungen unternommen, mit Ausnahme derjenigen, die in der Zulassung begriffen sind oder mit einem festgesetzten Termin dem Pruefer zur Behandlung vorliegen; der Anmelder hat drei Monate Zeit zur Erwiderung; nach einem in Belieben der Beteiligten stehenden Interview muss die Erwiderung auf die gemachten Zurueckweisungen, Einwaende und Forderungen begrenzt sein; der Pruefer trifft innerhalb eines Monats nach der Erwinderung seine endgueltige Anordnung. (R. 102, MPEP 708.01 and 708.02)

species claim—a single specifically different embodiment of an invention (MPEP 806.04(e)). Five species may be claimed in one application. (R. 141)

revendications de variantes—une incarnation unique, spécifiquement différente, d'une invention (MPEP 806.04(e)). On peut revendiquer cinq variantes dans une demande. (R. 141)

Gattungs-Anspruch—eine einzelne im besondern differenzierte Ausfuehrung einer Erfindung (MPEP 806.04(e)). Fuenf Gattungen koennen in einer Anmeldung beansprucht werden. (R. 141)

specification—a precise description of a preferred embodiment of an invention, distinguishing the invention from what is old. The specification must be full, clear, concise and exact, so that a person skilled in the art can make and use the invention; it comprises, in order, a title, an abstract of the disclosure, cross-reference to any related application, the background of the invention, a brief summary of the invention, a brief description of the views of the drawing, a detailed description, claims, and a signature. (R. 77)

spécification—une description précise d'une incarnation préférée de l'invention, distinguant l'invention de ce qui est vieille. La spécification doit être complète, nette, concise et exacte, afin qu'une personne adroite dans la technique puisse employer l'invention; elle comprend, en ordre, un titre, une abstraction de la divulgation, un renvoi à aucune invention relative, le fond de l'invention, un bref sommaire de l'invention, une brève description des vues des dessins, une description détaillée, les revendications et une signature. (R. 77)

Beschreibung (specification)—eine genaue Schilderung einer bevorzugten Ausfuehrungsform einer Erfindung, die diese von allem schon Dagewesenen unterscheidet. Die Beschreibung (specification) muss so vollstaendig, klar, knapp und exakt sein, dass ein Fachmann auf dem Gebiet sie ausfuehren und benutzen kann; gemaess nachstehender Reihenfolge umfasst sie einen Titel, einen Auszug aus der Offenbarung, Hinweise auf all verwandten Anmeldungen, den Hintergrund der Erfindung, eine kurze Zusammenfassung der Erfindung, eine kurze Schilderung der Ansichten der Zeichnung, eine ausfuehrliche Beschreibung, Ansprueche und eine Unterschrift. (R. 77)

state of the art—the data in an area of technical knowledge at a given time

état de la technique—les données dans un domaine de connaissance technique au moment donné

Stand der Technik—die Gegebenheiten auf einem Gebiet technischer Kenntnisse zu einer bestimmten Zeit

status letter—inquiry to the examiner about the present status of an application. Sent, advisably, when an unduly long time has elapsed since the Patent Office last acted on the case.

lettre de condition—une requête à l'examinateur au sujet de la condition présente d'une demande. Envoyée, judicieusement, quand il est passé une période de temps excessivement longue depuis que l'Office des Brevets a agi sur le cas.

Akten-Nachfrage (Status-Brief)—Anfrage an den Pruefer den gegenwaertigen Stand einer Anmeldung betreffend. Es ist ratsam diesen Brief zu senden, wenn eine ungewoehnlich lange Zeit vergangen ist, seit das Patentamt zuletzt etwas in dem Fall unternommen hat.

statutory—established by act of Congress duly enacted into law

statutaire—établi par un acte du Congrès proprement rendu une loi

rechtsverbindlich—durch Congress-Beschluss festgesetzt und ordnungsgemaess zum Gesetz erhoben

statutory bar—see bar to patent grant

interdiction statutaire—voir interdiction à la délivrance d'un brevet

gesetzlicher Hinderungsgrund—vgl. Hinderungsgrund zur Patenterteilung

streamlined continuation application – an application in which the drawings and specification are identical with those of a pending application of the same applicant, and the claims are directed to the same invention as that prosecuted in the pending application, and procedures for transferring the drawings and specification from the pending application to the new application have been followed (Notice 824 O.G. 1)

"streamlined continuation" demande—une demande où les dessins et la spécification sont identiques avec ceux d'une demande pendante du même demandeur, les revendications concernent la même invention que celles poursuivies dans la demande pendante, et on a suivi les procédés pour céder les dessins et la spécification de la demande pendante à la nouvelle demande (Notification 824 O.G. 1)

"streamlined" Fortfuehrungs-Anmeldung—eine Anmeldung in der die Zeichnungen und Beschreibung (specification) mit einer anhaengigen Anmeldung desselben Anmelders identisch sind; die Ansprueche beziehen sich auf dieselbe Erfindung, die in der anhaengigen Anmeldung verfolgt wurden, und die Durchfuehrungsvorschriften zur Uebertragung von Zeichnungen und Beschreibung (specification) von der anhaengigen Anmeldung zur neuen Anmeldung sind befolgt worden (Notice 824 O. G. 1)

subclass—the Patent Office numerical designation of the subject matter division of a patent or publication, in further particularization of a classification of such subject matter

sous-classe—la designation numérique de l'Office des Brevets de la division de matière d'un brevet ou d'une publication, dans une particularisation plus grande de la classification de telle matière

Unterklasse—die nummerische Bestimmung der Unterteilung der Gegenstaende eines Patents oder einer Veroeffentlichung durch das Patentamt zur weiteren Detailierung der Klassifizierung solcher Gegenstaende

submission—request by appellant that the Board of Appeals consider the appeal on the written record, the request being effected by failure of appellant to request oral hearing

soumission—requête de l'appelant que la Commission d'Appel considère l'appel sur le dossier écrit, la requête résulte de la manque de l'appelant de demander une audience orale

Vorlage—Antrag des Berufungsklaegers, der Board of Appeals moege die Berufung auf Grund von schriftlichen Unterlagen erwaegen; der Antrag ist durch die Unterlassung des Berufungsklaegers um eine muendliche Verhandlung nachzusuchen veranlasst

substantially—in claims, a qualification having a meaning that should be supported by illustration in the specification

"substantially"—dans les revendications, une qualification qui a une signification qu'on devrait soutenir par illustration ou par example dans la spécification

im Wesentlichen—in Anspruechen eine Einschraenkung, deren Bedeutung durch Illustration in der Beschreibung (specification) unterstuetzt werden sollte

substitute application—a duplicate of an application by the same applicant that was abandoned before the filing of the later case (MPEP 201.09)

demande substitute—un double d'une demande du même demandeur qui a été abandonnée avant le dépôt de la demande postérieure (MPEP 201.09)

Ersatz-Anmeldung—ein Duplikat einer Anmeldung von demselben Anmelder, die vor dem Einreichen des spaeteren Falles fallengelassen worden ist (MPEP 201.09)

summary of the invention—statement in general terms of the advance in the art, the advantages provided by the invention, and a brief, generalized functional description as to how the inventive concept attains the superior results, included in the specification after the statement of the background of the invention

sommaire de l'invention—une déclaration en termes généraux du progrès de la technique, les avantages fournis et produits par l'invention, et une brève description fonctionnelle et généralisée de comment le concept inventif achève des résultats supérieurs, incluse dans la spécification après la declaration du fond de l'invention

Zusammenfassung der Erfindung—eine allgemein gehaltene Darstellung des technischen Fortschritts, der Vorteile, welche die Erfindung mit sich bringt und eine kurze, verallgemeinerte, funktionelle Schilderung, wie die erfinderische Idee ueberragende Ergebnisse erzielt; enthalten in der Beschreibung (specification), nach der Darstellung des Hintergrundes der Erfindung

supplemental oath or declaration—an oath or declaration filed, optionally, in support of new claims for subject matter originally described but not claimed (R. 67)

serment ou déclaration supplémentaire—un serment ou une déclaration déposée, au choix, à l'appui de nouvelles revendications pour la matière originalement décrite mais pas revendiquée (R. 67)

Ergaenzungs-Eid oder eidesstattliche Erklaerung—ein nach freiem Ermessen geleisteter Eid oder eidesstattliche Erklaerung zur Unterstuetzung neuer Ansprueche fuer urspruenglich beschriebene, aber nicht beanspruchte Anmeldungsgegenstaende (R. 67)

suspension of action—postponement of action by the Patent Office for good cause, at the request of applicant or at the instance of the Patent Office, for a reasonable specified time (R. 103)

suspension d'action—tenir en suspens une action pour une bonne raison, à la requête du demandeur ou de l'Office des Brevets, pendant un temps raisonnable et spécifié (R. 103)

Aussetzung der Behandlung—angemessen befristeter Aufschub der Behandlung durch das Patentamt aus guten Gruenden, entweder auf Ansuchen des Anmelders oder auf Veranlassung des Patentamts (R. 103)

swearing back of reference—making an oath showing completion of the invention of the application in the United States before the effective date of the reference (R. 131)

"swearing back of reference"—exposé sous serment démontrant la complétion aux Etats-Unis d'une invention à une date antérieure à la date d'effet du renvoi (R. 131)

"swearing back of reference"—einen Eid leisten, mit dem die Vollendung der in der Anmeldung genannten Erfindung in den Vereinigten Staaten, vor dem Datum des Inkrafttretens des Hinweises beschworen wird (R. 131)

T

tabular claim—a claim in which the several clauses or subparagraphs are indented from the margin to provide columnar recital of the elements and sub-elements of the claim

revendication synoptique—une revendication dans laquelle les plusieurs clauses ou sous-paragraphes sont mis intérieurement dans la marge pour pourvoir le récit en colonne des éléments et des sous-éléments de la revendication

tabellarischer Anspruch—ein Anspruch, wobei die verschiedenen Klauseln oder Unterabschnitte vom Rand eingerueckt sind, um die Aufreihung der Elemente und Unterelemente des Anspruchs in Kolonnen anzuordnen

term of patent—period for which patent rights are granted. The period of utility patents and plant patents is 17 years from the date of grant; the period of design patents is 3½, 7 or 14 years from the date of grant, at the option of applicant.

terme du brevet—la période pour laquelle on a délivré les droits de brevet. La période des brevets d'utilité et de plantes est 17 ans de la date de délivrance; la période des brevets de dessin est 3½ ans, 7 ans ou 14 ans de la date de délivrance, au choix du demandeur.

Laufzeit des Patents—Zeitspanne fuer die Patentrechte erteilt werden. Die Dauer von Gebrauchsmuster- und Pflanzen-Patenten ist siebzehn Jahre vom Erteilungsdatum; die Dauer von Geschmacksmuster-Patenten ist 3½, 7 oder 14 Jahre vom Verleihungsdatum, nach Belieben des Anmelders.

terminal disclaimer—making a claimed invention available for free use for a terminal part of the period of the patent (Sec. 253)

renonciation terminale—rendre une invention revendiquée disponible à l'utilisation libre pendant une partie terminale de la période du brevet (Sec. 253)

Verzicht auf den Restteil—eine beanspruchte Erfindung fuer den Restteil ihrer Patentlaufzeit dem freien Gebrauch zugaenglich machen (Sec. 253)

title—the heading on the first page of the specification; a short description that is representative generally of the claimed improvement

titre—l'en-tête de la première page de la spécification; une courte description qui est généralement représentative du perfectionnement revendiqué

Titel—die Ueberschrift auf der ersten Seite der Beschreibung (specification); eine kurze Darstellung, die allgemein bezeichnend fuer die beanspruchte Verbesserung ist

trademark—a word or symbol used by a merchant to identify and distinguish his product from the product of others; use of a trademark in a patent application to define a product is normally not permitted

marque de fabrique—un mot ou un signe employé par un marchand pour identifier et distinguer son produit du produit d'autrui; on ne permet pas d'ordinaire l'emploi d'une marque de fabrique pour définir un produit dans une demande de brevet

Warenzeichen—von einem Kaufmann zur Identifizierung und Unterscheidung seines Erzeugnisses von den Erzeugnissen anderer benutztes Wort oder Zeichen; der Gebrauch eines Warenzeichens zur Definition eines Erzeugnisses ist in einer Patentanmeldung normalerweise nicht gestattet

traverse—argument that an action was not proper

"traverse"—argument qu'une action n'était pas juste

Rechtseinwand—das Argument, dass eine Klage nicht korrekt war

U

underlining—a horizontal line placed under a word or words in a claim as a direction to the examiner to add such word or words to the claim (R. 121)

souligner—une ligne horizontale mise sous un mot ou plusieurs mots dans une revendication, comme une directive à l'examinateur d'ajouter tel mot ou tels mots à la revendication (R. 121)

unterstreichen—eine waagrechte Linie unter einem Wort oder Worten in einem Anspruch ist eine Anweisung an den Pruefer solch ein Wort oder Worte dem Anspruch hinzuzufuegen (R. 121)

unfair competition—deception or fraud in business practice that violates the legal or equitable rights of a competitor or the public

concurrence injuste—une déception ou une fraude dans la pratique des affaires qui viole les droits légaux ou équitables d'un concurrent ou du public

unlauterer Wettbewerb—Taeschung oder Betrug im Geschaeftsgebaren, die die gesetzlichen oder billigen Rechte eines Konkurrenten oder der Allgemeinheit verletzen

unobviousness—differences between the subject matter sought to be patented and the prior art of such a nature that the subject matter as a whole would not have been obvious at the time the invention was made to a person having ordinary skill in the art involved (Sec. 103)

"unobviousness"—les différences entres la matière qu'on veut rendre brevetée et la technique antérieure, d'une telle nature que la matière entière n'aurait pas été évidente à une personne qui a une habileté moyenne dans la technique à l'heure où on a créé l'invention (Sec. 103)

Nicht-Selbstverstaendlichkeit—Unterschiede zwischen dem zu patentierended Erfindungsgegenstand und dem Stand der Technik, die solcher Art sind, dass der Erfindungsgegenstand als Ganzes zu der Zeit, als die Erfindung gemacht wurde, einem auf dem Gebiet des Erfindungsgegenstandes Sachverstaendigen nicht selbstverstaendlich gewesen waere (Sec. 103)

use—to put into practice

utilisation—mettre en pratique une invention

Benutzung—in die Praxis umsetzen

utility—operative and not frivolous, fraudulent or against public policy (MPEP 706.3(p))

utilité—opératif et pas frivole, frauduleux ou contre la politique publique (MPEP 706.3(p))

Nuetzlichkeit—wirksam und nicht frivol, betreugerisch oder gegen das Wohl der Oeffentlichkeit (MPEP 706.03(p))

V

vague and indefinite—lacking a reasonable degree of particularity and distinctness

vague et indéfini—manquant un degré raisonnable de particularité et de clarité

verschwommen und bestimmt—einen angemessenen Grad von Genauigkeit und Klarheit vermissen lassend

valid patent—a duly granted patent that complies with the conditions for patentability of Sec. 102 and 103

brevet valide—un brevet proprement délivré qui se conforme aux conditions de brevetabilité de Sec. 102 et 103

gueltiges Patent—ein ordnungsgemaess erteiltes Patent, das die Bedingungen zur Patentfaehigkeit unter Sec. 102 und 103 erfuellt

validity search—see search

recherche de validité—voir recherche

Gueltigkeits-Untersuchung—vgl. Untersuchung

W

whereby clause—an optional clause in a claim, usually the ultimate clause, setting forth the function of the claimed combination or process

"whereby" clause—une clause facultative dans une revendication, d'ordinaire la clause finale, qui présente la fonction de la combinaison ou du procédé revendiqué

"whereby clause"—eine im Belieben des Anmelders stehende Klausel in einem Anspruch—gewoehnlich die allerletzte Klausel—welche die Funktion der beanspruchten Zusammensetzung oder des Verfahrens darlegt

SECTION II

FRENCH

ENGLISH

GERMAN

GLOSSAIRE DE LA PRATIQUE DE BREVETS AMERICAINE

ABREVIATIONS

Sec. ——— La section indiquée de Titre 35, Code des Etats-Unis

R. ——— La règle indiquée des Règles de Pratique de l'Office des Brevets des Etats-Unis

MPEP ——— La section indiquée du Etats-Unis 'Patent Office Manual of Patent Examining Procedure, 3rd ed.' (Le Manuel de l'Office des Brevets de la Procedure d'Examiner les Brevets, 3e edition)

A

abandon actuel de l'invention—voir abandon de l'invention

actual abandonment of invention—see abandonment of invention

tatsaechliches Fallenlassen der Erfindung—vgl. Fallenlassen der Erfindung

abandon de contestation—la concession de la priorité ou l'abandon de l'invention par une partie de la "interférence". On a besoin de l'accord écrit du cessionnaire de propriété.

abandonment of contest—concession of priority or abandonment of the invention by a party in an interference. The written consent of the assignee is required when an assignment was made.

Aufgabe des Wettstreits—Zugestaendnis der Prioritaet oder Fallenlassen der Erfindung durch eine Partei in einer Interferenz. Hat eine Patent uebertragung stattgefunden, so ist die schriftliche Zustimmung des Rechtsnachfolgers erforderlich.

abandon d'invention—une déclaration explicite ou tacite du demandeur qu'il ne prétendra pas un droit de propriété industrielle dans l'invention (Sec. 102)

abandonment of invention—express or implied declaration by applicant that he will not assert a property right in the invention (Sec. 102)

Fallenlassen der Erfindung—ausdrueckliche oder stillschweigend verstandene Erklaerung des Patentanmelders, dass er kein Eigentumsrecht auf die Erfindung geltend machen wird (Sec. 102)

abstraction de la divulgation—une déclaration technique, qui est concise et non-légal, du contenu de la divulgation, incluse dans la spécification comme un instrument "cherchant-scrutant" immédiatement après le titre; une déclaration limitèe à environs cent mots, omettant de vastes détails mécaniques et désignatifs, mais comprenant l'organisation et l'opération d'une machine ou d'un appareil, ou la méthode de fabriquer une chose, ou l'identité et l'utilisation d'un composé chimique, ou les ingrédients d'une mixture, ou bien les démarches d'un procédé (R. 72(b))

abstract of the disclosure—a concise, non-legal technical statement of the contents of the disclosure, included in the specification as a searching-scanning tool immediately after the title; a statement limited to about 100 words, omitting extensive mechanical and design details but including the organization and operation of a machine or apparatus, or the method of making an article, or the identity and use of a chemical compound, or the ingredients of a mixture, or the steps of a process (R. 72(b))

Auszug aus der Offenbarung—eine knappe nichtjuristische technische Darstellung des Inhalts der Offenbarung, unmittelbar nach dem Titel in der Beschreibung (specification) als Untersuchungs und Pruefwerkzeug enthalten; eine auf ungefaehr hundert Worte begrenzte Darlegung, die ausfuehrliche mechanische und Muster Einzelheiten auslaesst, aber die Organisation und den Betrieb einer Maschine oder eines Apparates, oder die Methode zur Herstellung eines Artikels, oder die Identitaet und den Gebrauch einer chemischen Verbindung, oder die Bestandteile einer Mischung, oder die Stufen eines Vorgangs einschliesst (R. 72(b))

abstraction de titre—les archives de l'Office des Brevets qui indiquent le propriétaire d'un brevet

abstract of title—Patent Office record of ownership of a patent

Auszug aus dem Titel—Patentamt-Eintragung ueber das Eigentumsrecht an einem Patent

abus de brevet–l'utilisation d'un brevet par un titulaire de brevet pour contrôler des matières hors de l'étendue des droits dans le brevet, rendant une défense contre une revendication de contrefaçon du brevet

misuse of patent–employment of a patent by a patent owner to control matters outside the scope of the rights in the patent, providing a defense against a claim of infringement of the patent

Missbrauch eines Patents–Verwendung eines Patents durch einen Patentinhaber um dinge ausserhalb des Bereichs der Rechte in dem Patent zu lenken und eine Verteidigung gegen einen Patentverletzungs-Anspruch zu schaffen

acceptable–voir la notification de "allowability"

allowable–see notice of allowability

zulaessig–vgl. Zulaessigkeits-Benachrichtigung

acceptation–voir la notification d'acceptation

allowance–see notice of allowance

Zulassung–vgl. Zulassungsbenachrichtigung

action–voir action d'Office

action–see Office action

Behandlung–vgl. Behandlung durch das (Patent)amt

action d'office–un document de l'examinateur déclarant l'attitude de l'Office des Brevets au sujet de la demande, énumérant les rejets et/ou les objections

office action–a paper from the examiner setting forth the Patent Office position on the application, enumerating rejections and/or objections

Behandlung durch das Amt–ein Schriftsatz des Pruefers mit der Stellungnahme des Patentamts zu der Anmeldung, unter Aufzaehlung von Zurueckweisungen und/oder Einwaenden

administrateur—le représentant d'un inventeur légalement incapacité

administrator—the representative of a legally incapacitated inventor

Sachwalter—der Vertreter eines Erfinders, der sich vor dem Gesetz nicht selbst vertreten kann

adresse—l'adresse où le demandeur reçoit d'ordinaire son courrier (MPEP 605.03)

post office address—the address at which the applicant customarily receives his mail (MPEP 605.03)

Postanschrift—die Adresse, unter welcher der Anmelder ueblicherweise seine Post empfaengt (MPEP 605.03)

adroite dans la technique—la personne imaginaire qu'on assume est au courant de tous les enseignements de son domaine. Pour être brevetable, la différence de la technique antérieure doit être telle que la matière revendiquée, en tout, n'aurait pas été évidente, à l'heure où on a créé l'invention, à une personne qui a de l'habileté moyenne dans le domaine de l'invention. (Sec. 103)

skilled in the art—the imaginary person assumed to be familiar with all the teachings in his technical field. To be patentable, the difference from the prior art must be such that the claimed subject matter, as a whole, would not have been obvious, at the time the invention was made, to a person having ordinary skill in the field of the invention. (Sec. 103)

"wahrer Fachmann"—die nur in der Vorstellung vorhandene Person, von der angenommen wird, dass sie mit allen Kenntnissen auf ihrem Fachgebiet vertraut ist. Um patentfaehig zu sein, muss der Unterschied zum Stand der Technik derart sein, dass die beanspruchten Gegenstaende als Ganzes, zur Zeit als die Erfindung gemacht wurde, einem auf dem Gebiet des Erfindungsgegenstandes Sachverstaendigen nicht selbstverstaendlich gewesen waeren. (Sec. 103)

agent—voir agent de brevets

agent—see patent agent

Vertreter—vgl. Patent-Vertreter

agent de brevets—une personne, pas un avoué, qui a les qualifications exigées pour la pratique et qu'on a admise à la pratique aupres de l'Office des Brevets (R. 341)

patent agent—a person, not an attorney at law, who has the qualifications required for and who has been admitted to practice before the Patent Office (R. 341)

Patent-Vertreter—eine Person—kein Rechtsanwalt—die die Bedingungen erfuellt und die zugelassen ist vor dem Patentamt zu praktizieren (R. 341)

"aggregation"—l'absence d'une relation coopérative entre un élément d'une revendication et au moins un autre élément de la revendication (MPEP 706.03(i))

aggregation—the absence of a cooperative relation between an element of a claim and at least one other element of the claim. (MPEP 706.03(i))

Aneinanderreihung—die Abwesenheit einer zusammenwirkenden Beziehung zwischen einem Element eines Patentanspruches und mindestens einem zweiten (MPEP 706.03 (i))

"allowability"—voir la notification de "allowability"

allowability—see notice of allowability

Zulaessigkeit—vgl· Zulaessigkeits-Benach richtigung

amendement—directive à l'Office des Brevets d'ajouter et/ou de rayer quelque chose de la demande (R. 21(k), 33, 67, 85, 111, 115-119, 121-127, 135, 173, 174, 196, 203-206, 212, 222, 231, 312)

amendment—instruction to the Patent Office to add and/or delete matter from the application (R. 21(k), 33, 67, 85, 111, 115-119, 121-127, 135, 173, 174, 196, 203-206, 212, 222, 231, 312)

Berichtigung—Anweisung an das Patentamt dem Antrag etwas zuzufuegen oder von dem Antrag etwas zu streichen (R. 21(k), 33, 67, 85, 111, 115-119, 121-127, 135, 173, 174, 196, 203-206, 212, 222, 231, 312)

amendement de l'examinateur—un amendement à une demande, fait par l'examinateur, avec une notification au demandeur, pour corriger des "erreurs évidentes et des omissions" (MPEP 1302.04)

examiner's amendment—an amendment to an application made by the examiner, with notice to applicant, to correct "obvious errors and omissions" (MPEP 1302.04)

Pruefers Berichtigung—eine Berichtigung zu einer Anmeldung die von einem Pruefer unter Benachrichtigung des Anmelders gemacht wird, um "augenfaellige Irrtuemer und Auslassungen" zu korrigieren (MPEP 1302.04)

annulation des revendications—la rayure des revendications d'une demande

cancellation of claims—deleting of claims from an application

Streichung von Anspruechen—Loeschen von Anspruechen einer Patentanmeldung

antécédent—le récit positif d'un mot ou d'une phrase pour permettre l'identification abrégée de tel mot ou telle phrase plus tard dans la phrase ou dans la composition

antecedent—a positive recital of a word or phrase to permit abbreviated identification of such word or phrase at a later point in the sentence or paper

Vorhergehendes—bestimmte Anfuehrung eines Wortes oder eines Ausdrucks um die abgekuerzte Identifizierung eines solchen Wortes oder Ausdrucks im weiteren Verlauf des Satzes oder Schriftstuecks zu gestatten

antérioriser—établir qu'une invention alléguée n'est pas nouvelle

anticipate—to establish that an alleged invention is not novel

vorwegnehmen—Feststellung, dasse eine angebliche Erfindung nicht neu ist

antériorité—voir antérioriser

anticipation—see anticipate

Vorwegnahme—vgl· vorwegnehmen

Appel à la Commission d'Appel—voir la Commission d'Appel

appeal to Board of Appeals—see Board of Appeals

Berufung an den Board of Appeals (Berufungsinstanz)—vgl. Board of Appeals

appel à la Cour de Cassation—voir Cour de Cassation

appeal to Court of Appeals—see Court of Appeals

Berufung an den Court of Appeals (Berufungsgericht)—vgl. Court of Appeals

appel à la Cour de Réclamation—voir la Cour de Réclamation

appeal to Court of Claims—see Court of Claims

Berufung an den Court of Claims—vgl. Court of Claims

appel à la "Court of Customs and Patent Appeals"—voir Court of Customs and Patent Appeals

appeal to Court of Customs and Patent Appeals—see Court of Customs and Patent Appeals

Berufung an den Court of Customs and Patent Appeals—vgl. Court of Customs and Patent Appeals

application nouvelle—une classe de matière brevetable fournissant un procédé basé sur une utilisation inventive d'un procédé, sur une machine, sur une fabrication, et sur la composition connus de matière ou de matériel (Sec. 100)

new use—a class of patentable subject matter providing a process based on an inventive use of a known process, machine, manufacture, composition of matter or material Sec. 100)

neue Anwendung—eine Klasse patentfaehiger Gegenstaende, die ein auf dem erfinderischen Gebrauch eines bekannten Verfahrens, einer Vorrichtung, Herstellungsweise, Zusammensetzung von Gegenstaenden oder eines Stoffes, beruhendes Verfahren hervorbringen (Sec. 100)

audience—la présentation d'un argument, oral par le demandeur devant la Commission d'Appel; l'examinateur peut aussi choisir de présenter un argument oral (R. 194)

hearing—presentation by appellant of oral argument before the Board of Appeals; the examiner has the option of also presenting oral argument (R. 194)

muendliche Verhandlung—Vorbringung muendlicher Beweisgruende vor dem Board of Appeals durch den Beschwerde-Fuehrenden (Berufungsklaeger); es steht dem Pruefer frei auch seinerseits muendliche Beweisgrunde vorzubringen (R. 194)

autorisation étrangere de dépôt—permission du Commissaire des Brevets déposêr une demande dans un pays étranger dans moins de six mois après avoir déposé la même demande aux Etats-Unis. On ne concédera pas une licence pour déposer a l'étranger une demande frappée d'une decision de mise au secret, mais on peut la concéder rétroactivement dans les autres instances où on a déposé par inadvertance une demande à l'ètranger sans une telle licence. (Sec. 184)

foreign filing authorization—permission by the Commissioner of Patents to file an application in a foreign country in less than six months after the filing of such application in the United States. License to file abroad will not be granted for an application under a secrecy order, but may be granted retroactively in other cases where an application has been filed abroad inadvertently without such license. (Sec. 184)

Genehmigung ein Patent im Ausland anzumelden—Erlaubnis vom Commissioner of Patents ein Patent weniger als sechs Monate nach seiner Anmeldung in den Vereinigten Staaten im Ausland anzumelden. Die Genehmigung eine unter Geheimhaltungs-Befehl stehende Anmeldung im Ausland einzureichen wird nicht erteilt werden, wenn eine Anmeldung im Ausland versehentlich ohne Genehmigung eingereicht worden war. (Sec. 184)

avancement d'une demande—l'examen d'une demande avant son tour chronologique, fait à preuve de l'âge ou de l'infirmité du demandeur, ou de l'hasard aux droits commerciaux du demandeur

advancement of application—examination of an application in advance of its chronological turn, made on a showing of age or infirmity of applicant or jeopardy of commercial rights of the applicant

Bevorzugung einer Anmeldung—die vorzeitige Pruefung einer Anmeldung, ausserhalb der zeitlichen Reihenfolge, aus Alters-oder Gesundheitsgruenden des Anmelders, oder wegen Gefaehrdung der kommerziellen Ansprueche des Anmelders

avocat—voir avocat de brevets

attorney—see patent attorney

Anwalt—vgl. Patentanwalt

avocat de brevets—un membre d'un barreau Fédéral ou d'état qui a les qualifications exigées pour la pratique et qu'on a admis à la pratique auprès de l'Office des Brevets (R. 341). Cela comprend des personnes qui n'appartiennent à aucun barreau, qui etaient admises comme "avocats enregistrés de brevets" avant 1931.

patent attorney—a member of a Federal or State bar who has the qualifications required for and who has been admitted to practice before the Patent Office (R. 341). Includes persons not a member of any bar who were admitted as "registered patent attorneys" before 1931.

Patent-Anwalt—Mitglied einer Bundes- oder Landesanwaltskammer, der den Bedingungen entspricht und beim Patentamt zugelassen ist (R. 341). Dies schliesst Personen ein, die nicht Mitglieder einer Anwaltskammer sind, die vor 1931 als "eingetragene Patent-Anwaelte" zugelassen wurden.

avocat "of record"—l'agent de brevets ou l'avocat de brevets nommé par le demandeur pour fairs ses affaires avec l'Office des Brevets. Le pouvoir d'agir de l'avocat doit être enregistré dans la demande déposée.

attorney of record—the patent agent or patent attorney appointed by applicant to transact his business before the Patent Office. The attorney's power to act must be recorded in the filed application.

Zustaendiger Anwalt—der Patentvertreter oder Patentanwalt, der vom Anmelder bestellt ist seine Interessen vor dem Patentamt zu vertreten. Die Handlungsvollmacht des Anwalts muss in der eingereichten Anmeldung beurkundet sein.

B

Bibliothèque Scientifique—voir Salle Publique de Recherche

Scientific Library—see Public Search Room

wissenschaftliche Bibliothek—vgl. oeffentlicher Nachschlage-Saal

brevet—octroi par le Gouvernement du droit d'empêcher à autrui de fabriquer, d'employer ou de vendre l'invention définie dans les revendications du brevet

patent—a grant by the Government of the right to prevent others from making, using or selling the invention defined in the claims of the patent

Patent—ein von der Regierung erteiltes Recht andere zu verhindern die in den Patentanspruechen definierte Erfindung herzustellen, zu benutzen oder zu verkaufen

brevet de base—un brevet qui domine plusieurs brevets postérieurs, de sorte que l'emploi des brevets postérieurs constituent la contrefaçon du brevet de base. Voir brevet de pionnier.

basic patent—a patent that dominates many later patents, so that use of the later patents would constitute infringement of the basic patent. See pioneer patent.

Grund-Patent—ein Patent, das ueber viele spaetere Patente vorherrscht, so dass die Benutzung der spaeteren Patente eine Verletzun des Grund-Patentes ausmachen wuerded. Vgl. Pionier-Patent.

brevet de plantes—un brevet pour l'invention ou la découverte et pour la réproduction asexuelle d'une espèce de plante nouvelle et distincte (y inclus les variations des burgeons, les mutations, les hybrides cultivés, et les semis nouvellement trouvés, pas une plante tuberculeuse propagée ou une plante trouvée dans un état incultivé) (Sec. 161–164, R. 161–167)

plant patent—patent for the invention or discovery and asexual reproduction of a distinct and new variety of plant (including cultivated sports, mutants, hybrids and newly found seedlings, other than a tuber propagated plant or a plant found in an uncultivated state) (Sec. 161–164, R. 161–167)

Pflanzen-Patent—Patent fuer die Erfindung oder Entdeckung und Vermehrung ohne Befruchtung einer bestimmten und neuen Pflanzensorte (einschliesslich von Kulturabarten, Mutationen, Hybriden und neugefundenen Saemlingen, ausser einem Knollengewaechs oder einer in einem unkultivierten Stadium gefundenen Pflanze) (Sec. 161–164, R. 161–167)

brevet demandé—notification par un demandeur qu'une demande de brevet pour une invention a été déposée à l'Office des Brevets

patent applied for—notice by an applicant that an application for patent on an invention has been filed in the Patent Office

Patent angemeldet—Mitteilung eines Anmelders, dass eine Patentanmeldung an einer Erfindung beim Patentamt eingereicht worden ist

brevet dominant—voir brevet de base

dominating patent—see basic patent

vorherrschendes Patent—vgl. Grundpatent

brevet expiré—la désignation d'un brevet après la fin de la durée pour laquelle il a été délivré

expired patent—the denotation of a patent after the end of the term for which it was granted

abgelaufenes Patent—die Bezeichnung eines Patents nach Beendigung der Laufzeit, fuer die as erteilt war

brevet pendant—voir brevet demandé

patent pending—see patent applied for

Patent anhaengig—vgl. Patent angemeldet

brevet pionnier—le premier brevet d'un domaine, revendiquant les moyensou une fonction qu'on n'a jamais encore divulgée. On l'interprète libéralement et a droit à une large étendue d'équivalents.

pioneer patent—the first patent in a field, claiming means or a function never before disclosed. It is interpreted liberally and is entitled to a broad range of equivalents.

Pionier-Patent—das erste Patent auf einem Gebiet, das niemals vorher offenbarte Mittel oder eine Funktion mit Anspruch belegt. Es wird grosszuegig ausgelegt und ist zu einem weiten Bereich von Aequivalenzen berechtigt.

brevet valide—un brevet proprement délivré qui se conforme aux conditions de brevetabilité de Sec. 102 et 103

valid patent—a duly granted patent that complies with the conditions for patentability of Sec. 102 and 103

gueltiges Patent—ein ordnungsgemaess erteiltes Patent, das die Bedingungen zur Patentfaehigkeit unter Sec. 102 und 103 erfuellt

breveter double—où plusieurs demandes et/ou brevets ont la même entité inventive et une invention revendiquée dans un cas est la même que, ou n'est pas brevetablement distincte de, une invention dans l'autre cas (MPEP 804)

double patenting—where two or more applications and/or patents have the same inventive entity and an invention claimed in one case is the same as, or not patentably distinct from, an invention in the other case (MPEP 804)

Doppelpatentierung—zwei oder mehr Anmeldung und/oder Patente haben diesselbe erfinderische Einheit und eine beanspruchte Erfindung ist diesselbe, oder patentmaessig nicht verschieden, von der Erfindung im andern Fall (MPEP 804)

C

c. i. p.—voir continuation-en-partie

c. i. p.—see continuation-in-part

c. i. p.—vgl. Teilfortfuehrung

cédant—celui qui transfère les droits de propriété dans une invention

assignor—the transferor of property rights in an invention

Zedent—die Person, die die Eigentumsrechte an einer Erfindung uebertraegt

certificat de correction—la déclaration de l'Office des Brevets qui corrige une erreur matérielle dans un brevet délivré où l'erreur est par suite de la faute de l'Office des Brevets ou est par suite d'une faute pardonnable du demandeur

certificate of correction—statement by the Patent Office correcting a material error in an issued patent where the error is due to the fault of the Patent Office or is due to the excusable fault of the applicant

Korrektur-Beschernigung—Erklärung des Patentamts zwecks Korrektur eines sachlichen Irrtums in einem verliehenen Patent, wenn die Schuld an dem unterlaufenen Fehler beim Patentamt liegt, oder ein entschuldbarer Fehler des Patentanmelders vorliegt

cession—le document qui transfère les droits de propriété dans une invention

assignment—instrument transferring property rights in an invention

Rechtnachsfolge—das gesetzliche Instrument zur Uebertragung der Eigentumsrechte an einer Erfindung (auch Zession genannt)

cession conditionelle—une cession qui deviendra effective après l'accomplissement d'un acte ou événement; si elles sont enregistrées, de telles cessions sont regardées comme des cessions absolues selon les intentions de l'Office des Brevets (R. 333)

conditional assignment—an assignment provided to be effective on the performance of an act or event; if recorded, such assignments are regarded as absolute assignments for Patent Office purposes (R. 333)

bedingte Uebertragung—eine Uebertragung, welche auf Grund der Ausfuehrung einer Handlung oder eines Ereignisses in Kraft tritt; falls schriftlich niedergelegt, werden solche Uebertragungen fuer die Zwecke des Patentamts als definitive Uebertragungen betrachtet (R. 333)

cessionnaire—le cessionnaire des droits de propriété dans une invention

assignee—the transferee of property rights in an invention

Rechtsnachfolger(Gesamt)—die Person, auf die alle Eigentumsrechte an einer Erfindung uebertragen wurden (auch Zessionaer genannt)

charge de la preuve—le devoir d'introduire de la preuve pour soutenir une position prise au sujet d'une question. Dans les "interférences", la charge de la preuve reste avec le "junior party"; dans le litigies de contrefaçon, la charge de la preuve de contrefaçon reste avec le plaignant; où il s'agit de la validité d'une question, la charge de la preuve d'invalidité reste avec le défendeur.

burden of proof—the obligation to introduce evidence to sustain a position taken on an issue. In interferences, the burden of proof is on the junior party; in infringement suits, the burden of proof of infringement is on the plaintiff; where validity is an issue, the burden of proof of invalidity is on the defendant.

Last der Beweisfuehrung–die Verpflichtung Beweise zur Aufrechterhaltung eines eingenommenen Standpunkts zu erbringen. In Interferenz Faellen faellt die Last der Beweisfuehrung der Juniorpartei (mit dem spaeteren Anmeldetermin) zu; bei Patentverletzungsklagen muss der Klaeger den Beweis der Patentverletzung erbringen; wo die Gueltigkeit in Frage steht, muss der Angeklagte die Ungueltigkeit beweisen.

choix de variantes—choix d'un demandeur, en réponse à une action avançant qu'aucune revendication générique ne soit acceptable, de la variante de son invention à laquelle seront restreintes ses revendications, si on ne tient finalement aucune revendication générique comme acceptable (R. 146)

election of species–selection by applicant, in response to an action holding that no generic claim presented is allowable, of the species of his invention to which his claims shall be restricted if no generic claim is finally held allowable (R. 146)

Wahl der Gattung–Auswahl der Gattung seiner Erfindung durch den Anmelder in Erwiderung auf eine Klage, dass kein vorgebrachter umfassender Anspruch zulaessig ist. Durch Auswahl der Gattung soll der Anspruch auf diese Gattung beschraenkt bleiben, sofern kein umfassender Anspruch als endgueltig zulaessig anerkannt wird. (R. 146)

citation–état de la technique enregistré par l'examinateur comme antériorisé ou pertinent

citation–prior art listed by the examiner as anticipatory or pertinent

Entgegenhaltung–fruehere Technik, die vom Pruefer als vorwegnehmend oder einschlaegig angefuehrt wird

citation des sources—les lois, les affaires de tribunal, ou les publications auxquelles on fait allusion dans une action pour soutenir une position prise

citation of authorities—laws, court cases or publications referred to in an action to support a position taken

Anfuehrung von Autoritaeten—Hinweis auf Gesetze, Gerichtsfaelle order Veroeffentlichungen um eine im Klagefall eingenommene Position zu stuetzen

classification—la désignation numérique de l'Office des Brevets de la catégorie de la matière d'un brevet ou d'une publication das les diverses techniques. La classification est publiée dans le Manuel de Classification et dans les Bulletins de Classification.

classification—the Patent Office numerical designation of the subject matter division of a patent or publication in the various arts. Classification is published in the Manual of Classification and in Classification Bulletins.

Klassifizierung—die vom Patentamt bestimmte zahlenmaessige Einordnung eines Patentgegenstands oder einer Veroeffentlichung in die verschiedenen Sparten der Technik. Die Klassifizierung wird in einem Klassifizierungshandbuch und in Klassifizierungsbekanntmachungen veroeffentlicht.

clause de réserve—un effort d'affirmer ou de réserver la possession d'une matière divulguée mais pas revendiquée dans une demande; cela n'a pas d'effet légal dans les demandes des Etats-Unis

reservation clause—an effort to assert ownership of subject matter disclosed but not claimed in an application; has no legal effect in United States applications

Vorbehalts-Klausel—das Bestreben Eingetumsrechte auf die in einer Anmeldung offenbarten aber nicht mit Anspruch belegten Gegenstaende geltend zu machen; hat keinerlei gesetzliche Wirkung in Anmeldung in den Vereinigten Staaten

co-demandeurs—des co-inventeurs qui demandent un brevet

joint applicants—joint inventors who apply for a patent

Mitanmelder—Erfindergemeinschaft, die ein Patent anmeldet

co-inventeur—un de plusieurs inventeurs qui, ensemble, créent une invention

joint inventor—one of two or more inventors who, together, make an invention

Miterfinder—einer von zwei oder mehr Erfindern, die zusammen eine Erfindung machen

co-inventeurs—plusieurs qui ont créé ensemble une invention

co-inventors—two or more persons who jointly made an invention

Miterfinder—zwei oder mehr Personen, die gemeinsam eine Erfindung gemacht haben

combinaison—plusieurs éléments dont l'action est réciproque

combination—two or more interacting elements

Verbindung—zwei oder mehr aufeinander einwirkende Elemente

combinaison de renvois—la citation de plusieurs renvois qui, considérés ensemble, montrent tous les traits significatifs de la combinaison revendiquée et enseignent l'association de tels traits de la combinaison revendiquée

combination of references—citation of two or more references that, considered together, show all of the significant features of the claimed combination and teach the association of such features of the claimed combination

Verbindung von Hinweisen—Anfuehrung von zwei oder mehr Hinweisen, die zusammen betrachtet, alle kennzeichnenden Eigenschaften der beanspruchten Verbindung tragen und die Assoziation solcher Eigenschaften der beanspruchten Verbindung lehren

Commission d'Appel—le tribunal dans l'Office des Brevets qui a la juridiction de revoir la décision d'un examinateur sur l'appel d'un demandeur. Le tribunal consiste de trois membres choisis du groupe du Commissaire, des Commissaires Adjoints, et des Examinateurs-en-chef.

Board of Appeals—the court in the Patent Office having jurisdiction to review the decision of an examiner on appeal by an applicant. The court consists of three members selected from the group of Commissioner, Assistant Commissioners and Examiners-in-Chief.

Board of Appeals—die Instanz innerhalb des Patentamts, welche bei einer Berufung des Anmelders zustaendig ist, die Entscheidung eines Pruefers nachzupruefen. Diese Instanz besteht aus drei aus der Gruppe des Commissioner, der Assistant Commissioners, und der Hauptpruefer ausgewaehlten Mitgliedern.

Commissaire des Brevets—le chef de l'Office des Brevets, désigné par le Président avec l'accord du Sénat, pour servir pendant un nombre d'années indéfinies comme administrateur de l'Office des Brevets

Commissioner of Patents—the head of the Patent Office, designated by the President with the consent of the Senate, to serve for an indefinite term as administrator of the Patent Office

Commissioner of Patents—der Chef des Patentamts, vom Praesidenten mit der Zustimmung des Senats auf unbefristete Zeit als Verwaltungsbeamter ernannt

Commission des "Interférences" des Brevets—le tribunal dans l'Office des Brevets qui a la juridiction de décider les questions de "interférence"

Board of Patent Interferences—the court in the Patent Office having jurisdiction to decide interference issues

Board of Patent Interferences—die Instanz im Patentamt, der die Rechtsprechung in Interferenz Faellen obliegt

compensation—la restitution d'une perte

compensation—restitution for a loss

Abfindung—Rueckerstattung fuer einen Verlust

composition—une classe de matière brevetable qui comprend la mixture de plusieurs ingrédients pour produire un solide, un liquide, ou un gaz possédant les qualités différentes des, ou en addition aux qualités possédées par les plusieurs ingrédients, individuellement ou en commun

composition of matter—a class of patentable subject matter that involves the mixture of two or more ingredients to provide a solid, liquid or gas possessing properties different from or in addition to the properties possessed by the several ingredients, individually or in common

Stoffverbindung—eine Klase patentfaehiger Gegenstaende, welche die Mischung von zwei oder mehr Bestandteilen umfasst um eine feste Masse, eine Fluessigkeit oder ein Gas zu schaffen, mit Eigenschaften verschieden von, oder zusaetzlich zu den Eigenschaften, welche die individuellen Bestandteile im einzelnen oder gemeinsam aufweisen

"comprising"—une qualification qui laisse ouverte une revendication pour y inclure des ingrédients non-spécifiés, même dans des quantités majeures. "Comprising essentially" a la même signification.

comprising—a qualification that leaves a claim open for the inclusion of unspecified ingredients, even in major amounts. "Comprising essentially" has the same meaning.

inbegriffen—eine Qualifikation, welche einen Anspruch auf Einschluss sicht-spezifizierter Bestandteile selbst in groesseren Mengen offen laesst. "Im wesentlichen inbegriffen" bedeutet dasselbe.

compte de dépôt–une somme, maintenue à un minimum de $50.00, gardée sur dépôt avec l'Office des Brevets par un avocat ou un agent, chargée pour couvrir les taxes de délivrance, les taxes finales, les taxes d'appel et de pétition, et la coûte des services de l'Office des Brevets, tel que des requêtes des copies des archives, des histoires du brevet, et la correction des dessins (R. 25)

deposit account–a sum, maintained at a minimum of $50.00, kept on deposit with the Patent Office by an attorney or agent to be charged to cover filing, final, appeal and petition fees, and cost of Patent Office services such as requests for copies of records, file histories, and correction of drawings (R. 25)

Hinterlegungs–Konto–eine Summe von mindestens $50., die ein Anwalt oder gesetzlicher Vertreter zur Deckung von Anmelde–und Schluss–gebuehren, Berufungs–und Eingebegebuehren, sowie Kosten fuer Dienstleistungen des Patentamts, wie Gesuche um Abschriften einer Akte und Zeichnungs–Korrekturen, beim Patentamt unterhaelt (R. 25)

concédant–un demandeur ou un breveté qui accorde la licence

licensor–applicant or patentee who grants a license

Lizenzgeber–Anmelder oder Patentinhaber, der eine Lizenz erteilt

conception–la partie mentale de l'acte inventif, qui est accompli quand on reconnaît une incarnation active de l'invention. On doit pouvoir prouver la conception, au moyen des dessins ou de la communication faite à une autre personne, si on peut y compter. (MPEP 715.07)

conception–the mental part of the inventive act, which is completed when an operative embodiment of the invention is recognized. Conception must be capable of proof, such as by drawings or disclosure to another person, if it is to be relied upon. (MPEP 715.07)

gedankliche Erfassung—der geistige Teil des Erfindungsprozesses der vollendet ist, wenn eine wirksame Ausfuehrungsform der Erfindung anerkannt ist. Die gedankliche Erfassung muss z. B. durch Zeichnungen oder Offenbarung einem anderen gegenueber beweisfaehig sein um sich darauf stuezen zu koennen. (MPEP 715.07)

concurrence injuste—une déception ou une fraude dans la pratique des affaires qui viole les droits légaux ou équitables d'un concurrent ou du public

unfair competition—deception or fraud in business practice that violates the legal or equitable rights of a competitor or the public

unlauterer Wettbewerb—Taeschung oder Betrug im Geschaeftsgebaren, die die gesetzlichen oder billigen Rechte eines Konkurrenten oder der Allgemeinheit verletzen

congé—un jour officiel où on ne travaille pas dans le District of Columbia: le Jour de l'An, le 1er janvier; l'anniversaire de Washington, le 22 février; le Jour Commémoratif, le 30 mai; le Jour d'Indépendance, le 4 juillet; le Jour de Travail, le premier lundi de septembre; le Jour des Anciens Combattants, de 11 novembre; le Jour des Actions de Grâce, le quatrième jeudi de novembre; le Jour de Noël, le 25 décembre; et le Jour de l'Inauguration, le 20 janvier, tous les quatre ans. Quand le congé est le samedi, on observe le vendredi précédant comme jour de congé.

holiday—an official non-work day in the District of Columbia: New Year's Day, January 1; Washington's Birthday, February 22; Memorial Day, May 30; Independence Day, July 4; Labor Day, first Monday in September; Veterans Day, November 11; Thanksgiving Day, fourth Thursday in November; Christmas Day, December 25; and Inauguration Day, January 20 every four years; when the holiday falls on a Saturday, the preceding Friday is observed as a holiday

Feiertag—ein amtlicher Nicht-Arbeitstag im District of Columbia: der Neujahrstag am 1. Januar; Washington's Geburtstag am 22. Februar; Memorial Day am 30. Mai; Unabhaengigkeitstag am 4. Juli; Labor Day am ersten Montag im September; Tag der Veteranen am 11. November; Weihnachten am 25. Dezember; und alle vier Jahre der 20. Januar, die Amtseinsetzung des Praesidenten; faellt der Feiertag auf einen Samstag, ist der vorhergehende Freitag ein Feiertag

connaissance ou usage antérieur—voir antériorité

prior knowledge or use—see anticipation

fruehere Kenntnis oder Benutzung—vgl. Vorwegnahme

"consisting of"—une qualification qui ferme une revendication à l'inclusion des substances ou des matériels hors de ceux qui sont énumérés, sauf les impuretés associées ordinairement avec les substances ou matériels énumérés. En ajoutant "essentiellement" à "consisting of" on ouvre la revendication aux ingrédients, qui n'influencent pas matériellement les caractéristiques fondamentales et nouvelles de la composition.

consisting of—a qualification that closes a claim to the inclusion of materials other than those recited, except for impurities ordinarily associated with the recited materials. Adding "essentially" to "consisting of" opens the claim to ingredients that do not materially affect the basic and novel characteristics of the composition.

bestehend aus—eine Einschraenkung, welche einen Anspruch vom Einschluss von Materialien ausser den genannten ausschliesst, mit Ausnahme von Unreinheiten, welche im Allgemeinen mit den genannten Materielien verbunden sind. Wird "wesentlich" zu "bestehend aus" hinzugefuegt, so wird damit der Anspruch Bestandteilen geoeffnet, die die grundlegenden und neuartigen Eigentuemlichkeiten der Zusammensetzung nicht wesentlich beeintrachtigen.

continuation—une deuxième demande pour la même invention revendiquée ou divulguée dans une demande antérieure, où la deuxiéme demande est déposée avant que la demande originale soit abandonnée, par le même demandeur, et il n'y introduit aucune matière nouvelle. On peut employer une continuation pour introduire un nouvel ensemble de revendications après le rejet final pour un autre examen par l'examinateur Primaire (MPEP 201.07) at a droit à la date de dépôt de la demande originale. (MPEP 201.11)

continuation—a second application for the same invention claimed or disclosed in a prior application, where the second application is filed, before the original application is abandoned, by the same applicant, and no new matter is introduced. A continuation may be used to introduce a new set of claims after final rejection for further examination by the Primary Examiner (MPEP 201.07) and is entitled to the benefit of the filing date of the original application. (MPEP 201.11)

Fortfuehrung—eine zweite Anmeldung fuer die gleiche, in einer frueheren Anmeldung beanspruchte und offenbarte Erfindung, bei der die zweite Anmeldung von demselben Anmelder eingereicht wurde, ehe die Erst-Anmeldung aufgegeben war, und kein neues Material eingefuehrt wird. Eine Fortfuehrung kann dazu benutzt werden, eine neue Serie von Anspruechen—nach der endgueltigen Ablehnung des Vorpruefers—zur weiteren Pruefung einzureichen (MPEP 201.07); die Fortfuehrung berechtigt von dem Einreichungstermin der Erst-Anmeldung zu profitieren. (MPEP 201.11)

contrefaçon—l'utilisation ou la vente d'une invention brevetée sans autorisation, ou l'encouragement actif d'une telle utilisation ou vente (Sec. 271)

infringement—use or sale of a patented invention without authority, or active inducement of such use or sale (Sec. 271)

Verletzung—Benutzung oder Verkauf einer patentierten Erfindung ohne Berichtigung oder taetige Veranlassung zu solchem Gebrauch oder Verkauf (Sec. 271)

contribuant à la contrefaçon—encourageant l'utilisation d'une invention revendiquée par une personne sans autorisation, ou vendant une partie constituante d'une invention brevetée ou d'un matériel ou d'un appareil employé dans la partique d'un procédé breveté, tout en sachant qu'il était fabriqué et adapté spécialement pour l'employer dans un contrefaçon d'un tel brevet, à moins que la partie constituante soit un article régulaire ou établi à un grand emploi non-contrefaisant (Sec. 271)

contributory infringement—inducing the practice of a claimed invention by an unauthorized person, or selling a component of a patented invention or a material or apparatus used in practising a patented process while knowing it was specially made and adapted for use in an infringement of such patent, unless the component is a staple article suitable for substantial non-infringing use (Sec. 271)

Beihilfe zur Patentverletzung—die Veranlassung zur Ausfuehrung einer beanspruchten Erfindung durch Unbefugte; oder der Verkauf eines Teiles einer patentierten Erfindung, oder eines Stoffes, oder Apparates, die der Ausuebung eines patentierten Verfahrens dienen, wohlwissend, dass sie eigens zur Benutzung bei der Verletzung eines solchen Patents hergestellt oder dazu besonders angepasst wurden, sofern der Teil keine zu wesentlicher nicht-patent-verletzender Benutzung geeignete Stapelware ist (Sec. 271)

Convention de Paris—la Convention Internationale pour la Protection de la Propriété Industrielle

Paris Convention—the International Convention for Protection of Industrial Property

Pariser Verbandsuebereinkunft—die internationale Verbandsuebereinkunft zum Schutz gewerblichen Eigentums

Convention Internationale pour la Protection de la Propriété Industrielle—un acord au sujet des brevets et des marques de fabrique, concédant à un demandeur d'un pays unioniste la même date d'effet de dépôt dans d'autres pays unionistes pour une demande déposée dans le délai d'une année de la première date de dépôt. La demande doit acceder aux lois des brevets du pays où on veut le déposer.

International Convention for Protection of Industrial Property—an agreement respecting patents and trademarks giving an applicant in one member country the same effective filing date in other Convention Countries for an application filed within a year of the first filing date. The application must comply with the patent laws of the country in which filing is sought.

Internationale Uebereinkunft zum Schutz gewerblichen Eigentums—eine Vereinbarung ueber Patente und Warenzeichen, die Anmeldern in einem Mitgliedsland dasselbe Einreichungsdatum als Termin des Inkrafttretens, wie in anderen Uebereinkunftslaendern, fuer eine innerhalb eines Jahres vom ersten Einreichungsdatum eingereichte Anmeldung, zugesteht. Die Anmeldung muss den Patentgesetzen des Landes, in dem um die Einreichung nachgesucht wird, genuegen.

co-pendant—des demandes viables qui sont simultanément à l'Office des Brevets

copending—applications that are on file and active in the Patent Office at the same time

gleichzeitig anhaengig—Anmeldungen, die zur gleichen Zeit in den Akten vorhanden und aktiv sind

copiant une revendication—faisant des amendements à une demande pour y inclure une revendication faite à un autre, dans le but de décider ce lui qui est le premier inventeur de ce que décrit la revendication copiée

copying a claim—amending an application to include a claim of another for the purpose of the declaring of an interference, to determine who is the first inventor of what the copied claim describes

Abschrift eines Anspruchs—eine Anmeldung dahingehend zu berichtigen, dass der Anspruch eines anderen zum Zwecke einer Interferenz Erklaerung eingeschlossen wird, um festzustellen, wer der erste Erfinder dessen ist, was in der Abschrift des Anspruchs beschrieben wird

copie certifiée—une copie portant l'attestation de l'Office des Brevets qu'elle est une vraie copie, qu'on peut exiger dans des affaires de priorité (Sec. 119) ou pour des autres intentions

certified copy—a copy bearing the attestation of the Patent Office that it is a true copy, as may be required in priority cases (Sec. 119) or for other purposes

beglaubigte Abschrift—eine Abschrift mit der Bestaetigung des Patentamts, dass es sich um eine wortgetreue Kopie handelt, wie sie in Prioritaetsfaellen (Sec. 119) oder zu anderen Zwecken verlangt wird

copyright (droit d'auteur)—une restriction à l'initiateur ou à son successeur en intérêt, du droit de reproduire une oeuvre littéraire ou artistique, telle restriction étant protégée par conformité des stipulations des statuts des droits d'auteur et soutenant les règlements administratifs

copyright—a reservation to the originator, or to his successor in interest, of the right to reproduce a literary or artistic work, such reservation being protected by compliance with the provisions of the copyright statutes and supporting administrative regulations

Copyright (Urheberrecht)—ein Reservatsrecht des Urhebers oder seines Interessen-Nachfolgers ein literarisches oder kuenstlerisches Werk zu reproduzieren; dieses Reservatsrecht ist durch Erfuellung der Bestimmungen der Copyright Statuten und der Ausfuehrungsbestimmungen geschuetzt

corroboration d'un inventeur—la preuve des déclarations faites du part d'un inventeur

corroboration of an inventor—evidence to prove statements made by an inventor

Bestaetigung—Beweismaterial zur Bezeugung der Darlegung eines Erfinders

"**count**"—dans la practique d'interférence une revendication qui intervient (une réclamation faite des parties d'une "interference")

count—in interference practice, an interfering claim (a claim made by the parties to an interference)

Klagepunkt—in Interferenz Praxis, ein kollidierender Anspruch (ein von den Parteien in einer Interferenz gemachter Anspruch)

coupon—an garant vendu, par l'Office des Brevets, individuellement ou dans les livrets en dénominations de vingt ou cinquante cents, emploé pour l'achat des copies de brevets, des brevets de dessein et de plante, et des dépôts de marque de fabrique (R. 24)

coupon—a voucher sold by the Patent Office individually or in books in denominations of twenty cents and fifty cents for use in purchasing copies of patents, design and plant patents, and trademark registrations (R.24)

Kupon—ein vom Patentamt einzeln oder in Heften mit Werten von 20 und 50 cents verkaufter Bezugschein zur Benutzung beim Erwerb von Patentabschriften, Geschmacksmuster und Pflanzen Patenten, sowie Registrierung von Warenzeichen (R. 24)

Court of Appeals (cour de cessation)—un tribunal qui a la jurisdiction dans son domaine sur des appels des décisions finales des United States District Courts

Court of Appeals—a court having jurisdiction in its area over appeals from final decisions of U. S. District Courts

Berufungsgericht (Court of Appeals)—ein Gericht, welches in seinem Gebiet fuer die Einlegung von Berufung gegen endgueltige Entscheidungen des U. S. District Courts zustaendig ist

Court of Claims (cour des réclamation)—un tribunal qui entend des plaintes contre le Gouvernement des Etats-Unis; en matières des brevets, une telle plainte pourrait être une réclamation pour restitution, à cause d'un emploi sans autorisation d'un brevet par le Gouvernement des Etats-Unis

Court of Claims—a court that hears cases against the Government of the United States; in patent matters, such a case could be a claim for compensation for unauthorized use of a patent by the Government of the United States

Court of Claims—ein Gerichtshof, in dem Klagen gegen die Regierung der Vereinigten Staaten zur Verhandlung kommen; in Patentangelegenheiten koennte dies eine Schadenersatzklage wegen unbefugter Benutzung eines Patents durch die Regierung der Vereinigten Staaten sein

Court of Customs and Patent Appeals—un tribunal à Washington, D. C. qui entend des appels des décisions de la Commission d'Appel et de la Commission des Examineteurs d'Interférence par le témoignage produit devant l'Office des Brevets (Sec. 141)

Court of Customs and Patent Appeals—a court in Washington, D. C. that hears appeals from decisions of the Board of Appeals and the Board of Interference Examiners, on the evidence produced before the Patent Office (Sec. 141)

Court of Customs and Patent Appeals—ein Gerichtshof in Washington, D. C., in dem Berufungen gegen die Entscheidungen des Board of Appeals und des Board of Interference Examiners zur Verhandlung kommen, auf Grund von Beweismaterial, das vor dem Patentamt erbracht wurde (Sec. 141)

cross-reference—renvoi à une demande relative—la déclaration dans une spécification, suivant immédiatement l'abstraction de la divulgation, identifiant une demande copendante, antérieurement déposée par le même demandeur pour la même invention par nombre successif, le date de dépôt et relation, dans le but d'obtenir l'avantage de la date de dépôt de la demande antérieure

cross-reference to a related application—the statement in a specification, immediately after the abstract of the disclosure, identifying an earlier filed co-pending application of the same applicant for the same invention by serial number, filing date and relationship, for the purpose of getting the benefit of the filing date of the prior application

Hinweis auf eine verwandte Anmeldung—die Angabe in einer Beschreibung (specification) sofort nach dem Auszug aus der Offenbarung, welche eine frueher eingerichte, gleichzeitig schwebende Anmeldung des gleichen Anmelders fuer die gleiche Erfindung mit laufender Nummer, Einreichungsdatum und Beziehung identifiziert, um in die Nutzniessung des Einreichungsdatums der frueheren Anmeldung zu gelangen

D

date d'antériorité—voir droit de priorité

priority date—see priority right

Prioritaetsdatum—vgl. Prioritaetsrecht

date de délivrance—la date de la délivrance d'un brevet

date of grant—date of issue of a patent

Erteilungsdatum—Datum der Patentverleihung

date de demande—voir date de dépôt

application date—see filing date

Anmeldedatum—vgl. Einreichungsdatum

date d'effet de demande—la date de dépôt d'une "parent" demande, ou d'une demande déposée de la même personne pour la même invention dans un pays étranger unioniste et accédant aux conditions de Sec. 119

effective date of application—the date of filing of a parent application, or of an application filed by the same person for the same invention in a foreign convention country and complying with the provisions of Sec. 119

Datum des Inkrafttretens einer Anmeldung—das Einreichungsdatum einer Stamm-Anmeldung oder einer Anmeldung, die von derselben Person fuer diesselbe Erfindung in einem auslaendischen Verbandsstaat eingereicht wurde und die Vorschriften unter Sec. 119 erfuellt

date de dépôt—la date où la demande entière ou la dernière partie d'une demande, dans une forme acceptable pour l'examen, est reçue dans l'Office des Brevets (R. 55)

filing date—the date on which the complete or the last part of an application, in form acceptable for examination, is received in the Patent Office (R. 55)

(offizielles) Einreichungsdatum—das Datum, an dem die vollstaendige Anmeldung oder der letzte Teil derselben, in zur Pruefung annehmbarer Form, im Patentamt empfangen wird (R. 55)

date de priorité conventionnelle ou unioniste—la date de priorité d'une demande, et du brevet y inclus, déposée sous le bénéfice de la Convention d'Union de Paris

convention date—priority date of an application, and of the patent thereon, filed under the provisions of the Union Convention of Paris

Datum der Verbands-Prioritaet—Prioritaetsdatum einer Anmeldung und des darauffolgenden Patents, eingereicht gemaess den Bestimmungen der Pariser Union Verbandsuebereinkunft

date due—le dernier jour de la période de temps dans laquelle le demandeur doit répondre à une action de l'Office des Brevets

due date—the last day of the time period in which applicant must answer an action by the Patent Office

Faelligkeitstermin—der letzte Tag der Frist, innerhalb welcher der Anmelder auf eine Klage des Patentamts antworten muss

déchéance du brevet—la terminaison de la durée du brevet parce qu'on a manqué de payer le solde de la taxe de délivrance dans le délai de trois mois de la date du brevet (860 OG 2)

lapse of patent—termination of patent term by reason of failure to pay the balance of the issue fee due within three months of the date of the patent (860 OG 2)

Verfallen des Patents—Beendigung der Laufzeit des Patents durch Versaeumnis die Restsumme der Erteilungsgebuehr, die innerhalb von drei Monaten von Datum des Patents faellig ist, zu bezahlen (860 O. G. 2)

déclaration—déclaration du demandeur qu'il a accédé aux stipulations de Sec. 101 et Sec. 102, acceptée au lieu d'un serment si elle comprend les affirmations que les déclarations faites de sa propre connaissance sont vraies, que les déclarations faites des renseignements et de la croyance sont crues d'être vraies, et qu'on punira les déclarations fausses faites volontairement par amende et/ou incarcération (18 USC 1001) et que telles déclarations peuvent nasarder la validité de la déclaration ou d'aucun brevet qui est délivré d'une telle déclaration. On peut aussi employer la déclaration quand on présente une revendication pour la matière qui n'était pas originalement revendiquée (R. 67), quand on demande un brevet "reissue" (R. 171, 172), quand on demande un brevet de dessein (R. 151, 153), quand on demande un brevet de plante (R. 161, 162), et quand on dépose une déclaration exigée de 42 USC 2182 ou 2457 (c) (comme les inventions sous les règlements de la Commission d'Energie Atomique ou le Programme de l'Espace Nationale).

declaration—statement of the applicant that he has complied with the provisions of Sec. 101 and Sec. 102, accepted in lieu of oath if it includes the averments that statements made of his own knowledge are true, that statements made on information and belief are believed to be true, and there is included the notice that willful false statements are punishable by fine and/or imprisonment (18 USC 1001) and may jeopardize the validity of the application or any patent issuing on such declaration. Declaration can also be used when presenting a claim for matter not claimed originally (R. 67), when applying for a reissue patent (R. 171, 172), when applying for a design patent (R. 151, 153), when applying for a plant patent (R. 161, 162) and when filing a statement required by 42 USC 2182 or 2457(c) (as to inventions under Atomic Energy Commission or National Space Program regulations).

eidesstattliche Erklaerung—Mitteilung des Anmelders, dass er die Vorschriften unter Sec. 101 und Sec. 102 erfuellt hat angenommen an Eides statt, sofern diese die Versicherung enthaelt, dass die aus eigener Kenntnis gemachten Behauptungen wahr sind und, dass Behauptungen begruendet auf Auskuenften und Glauben fuer wahr gehalten werden. Auch ist die Benachrichtigung, dass absichtlich gemachte falsche Aussagen mit Geldstrafe und/oder Gefangenschaft strafbar sind enthalten (18 USC 1001) und die Gueltigkeit der Anmeldung oder eines auf der Erklaerung begruendeten Patents gefaehrden. Eine eidesstattliche Erklaerung kann auch dann benuetzt werden, wenn ein Anspruch auf urspruenglich nicht beanspruchte Materie geltend gemacht wird (R. 67), beim Anmelden eines Wiedererteilungs-Patents (R. 171, -172), beim Anmelden eines Geschmacksmusters (R. 151, 153), beim Anmelden eines Pflanzenpatents (R. 161, 162), und beim Einreichen einer vom 42 USC 2182 oder 2457 (c) verlangten Aufstellung (mit Hinsicht auf Erfindungen, die unter die Vorschriften der Atomic Energy Commission oder des National Space Program fallen.

déclaration préliminaire—pour chaque "count" d'une "interférence", au sujet d'une invention créée aux Etats-Unis, une déclaration des faits et des actes qui établissent la date où on a fait le premier dessin de l'invention (ou une déclaration qu'on n'a fait aucun dessin de l'invention avant de déposer), la date où on a fait la première description écrite de l'invention (ou une déclaration qu'on n'a fait aucune description écrite avant de déposer), la date de la première divulgation de l'invention à autrui (ou une déclaration qu'il n'y avait aucune divulgation faite avant de déposer), la date et la nature des premiers actes prouvables qui établiraient la conception de l'invention (ou une déclaration qu'il n'y avait pas de teks actes), la date de la réduction actuelle à la pratique de l'invention (ou une déclaration qu'il n'y avait pas de réduction à la pratique avant de déposer), et la date où il a commencé l'exercice actif pour réduire à la pratique l'invention. Si une partie dépend uniquement d'une demande antérieure des Etats-Unis, ou étrangère, la déclaration préliminaire peut le proclamer et ne doit pas être signée (R. 216).

Quand on a créé l'invention à l'étranger, la déclaration devrait proclamer l'heure où on a introduit l'invention aux Etats-Unis, énumérant les circonstances et les dates de l'activité aux Etats-Unis. (R. 217)

preliminary statement—as to each count of an interference, on an invention made in the United States, a statement of the facts and acts that establish the date on which the first drawing of the invention was made (or a statement that no drawing was made prior to filing), the date on which the first written description of the invention was made (or a statement that no written description was made prior to filing), the date of first disclosure of the invention to another (or a statement that there was no disclosure prior to filing), the date and nature of the first provable acts that would establish conception of the invention (or a statement that there were no such acts), the date of actual reduction to practice of the invention (or a statement that there was no actual reduction to practice prior to filing), and the date when active exercise of reasonable diligence toward reducing the invention to practice began. If a party relies solely on a prior domestic or foreign application, the preliminary statement may so state, and need not be signed. (R. 216)

When the invention was made abroad, the preliminary statement should state when the invention was introduced into the United States, giving the circumstances and dates of activity in the United States. (R. 217)

Vorerklaerung—in Bezug auf jeden Klagepunkt in einer Interferenz bei einer in den Vereinigten Staaten gemachten Erfindung: eine Darstellung des Sachverhalts und Verhaltens, die das Datum an dem die erste Zeichnung fuer die Erfindung gemacht wurde, festlegen (oder eine Erklaerung, dass keine Zeichnung vor dem Einreichen gemacht wurde), das Datum an dem die erste schriftliche Schilderung gemacht wurde (oder eine Erklaerung, dass keine schriftliche Schilderung vor dem Einreichen gemacht wurde), das Datum der ersten Offenbarung der Erfindung einem andern gegenueber (oder eine Erklaerung, dass vor dem Einreichen keine Offenbarung gemacht wurde); das Datum und die Beschaffenheit der ersten beweisfaehigen Handlungen, die die gedankliche Erfassung der Erfindung festlegen (oder eine Erklaerung, dass solche Handlungen nicht stattgefunden haben), das Datum des tatsaechlichen Umsetzens der Erfindung in die Praxis (oder eine Erklaerung, dass ein tatsaechliches Umsetzen in die Praxis vor dem Einreichen nicht stattgefunden hat), und das Datum an dem die taetige Aufwendung angemessener Sorgfalt um die Erfindung in die Praxis umzusetzen, began. Wenn eine Partei sich ausschliesslich auf eine fruehere in- oder auslaendische Anmeldung stuetzt, so kann dies in der Vorerklaerung angegeben und braucht nicht unterzeichnet zu werden (R. 216). Falls die Erfindung im Ausland gemacht wurde, sollte in der Vorerklaerung—unter Angabe der Umstaende und Betaetigungsdaten in den Vereinigten Staaten—angegeben werden wann die Erfindung in die Vereinigten Staaten eingefuehrt wurde (R. 217).

déclaration sour serment—la declaration des faits sous serment pour surmonter un brevet cité ou une publication (R. 131), pour nier une raison de rejet (R. 132), pour soutenir une demande pour "reissue" (R. 175), avant une déclaration de "interférence" (R. 202, 204), ou après un appel (R. 195)

affidavit—statement of facts under oath to overcome a cited patent or publication (R. 131), to traverse a ground of rejection (R. 132), in support of an application for reissue (R. 175), before a declaration of interference (R. 202, 204), or after appeal (R. 195)

beschworene schriftliche Erklaerung—Darlegung von Tatsachen unter Eid um ein angefuehrtes Patent oder eine Veroeffentlichung ausser Kraft zu setzen (R. 131), einen Grund zur Ablehnung zu ueberbruecken (R. 132), zur Unterstuetzung einer Anmeldung zur Wiedererteilung (R. 175), vor einer Interferenz Erklaerung (R. 202, 204), oder nach einer Berufung (R. 195)

dédicace—rendant disponible une invention pour l'utilisation libre. Accompli par une déclaration directe, ou en divulguant et ne revendiquant pas une invention d'une telle manière qu'il opère une interdiction statutaire de breveter.

dedication—making an invention available for free use. Accomplished by direct statement, or by disclosing and not claiming an invention in such a manner that a statutory or other bar to patenting takes effect.

Verzicht zu Gunsten der Allgemeinheit—eine Erfindung zum freien Gebrauch zur Verfuegung stellen. Ausfuehrbar entweder durch deutliche Erklaerung oder durch Offenbarung und Nicht-Beanspruchung der Erfindung in einer Weise, die einen gesetzlichen oder anderen Hinderungsgrund zur Patentierung in Kraft treten laesst.

délivrance—l'octroi d'un brevet

issue—the grant of a patent

Ausgabe—die Erteilung eines Patents

demande abandonnée—une plainte que le demandeur n'a pas poursuivie pendant le temps détérminé, ou une plainte que le demandeur a declarée, d'une manière expressive, ne sera pas revendiquée (R. 135)

abandoned application—a case that applicant has failed to prosecute within the time fixed, or a case that applicant has declared expressly will not be further prosecuted (R. 135)

Fallengelassene Anmeldung—ein Fall, den der Anmelder innerhalb der festgesetzten Frist zu verfolgen versaeumt hat; oder ein Fall, der nach ausdruecklicher Erklaerung pas revendiquée (R. 135)

une demande de continuation—en-partie—une demande déposée pendant la vie d'une demande antérieure par le même demandeur, répétant quelque partie significative de la demande antérieure et ajoutant quelque chose qui n'était pas inclus dans l'affaire antérieure (MPEP 201.8) ou rayant quelque chose divulgé dans l'affaire antérieure

continuation-in-part application—an application filed during the lifetime of an earlier application by the same applicant, repeating some substantial portion of the earlier application and adding matter not disclosed in the earlier case (MPEP 201.8) or deleting matter disclosed in the earlier case

Teilfortfuehrungs-Anmeldung—eine Anmeldung, die weahrend der Laufzeit einer frueheren Anmeldung von demselben Anmelder eingereicht wurde, unter Wiederholung eines betraechtlichen Teils der frueheren Anmeldung und unter Hinzufuegung von in dem vorhergehenden Fall nicht offenbartem Material (MPEP 201.8), oder unter Streichung von in dem vorhergehenden Fall offenbartem Material

demande divisionnaire—une demande présentant une invention indépendante et distincte qu'on a incluse dans une demande présentant une autre invention indépendante et distincte

divisional application—an application setting forth an independent and distinct invention that had been included in an application setting forth another independent and distinct invention

Ausgeschiedene Anmeldung—eine Anmeldung, die eine von einer andern unabhaengige und verschiedene Erfindung darlegt, die in einer Anmeldung eingeschlossen war, welche eine andere unabhaengige und verschiedene Erfindung darlegt

demande d'un brevet—un pétition ou une requête pour un brevet (R. 61), la spécification et les revendications (R. 71-77), le serment ou la déclaration (R. 65), les dessins nécessaires (R. 81-88) et la taxe de dépôt nécessaire (R. 21)

application for patent—a petition or request for a patent (R. 61), specification and claims (R. 71-77), oath or declaration (R. 65), necessary drawings (R. 81-88) and prescribed filing fee R. 21)

Patentanmeldung—ein Antrag oder Gesuch um Erteilung eines Patents (R. 61), Beschreibung (specification) und Ansprueche (R. 71-77), Eid oder eidesstattliche Erklaerung (R. 65), notwendige Zeichnungen (R. 81-88) und die vorgeschriebene Anmeldegebuehr (R. 21)

demande substitute—un double d'une demande du même demandeur qui a été abandonnée avant le dépôt de la demande postérieure (MPEP 201.09)

substitute application—a duplicate of an application by the same applicant that was abandoned before the filing of the later case (MPEP 201.09)

Ersatz-Anmeldung—ein Duplikat einer Anmeldung von demselben Anmelder, die vor dem Einreichen des spaeteren Falles fallengelassen worden ist (MPEP 201.09)

demandeur—l'inventeur ou les co-inventeurs qui ont demandé un brevet; ou le représentant légal (R. 42, 43) ou le co-inventeur (R. 47 (a)) ou l'intérêt propriétaire (R. 47(b)) qui a demandé un brevet au lieu de l'inventeur

applicant—the inventor or the joint inventors who have applied for a patent; or the legal representative (R. 42, 43) or joint inventor (R. 47(a)) or proprietary interest (R. 47(b)) who has applied for a patent in place of the inventor

Anmelder—der Erfinder oder die Erfindergemeinschaft, die ein Patent eingereicht haben; oder der gesetzliche Vertreter (R. 42, 43), oder der Miterfinder (R. 47(a)), oder der rechtliche Eigentuemer (R. 47(b)) der an Stelle des Erfinders ein Patent zur Anmeldung eingereicht hat

démarches mentales—les démarches dans un procédé qu'on peut exécuter dans l'esprit humain, tel que calculer, comparer, déterminer, compter, observer, enregistrer et supputer

mental steps—steps in a process that can be performed in the human mind, such as calculating, comparing, determining, counting, observing, recording and computing

geistige Schritte—Schritte in einem Vorgang, die im menschlichen Verstand geleistet werden koennen, wie zum Beispiel, rechnen, vergleichen, bestimmen, zaehlen, beobachten, registrieren und auswerten

demeure—la ville et l'état ou le pays où demeure le demandeur (MPEP 605.02)

residence—the city and state or country in which the applicant lives (MPEP 605.02)

Wohnort—die Stadt, oder der Staat, oder das Land in dem der Anmelder wohnhaft ist (MPEP 605.02)

dépôt—la transcription des épreuves orales d'un temoin dans une "interférence sous les conditions de R. 272 et seq.

deposition—the record of the oral examination of a witness in an interference under the provisions of R. 272 et seq.

eidliche Aussage—Protokoll des muendlichen Verhoers eines Zeugen in einer Interferenz unter den Bestimmungen von R. 272 et seq.

dessin—une représentation de chaque trait de l'invention spécifiée dans les revendications, préparée en accord avec les R. 81-88 des Règles de la Preatique

drawing—a showing of every feature of the invention specified in the claims, prepared in accordance with Rules 81-88 of the Rules of Practice

Zeichnung—das Aufzeigen eines jeden Merkmals der im Patentanspruch beschriebenen Erfindung, angefertigt in Uebereinstimmung mit den Vorschriften 81-88 der Rules of Practice

dessin casuel—un dessin qui ne conforme par aux exigences de R. 81–84, qu'on peut admettre pour l'examen mais on doit le corriger ou en présenter un nouveau dessin, comme exigé

informal drawing—a drawing that fails to comply with the requirements of R. 81-84, which may be admitted for purpose of examination but must be corrected or a new drawing furnished, as required

nicht-formgerechte Zeichnung—eine Zeichnung, die mit den Anforderungen von R. 81–84 nicht uebereinstimmt, die zum Zweck der Pruefung zugelassen werden darf, aber korrigiert werden muss, oder—nach jeweiligem Verlangen —durch eine neue Zeichnung ersetzt werden muss

dessin ou modèle déposé—un brevet sur un dessin nouveau, original et ornémental, conçu pour un produit industriel, délivré pour une période de trois et demie, sept ou quatorze ans, la durée est au choix du demandeur (R. 151-155)

design patent—patent on a new, original and ornamental design for an article of manufacture, granted for a period of three and one-half, seven or fourteen years, the term being at the option of applicant (R. 151-155)

Geschmacksmusterpatent—Patent fuer ein neues, eigenartiges und ornamentales Muster fuer einen gewerblichen Artikel, das fuer eine Zeitspanne von dreieinhalb, sieben oder vierzehn Jahren erteilt wird; die Dauer der Laufzeit liegt beim Anmelder (R. 151-155)

diligence—activité continue d'un progrès raisonnable en réduisant à la pratique une invention, ou en agissant pour corriger une erreur dans un brevet octroyé

diligence—continuous activity at a reasonable rate in reducing an invention to practice or in acting to correct an error in an issued patent

Sorgfalt—in angemessenem Grad andauernde Taetigkeit die Erfindung in die Praxis umzusetzen, oder einen Irrtum in einem schon erteilten Patent zu korrigieren

dissimulation—garder secrète une invention

concealment—keeping an invention secret

Verheimlichung—eine Erfindung geheimhalten

District Court—un tribunal Fédéral qui a la juridiction d'une action relative aux brevets. On peut présenter les procès de contrefaçon dans le district où demeure le défendeur, ou dans le district, où il a commis des actes de contrefaçon et où il a établi ses affaires. (28 USC 1338, 1400)

District Court—a Federal court having jurisdiction of an action relating to patents. Infringement suit can be brought in the district where the defendant resides, or has committed acts of infringement and has an established business. (28 USC 1338, 1400)

District Court—ein Bundesgerichtshof (Federal Court), der die Gerichtsbarkeit in Zivilklagen mit Bezug auf Patente hat. Patentverletzungsklagen koennen im Wohnbezirk des Angeklagten angestrengt werden oder dort, wo er das Patent verletzt hat oder ein eingefuehrtes Geschaeft besitzt. (28 USC 1338, 1400)

District Court for District of Columbia—un tribunal Fédéral qui a la juridiction des appel d'une décision de la Commision d'Appel et de la Commission des "Interférences" des Brevets, quant des parties opposées habitent des districts judiciaux différents, pas dedans un état ou habitent un pays étranger, et quand l'appel n'est pas déposé avec la Court of Customs and Patent Appeals (Sec. 145, 146)

District Court for District of Columbia—a Federal court having jurisdiction of appeals from decisions of the Board of Appeals and the Board of Patent Interferences, when adverse parties reside in different judicial districts not within one state or in a foreign country, and when the appeal is not filed with the Court of Customs and Patent Appeals (Sec. 145, 146)

District Court for District of Columbia—ein Bundesgerichtshof (Federal Court), der die Gerichtsbarkeit in Berufungen gegen Entscheidungen des Board of Appeals und des Board of Patent Interferences hat, wenn die Gegenparteien in verschiedenen Gerichtsbezirken, nicht innerhalb desselben Bundesstaates, oder im Ausland wohnhaft sind und, wenn beim Court of Customs and Patent Appeals keine Berufung eingelegt wurde (Sec. 145, 146)

division—voir demande divisionnaire

division—see divisional application

Ausscheidung—vgl. ausgeschiedene Anmeldung

divulgation—la déclaration d'une invention présentée, i.e. présentée dans la spécification, les dessin ou les revendications

disclosure—statement of the invention as set forth in any evidence, i.e. as set forth in the specification, drawings or claims

Offenbarung—Darlegung der Erfindung durch jede Art von Beweismaterial, wie durch Beschreibung (specification), Zeischnungen oder Ansprueche

divulgation document—la déclaration d'une invention avec signature de l'inventeur, dépôt dans l'Office des Brevets par l'inventeur ou son cessionnaire avec la taxe de $10., une enveloppe timbrée addressé à l'inventeur, et une lettre signé par l'inventeur demandant dépôt et maintenance de la déclaration pendant deux ans dans l'Office de Brevets Programme de Divulgation des Documents en evidence de conception

disclosure document—an invention disclosure signed by the inventor and forwarded to the Patent Office by the inventor or his assignee, with the $10. fee, a stamped self-addressed envelope and the inventor's separate signed request that the invention disclosure be accepted and preserved for two years under the Patent Office Disclosure Document Program as proof of conception

Offenbarungs–Urkunde—eine Erfindungs–Offenbarung, vom Erfinder unterzeichnet und vom Erfinder oder seinem Rechtnachsfolger dem Patentamt mit der Gebuehr von $10. zugesandt, einem an den Absender zurueckadressierten Freiumschlag—und getrennt davon—das unterzeichnete Ersuchen des Erfinders die Erfindungs–Offenbarung anzunehmen und sie zwei Jahre unter dem Patentamt Offenbarungs–Urkunden–Programm als Beweis fuer die geistige Erfassung aufzubewahren

divulgation insuffisante—une divulgation qui manque d'inclure les données qui permettraient à une personne habile dans la technique à laquelle rapporte l'invention, de fabriquer et d'employer l'invention (MPEP 608.01 (p))

insufficient disclosure—a disclosure that fails to include data that would enable a person skilled in the art to which the invention relates to make and use the invention (MPEP 608.01(p))

ungenuegende Offenbarung—eine Offenbarung, welche versaeumt Daten einzuschliessen, die jemanden, der mit der Technik auf die sich die Erfindung bezieht vertraut ist, in den Stand setzen wuerde die Erfindung herzustellen und zu benutzen (MPEP 608.01 (p))

domaine de l'invention—voir fond de l'invention

field of the invention—see background of the invention

Gebiet der Erfindung—vgl. Hintergrund der Erfindung

dominer—avoir une étendue de revendication qui comprend un autre développement

dominate—having a claim scope that includes another development

vorherrschen—einen Anspruchsbereich haben, der eine andere Entwicklung einschliesst

dommages pour la contrefaçon—de l'argent pour restituer l'emploi sans autorisation des droits de brevet. La décision compensatrice comprend une somme qui n'est pas moins que les redevenances raisonnables pour l'emploi, avec l'intérêt et les frais du tribunal (les frais ne comprennent pas les frais d'un avocat). (Sec. 284)

damages for infringement—an award in dollars to compensate for unauthorized use of patent rights. Compensatory award includes a sum that is not less than a reasonable royalty for use, with interest and court costs. (Sec. 284)

Schadenersatz fuer Patentverletzung—eine Dollarpraemie als Entschaedigung fuer die unbefugte Benutzung von Patentrechten. Die zuerkannte Verguetung umfasst eine Summe, die nicht geringer als eine angemessene Gebuehr fuer die Benutzung inklusive Zinsen und Gerichtskosten ist. (Sec. 284)

dossier—une déclaration des faits, des raisons et des sources sur lesquels on a comptés pour soutenir une procédure, un pétition, un appel, une action de "interférence" ou les procédés d'un tribunal (R. 181, 192, 243, 244)

brief—statement of the facts, reasons and authorities relied upon to support a motion, petition, appeal, interference action or court proceeding (R. 181, 192, 243, 244)

Schriftsatz—Darlegung der Tatsachen, Gruende und Autoritaeten zur Unterstuetzung eines Antrags, Gesuchs, einer Berufung, eines Interferenz-oder Gerichtsverfahrens (R. 181, 192, 243, 244)

dossier de réplique—réponse aux nouveaux points d'argument posés par la réponse de l'examinateur, qui doit être déposée dans le délai de vingt jours de la date de telle réponse (R. 193)

reply brief—response to new points of argument raised by the examiner's answer, to be filed within twenty days from the date of such answer (R.193)

Erwiderungs-Schriftsatz—Entgegnung auf neue Argumente, die durch die Antwort des Pruefers hervorgerufen wurden; sie ist innerhalb von zwanzig Tagen vom Datum dieser Antwort einzureichen (R. 193)

droit conventionnel ou unioniste—voir période conventionnelle ou unioniste

convention rights—see convention period

Uebereinkunfts-Recht—vgl. Uebereinkunfts-Frist

droit de priorité—le droit d'avancer la date d'effet de dépôt d'une demande à la date de dépôt de la première demande correspondante et étrangère, pourvu que le pays étrangèr soit un pays "unioniste" et que la date de dépôt dans ce pays—la ne soit plus qu'un an antérieur à la date de dépôt aux Etats-Unis

priority right—the right to promote the effective date of filing an application to the filing date of the first corresponding foreign application, provided the foreign country is a "treaty" country and the filing date in that country is not more than one year prior to the date of filing in the United States

Prioritaetsrecht—das Recht den Termin des Inkrafttretens fuer das Einreichen einer Anmeldung auf das Einreichungsdatum der ersten entsprechenden auslaendischen Anmeldung vorzuverlegen, vorausgesetzt der auslaendische Staat ist ein "Vertragsland" und das Einreichungsdatum in diesem Land liegt nicht mehr als ein Jahr vor dem Einreichungsdatum in den Vereinigten Staaten

E

enjoindre—imposer à un litigant, par ordonnance d'un tribunal, de cesser d'exécuter des actes détérminés

enjoin—to require a litigant, by court order, to desist from performing specified acts

verwarnen—einen Prozessfuehrnden durch Gerichtsbescheid dazu auffordern von der Ausfuehrung bestimmter Handlungen Abstand zu nehmen

entré—fait une partie permanente de l'histoire du brevet (MPEP 717)

entered—made a permanent part of the file wrapper (MPEP 717)

eingetragen—zu einem permanenten Teil der Akte gemacht (MPEP 717)

entrevue—discussion orale des objections et des rejets, avec l'examinateur à l'Office des Brevets, d'ordinaire à la requête de l'examinateur, pour expédier la résolution des questions (R. 133)

interview—oral discussion of objections and rejections with the examiner in the Patent Office, usually at the request of the examiner, to expedite resolution of issues (R. 133)

Interview—muendliche Eroerterung der Einwaende und Zurueckweisungen mit dem Pruefer im Patentamt—gewoehnlich auf Wunsch des Pruefers—um die Loesung von Streitfragen zu beschleunigen (R. 133)

équivalent–technologie enseignée par la technique antérieure et pertinente

equivalent–functionally duplicate technology taught by the pertinent prior art

gleichwertig–durch den zutreffenden Stand der Technig gelehrtes technisches Koennen

estop–voir estoppel

estop–see estoppel

Ausschliessung–vgl. Untersagung

estoppel–une interdiction d'alléguer ou de nier un fait, l'interdiction ayant été créée par une déclaration ou une action antérieure de la personne "estopped"; un acte antérieure qui défend certaines actions postérieures. Par exemple, la publication d'une invention pendant plus d'une année agit comme une interdiction ou "estoppel" d'obtenir un brevet pour telle invention.

estoppel–a prohibition against alleging or denying a fact, the prohibition having been created by some previous action or statement by the person estopped; a prior act that bars certain subsequent actions. For example, publication of an invention for more than one year acts as a bar or estoppel to obtaining a patent for such invention.

Untersagung–ein Verbot gegen die Behauptung oder Verneinung einer Tatsache. Das Verbot wurde durch eine vorhergehende Handlung oder Aussage der mit der Untersagung belegten Person hervorgerufen; ein frueheres Handeln, das gewisse folgende Handlungen ausschliesst. Die Veroeffentlichung einer Erfindung seit mehr als einem Jahr stellt, zum Beispiel, einen Hinderungsgrund oder eine Untersagung zur Erlangung eines Patents fuer eine solche Erfindung dar.

état de la technique—les données dans un domaine de connaissance technique au moment donné

state of the art—the data in an area of technical knowledge at a given time

Stand der Technik—die Gegebenheiten auf einem Gebiet technischer Kenntnisse zu einer bestimmten Zeit

état de la technique—toute matière pertinente à la nouveauté de l'invention revendiquée sous Sec. 102

prior art—all subject matter that is pertinent to the novelty of a claimed invention under Sec. 102

Stand der Technik—Alles aus dem Fachgebiet, das auf die Neuheit einer beanspruchten Erfindung Bezug hat

évident—voir la définition de "unobviousness"

obvious—see definition of unobviousness

selbstverstaendlich—zur Erklaerung vgl. Nicht-Selbstverss-taendlichkeit

examen—voir examinateur

examination—see examiner

Pruefung—vgl. Pruefer

examinateur—un employé de l'Office des Brevets qui revoit les demandes de brevets pour déterminer la brevetabilité et l'étendue d'une invention et, avec des autres examinateurs, la question de la priorité entre des demandeurs rivaux revendiquant la même matière

examiner—a Patent Office employee who reviews patent applications to determine the patentability and the scope of inventions and, with other examiners, the question of priority between rival applicants claiming the same subject matter

Pruefer—ein Beamter der Patentamts, der Patentanmeldungen nachprueft um die Patentfaehigkeit und den Umfang von Erfindungen zu bestimmen und, mit andern Pruefern, die Frage der Prioritaet zwischen konkurrierenden Anmeldern, die den gleichen Gegenstand beanspruchen, zu entscheiden

examinateur primaire—le chef d'un groupe d'examinateurs à l'Office des Brevets

primary examiner—the chief of an examining group in the Patent Office

Hauptpruefer—der Chef einer Pruefungsgruppe im Patentamt

examinateur principal—voir examinateur primaire

principal examiner—see primary examiner

erster Pruefer—vgl. Hauptpruefer

examinateurs-en-chef—"senior" examinateurs des brevets qui, avec le Commissaire des Brevets et les Commissaires Auxiliaires, constituent la Commission d'Appel

examiners-in-chief—senior patent examiners who, with the Commissioner of Patents and the Assistant Commissioners, constitute the Board of Appeals

Haupt-Pruefer—"Oberpatentpruefer" (dienstaeltere Pruefer), die zusammen mit dem Commissioner of Patents und den Assistant Commissioners den Board of Appeals bilden

exécuteur—le représentant d'un inventeur légalement incapacité

executor—the representative of a legally incapacitated inventor

Treuhaender—der Vertreter eines vor dem Gestz unfaehigen Erfinders

exécution de demande—signature d'une demande devant un notaire, ou une autre personne autorisée aux Etats-Unis. Une demande exécutée à l'étranger devant un notaire ou une autre personne autorisée doit être légalisée par un consulat ou par un officier diplomatique des Etats-Unis. Alternativement, on peut faire une déclaration (R. 68) au lieu d'une signature devant un notaire ou une autre personne autorisée.

execution of application—signature of an application before a notary or other authorized person in the United States. An application executed abroad before a notary or other authorized person must be legalized by a United States consular or diplomatic officer. Alternatively, a declaration (R. 68) may be made instead of signature before a notary or other authorized person.

Ausfertigung der Anmeldung—Leistung der Anmeldungsunterschrift vor einem Notar oder einer andern dazu befugten Person in den Vereinigten Staaten. Eine Anmeldung, die im Ausland vor einem Notar oder einer andern dazu befugten Person ausgefertigt wurde, muss durch einen Konsulats-oder Botschaftsbeamten der Vereinigten Staaten beglaubigt werden. Andern Falls kann auch eine eidesstattliche Erklaerung (R. 68) an Stelle der Unterschrift vor einem Notar oder einer anderen dazu befugten Person abgegeben werden.

"exhausted combination"—une combinaison d'éléments démontrée d'être antériorisée par la technique antérieure

exhausted combination—a combination of elements shown by the prior art to be anticipated

ausgeschoepfte Verbindung—eine Verbindung von Elementen, die sich durch den Stand der Technik als vorweggenommen erweist

expression alternative—la définition d'un élément dans une revendication par plusieurs mots ou par une phrase (MPEP 706.03(d))

alternative expression—definition of one element, in a claim, by more than one word or phrase (MPEP 706.03(d))

alternative Ausdrucksweise—Definition **eines** Elements in einem Patentanspruch durch mehr als **ein** Wort oder **einen** Ausdruck (MPEP 706.03 (d))

F

fabrication—une classe de matière brevetable rendant une chose physìque et tangible

manufacture—a class of patentable subject matter providing a physical tangible thing

Herstellungsweise—eine Klasse von patentfaehigen Gegenstaenden, die ein koerperlich greifbares Objekt liefern

fond de l'invention—une déclaration générale de la technique dans laquelle se trouve l'invention, de la branche (partie) spécifique de cette technique avec une caractérisation de l'invention, une brève description de la technique antérieure, et les désavantages spécifiques de la technique antérieure, incluse dans la spécification immédiatement après un renvoi à aucune demande relative

background of the invention—a general statement of the art in which the invention lies, of the specific branch of that art with a characterization of the invention, a brief description of the prior art, and the specific disadvantages of the prior art, included in the specification immediately after a cross-reference to any related application

Hintergrund der Erfindung—eine allgemeine Darstellung der Technik, auf deren Gebiet die Erfindung liegt, des bestimmten Zweiges dieser Technik mit einer Charakterisierung der Erfindung, einer kurzen Beschreibung der bisherigen Technik und der besonderen Nachteile derselben; diese Darstellung ist in der Beschreibung (specification) eingeschlossen und folgt unmittelbar einem Hinweis auf alle verwandten Anmeldungen

forfeited application (demande)—une demande sur laquelle on n'a pas délivré le brevet parce que le demandeur a manqué de payer la taxe finale (R 316). Si la taxe finale n'est pas acceptée dans le delai imparti d'une année après que la periode de paiement de six mois est passée, on considère la demande comme abandonnée de la date de "forfeiture."

forfeited application—an application on which the patent did not issue because applicant failed to pay the final fee (R. 316). If the final fee is not accepted within one year after the six months period for payment has passed, the application stands abandoned as of the date of forfeiture.

verfallene Anmeldung—eine Anmeldung, zu der das Patent nicht verliehen wurde, da der Anmelder versaeumte die Schlussgebuehr zu bezahlen (R. 116). Falls die Schlussgebuehr innedhalb eines Jahres and Ablauf der sechs Monatsfrist nicht angenommen wird, gilt die Anmeldung vom Verfallsdatum an als fallengelassen.

forme avec une signature—une pétition, serment ou déclaration, et le pouvoir d'avocat combinés attaché à la spécification comme la dernière page, pour la signature par l'inventeur

single signature form—a combined petition, oath or declaration, and power of attorney attached to the specification as the last page, for execution by the inventor

Alleinunterschrifts-Formblatt—eine Kombination von Gesuch, Eid oder eidesstattlicher Erklaerung und gesetzlicher Vollmacht, als letzte Seite der Beschreibung (specification) zur Ausfuehrung durch den Erfinder angehaftet

G

Gazette Officielle—la publication officielle hebdomadaire de l'Office des Brevets qui contient une abstraction de la divulgation de chaque brevet délivré ce jour-là; des renseignements au sujet des brevets, marques de fabrique, brevets de dessin et de plante; et des ordonnances, des notifications, des litigies déposées et des décisions choisies du tribunal dans le domaine des brevets et des marques de fabrique

Official Gazette—the official weekly publication of the Patent Office that contains an abstract of the disclosure of each patent issued that day; information on patents, trademarks, designs and plant patents; and orders, notices, suits filed and selected court decisions in the patent and trademark fields

Amtsblatt—woechentliche, amtliche Veroeffentlichung des Patentamts mit einem Auszug aus der Offenbarung jeden, an diesem Tag erteilten Patents; mit Information ueber Patente, Warenzeichen, Geschmacksmuster- und Pflanzenpatente; mit Verfuegungen, Amtsbescheiden, eingereichten Klagen und ausgewaehlten Gerichtsentscheiden auf dem Patent- und Warenzeichengebiet

genre—une classe qui est plus large que, ou comprend plus d'une variante

genus—a class that is broader than or includes more than one species

Art (genus)—ein Klasse, die umfangreicher ist und mehr als eine Gattung umfasst

H

habileté mécanique—l'habileté d'un technicien dans son propre domaine. Une épreuve négative d'invention, dans la croyance que les habiletés d'un technicien moyen ne soient pas au niveau d'invention.

mechanical skill—the skill of a technician in his own field. A negative test for invention, in the holding that the abilities of an ordinary mechanic are not at the level of invention.

technische Geschicklichkeit—die Geschicklichkeit eines Technikers auf seinem Fachgebiet. Eine negative Probe auf's Exempel—der Erfindung naemlich: die feste Annahme, dass die Fertigkeit eines Durchschnittsfachmanns nicht an das Niveau von Erfindungen heranreicht.

habileté moyenne dans la technique—voir habileté mécanique

ordinary skill in the art—see mechanical skill

uebliche Fachkenntnis—vgl. technische Geschicklichkeit

hachure—illustration d'une section coupée d'un dessin par lignes obliques et parallèles qui ne se séparent pas de moins d'une vingtième d'une pouce (R. 84 (d))

hatching—illustration of a cut section in a drawing by oblique parallel lines not less than about one-twentieth of an inch apart (R. 84(d))

Schraffierung—Illustration eines Schnitts in einer Zeichnung durch schraege Parallellinien, die nicht weniger als ungefaehr einen zwanzigstel Zoll (inch) auseinander sind (R. 84 (d))

histoire du brevet—tous les archives écrits dans le dépôt d'une demande à l'Office des Brevets

file wrapper—the total written record in the Patent Office file of an application

Akte—die gesamten schriftlichen Aufzeichnungen ueber eine Anmeldung im Archiv des Patentamts

histoire du brevet "estoppel"—l'interdiction établie par une concession faite du demandeur dans le cours de la poursuite d'une demande. Par example, quand l'étendue d'une revendication est limitée en réponse au rejet de la revendication par l'examinateur, il y a un hisoire du brevet "estoppel" (file wrapper estoppel) défendant la nouvelle assertion d'une revendication qui est plus large que la revendication limitée.

file wrapper estoppel—the prohibition established by a concession made by an applicant in the course of prosecution of an application. For example, when the scope of a claim is narrowed in response to the examiner's rejection of that claim, there is a file wrapper estoppel prohibiting the reassertion of a claim that is broader than the narrowed claim.

Untersagung in der Akte—ein Verbot begruendet auf einem Zugestaendnis, das von einem Anmelder im Verlauf der Verfolgung einer Anmeldung gemacht wurde. Wenn, zum Beispiel, der Umfang eines Anspruches in Erwinderung auf die Ablehnung des Pruefers dieses Anspruchs enger gehalten wird, dann befindet sich eine Untersagung in der Akte, welche die Wiedergeltendmachung eines Anspruchs, der umfassender als der verengte Anspruch ist, verbietet.

I

inclusion positive d'éléments—le récit dans une revendication, dans un mot ou une phrase positive, de chaque trait dont dépend la revendication pour être brevetable

positive inclusion of elements—recital in a claim, in a positive word or phrase, of every feature on which the claim depends for patentability

ausdruecklicher Einschluss von Elementen—Aufzaehlung mittels eines ausdruecklichen Wortes oder Satzes jeder Eigenschaft in einem Anspruch, von der die Patentfaehigkeit des Anspruche abhaengt

incomplet—une revendication ou une divulgation qui omet un élément, une démarche, ou une relation structurele coopérative essentielle des éléments

incomplete—a claim or disclosure that omits an essential element, step, or structural cooperative relationship of elements

unvollstaendig—ein Anspruch oder eine Offenbarung, welche einen wesentlichen Bestandteil, eine Stufe, oder eine strukturell zusammenwirkende Beziehung von Elementen auslassen

incorporation par renvoi—inclure dans une demande des données au moyen d'une déclaration sommaire identifiant les renseignements d'une facon si détaillée qu'on peut l'obtenir; exclues de la matière qu'on peut incorporer par renvoi sont les matières secrètes ou privilégiées, comme des demandes abandonnées, et de la matière qui n'est pas facilement disponible au public, tel que des études inédites, des publications étrangères et obscures, des publications auxquelles il n'y a pas de traductions disponibles en anglais. La matière essentielle (matière qui est nécessaire pour soutenir les revendications ou pour une divulgation suffisante de l'invention) peut être incorporée par renvoi à un brevet des Etats-Unis, ou une demande acceptée des Etats-Unis. La matière qui n'est pas essentielle peut être incorporée par renvoi aux brevets étrangers ou des Etats-Unis, des demandes des Etats-Unis antrieurement déposées, du même propriétaire, et des publications qui ne sont pas brevetées pour indiquer le fond de l'invention ou l'état de la technique. (MPEP 608.01))

incorporation by reference—including data in an application by means of a summary statement identifying the information in such detail that it can be retrieved; excluded from matter that can be incorporated by reference are secret or privileged materials such as some abandoned applications, and material not easily available to the public or the Patent Office such as unpublished papers, obscure foreign publications, and publications on which there are no available English translations. Essential material (subject matter that is necessary to support the claims or for adequate disclosure of the invention) may be incorporated by reference to a United States patent or an allowed United States application. Non-essential material may be incorporated by reference to United States or foreign patents, prior filed commonly owned United States applications and non-patent publications to indicate the background of the invention or the state of the art. (MPEP 608.01(p))

Eingliederung durch Hinweis—Einschluss von Daten in einer Anmeldung mittels einer Zusammenfassung, welche die Information in genuegender Einzelheit identifiziert, um sie wieder auffinden zu koennen; ausgenommen von der Materie, die durch Hinweis eingegliedert werden kann, sind geheime oder privilegierte Materialien, wie einige fallengelassene Anmeldungen, und Material, das der Oeffentlichkeit oder dem Patentamt nicht ohne Weiteres zugaenglich ist, wie unveroeffentlichte Schriften, wenig bekannte auslaendische Veroeffentlichungen und Veroeffentlichungen, von denen keine englischen Uebersetzungen vorhanden sind. Wesentliches Material (Gegenstaende, die zur Unterstuetzung der Ansprueche oder ausreichender Offenbarung der Erfindung notwendig sind) duerfen durch Hinweis auf ein amerikanisches Patent oder eine angenommene amerikanische Anmeldung eingegliedert werden. Nicht-wesentliches Material darf durch Hinweis auf amerikanische oder auslaendische Patente, auf früher eingereichte amerikanische Anmeldungen in gemeinsamen Besitz und auf nicht-Patent-Veroeffentlichungen eingeordnet werden, um den Hintergrund der Erfindung oder den Stand der Technik anzudeuten. (MPEP 608.01 (p))

indefini—voir vague et indéfini

indefinite—see vague and indefinite

unbestimmt—vgl. verschwommen und unbestimmt

index des brevets et de brevetés—une publication annuelle, vendue par le Directeur des Documents, l'Office d'Imprimerie du Gouvernement des Etats-Unis, Washington, D. C. 20402, qui enregistre les brevetés (y inclus les "reissue" brevetes), les brevetés de dessin, les brevetés de plante, les renonciations et les dédicaces, et les décisions publiées dans la Gazette Officielle

index of patents and patentees—an annual publication, sold by the Superintendent of Documents, U. S. Government Printing Office, Washington, D. C. 20402, that lists patentees (including reissue patentees), design patentees, plant patentees, disclaimers and dedications, and decisions published in the Official Gazette

Verzeichnis von Patenten und Patentinhabern—eine jaehrliche Veroeffentlichung, die vom Superintendent of Documents, U. S. Government Printing Office, Washington, D. C. 20402, verkauft wird; darin sind die Patentinhaber (inklusive Inhaber von Wiedererteilungs-Patenten), Geschmacksmuster-und Pflanzenpatentinhaber, Widerrufe und Verzichte zu Gunsten der Allgemeinheit, und im oeffentlichen Amtsblatt (Official Gazette) veroeffentlichte Entscheidungen aufgezaehlt

injonction—une ordonnance d'un tribunal imposant à une partie de cesser de contrfaire un brevet

injunction—a court order directing that a party desist from further infringement of a patent

Verfuegung—eine gerichtliche Verfuegung, die anordnet, dass eine Partei von weiterer Verletzung eines Patents Abstand zu nehmen hat

injonction préliminaire—ordonnance conservatoire délivrée par un tribunal, exigeant qu'un litigant cesse d'exécuter des actes spécifiés jusqu'à ce que le tribunal puisse entendre les preuves et déterminer s'il a droit à exécuter de tels actes

preliminary injunction—a restraining order issued by a court, requiring a litigant to desist from performing specified acts until the court can hear evidence and determine whether he has the right to perform such acts

einstweilige Verfuegung—eine gerichtliche Verhinderungs-Verfuegung, die von einer prozessierenden Partei verlangt von der Ausfuehrung bestimmter Handlungen Abstand zu nehmen, bis das Gericht Beweismaterial aufnehmen und bestimmen kann, ob die Partei das Recht hat solche Handlungen auszufuehren

inspection—le droit du public d'examiner et d'obtenir des copies d'un brevet délivré et ses dessin de spécification et tous les histoires du brevet de la demande, et d'examiner et d'obtenir des copies des archives d'une "interférence" terminée entraînant un brevet ou une demande sur laquelle on a délivrée un brevet (R. 11, 15)

inspection—the right of the public to inspect and obtain copies of an issued patent and its specification, drawings and all papers of record relating to the case, and to inspect and obtain copies of the file of a terminated interference involving a patent or an application on which a patent issued (R. 11, 15)

Inspektion—das Recht der Oeffentlichkeit ein erteiltes Patent einzusehen, sowie Kopien desselben und seiner Beschreibungs- (specification) Zeichnungen und aller zu den Akten genommenen Schriftstuecke zu erhalten—soweit sie sich auf den Fall beziehen; die Akte einzusehen und Kopien zu erhalten von einer beendeten Interferenz, bei der es sich um ein Patent oder um eine Anmeldung, zu der ein Patent erteilt wurde, behandelt (R. 11, 15)

interdiction à la délivrance d'un brevet—une condition qui défend la délivrance d'un brevet; une condition établie dans la Sec. 102 (nouveauté et perte du droit d'un brevet) ou dans la Sec. 103 (de la matière non-évidente)

bar to patent grant—a condition that prohibits the grant of a patent; a condition set forth in Sec. 102 (novelty and loss of right to patent) or in Sec. 103 (non-obvious subject matter)

Hinderungsgrund zur Patentverleihung—ein die Patentverleihung verbietender Umstand; Umstaende, die in Sec. 102 (Neuheit und Verlust des Rechts auf ein Patent) oder in S. 103 (nicht-selbstverstaendlicher Erfindungsgegenstand) dargelegt sind

interdiction statutaire—voir interdiction à la délivrance d'un brevet

statutory bar—see bar to patent grant

gesetzlicher Hinderungsgrund—vgl. Hinderungsgrund zur Patenterteilung

"interférence"—une procédure tendant à déterminer lequel des plusieurs demandeurs de brevet est le premier inventeur. "Interférence" peut s'agir d'une demande et d'un brevet, pourvu que la revendication soit faite dans la demande avant une année de la date sur laquelle le brevet a été délivré. (Sec. 135)

interference—a proceeding to determine which of two or more applicants for a patent is the first inventor. The interference may involve an application and a patent, provided the claim is made in the application prior to one year from the date on which the patent issued. (Sec. 135)

Interferenz—ein Verfahren, das dazu dient zu bestimmen, welcher von zwei oder mehr Patentanmeldern der Erst-Erfinder ist. Es kann sich bei der Interferenz um eine Anmeldung und ein Patent handeln, vorausgesetzt der Anspruch in der Anmeldung ist mehr als ein Jahr vor dem Datum der Patenterteilung gemacht. (Sec. 135)

inventeur unique—une personne qui seule a créé une invention

sole inventor—a person who singly made an invention

alleiniger Erfinder—eine Person, die allein eine Erfindung gemacht hat

invention—voir invention brevetable

invention—see patentable invention

Erfindung—vgl. patentfaehige Erfindung

invention brevetable—un procédé, une machine, la fabrication ou la composition de matière, ou le perfectionnement de cela, qui est nouveau, utile et non évident

patentable invention—a new, useful and unobvious process, machine, manufacture or composition of matter, or improvement thereof

patentfaehige Erfindung—ein neues, nuetzliches und nichtselbstverstaendliches Verfahren, Vorrichtung, Herstellungsweise oder Zusammensetzung von Gegenstaenden, oder eine Verbesserung davon

J

jugement déclaratif—une décision par un tribunal, dans une action commencée par une partie menacée d'un procès de contrefaçon, au sujet de la validité ou de la contrefaçon d'un brevet

declaratory judgment—a decision by a court, in an action started by a party threatened with infringement suit, as to whether the patent is valid and/or infringed

Feststellungs-Urteil—ein Gerichtsentscheid ueber Patentgueltigkeit oder Patentverletzung in einer Klage, die von einer mit Patentverletzung bedrohten Partei angestrengt wurde

"junior party"—dans une "interférence", le demandeur qui a la date d'effet de dépôt la plus postérieure

junior party—in an interference, the applicant having the later established effective filing date

juengere Partei (Junior Partei)—in einer Interferenz der Ansmelder, der den spaeter festgesetzten Termin fuer das Inkrafttreten des Einreichungsdatums hat

L

laches—négligence, manque ou délai déraisonnable en agissant pour faire valoir un droit; le droit est défendu pour empêcher le traitement inéquitable de la partie qui présente des "laches"

laches—neglect, failure or unreasonable delay in acting to enforce a right; enforcement of the right is barred to prevent inequitable treatment of the party asserting laches

Verzug—Vernachlaessigung, Versaeumnis oder unbillige Verzoegerung in der Durchsetzung eines Rechts; es ist untersagt Durchsetzung des Rechts zur Verhinderung ungerechter Behandlung der Partei, die Verzug geltend macht, anzuwenden

largeur de la revendication—l'étendue à laquelle une revendication domine une technique

breadth of claim—the extent to which a claim dominates an art

Ausmass des Anspruchs—der Umfang in welchem ein Anspruch ueber eine Technik vorherrscht

lettre de condition—une requête à l'examinateur au sujet de la condition présente d'une demande. Envoyée, judicieusement, quand il est passé une période de temps excessivement longue depuis que l'Office des Brevets a agi sur le cas.

status letter—inquiry to the examiner about the present status of an application. Sent, advisably, when an unduly long time has elapsed since the Patent Office last acted on the case.

Akten-Nachfrage (Status-Brief)—Anfrage an den Pruefer den gegenwaertigen Stand einer Anmeldung betreffend. Es ist ratsam diesen Brief zu senden, wenn eine ungewoehnlich lange Zeit vergangen ist, seit das Patentamt zuletzt etwas in dem Fall unternommen hat.

"letters patent"—accorder à un inventeur le droit d'exclure autrui, pendant un terme limité, d'utiliser son invention. Cela fait aussi référence au certificat de la délivrance du brevet.

letters patent—the grant to an inventor of the right to exclude others, for a limited time, from using his invention. Also refers to the certificate of the patent grant.

Patenturkunde—einem Erfinder das Recht erteilen andere auf begrenzte Zeit vom Gebrauch seiner Erfindung auszuschliessen. Weist auch auf den Patenterteilungs-Schein (Patentverleihungs-Schein) hin.

licence—la cession d'un droit d'utiliser une invention aux conditions spécifiées

license—the grant of a right to practice an invention on terms specified

Lizenz—die Erteilung eines Rechts eine Erfindung zu bestimmten Bedingungen praktisch auszufuehren

licence de déposer à l'étranger—void autorisation de déposer à l'étranger

license for foreign filing—see foreign filing authorization

Lizenz zur Einreichung im Ausland—vgl. Genehmigung ein Patent im Ausland anzumelden

licence exclusive—voir licence

exclusive license—see license

ausschliessliche Lizenz—vgl. Lizenz

licence non-exclusive—une licence d'un brevet qui est limitée de la durée ou de l'étendue géographique ou autre, et ainsi ne défend pas la cession des droits à autrui sous le brevet

non-exclusive license—a license under a patent that is limited as to duration or geographical or other scope, and thus does not prohibit the granting of rights to others under the patent

nicht-ausschliessliche Lizenz—Lizenz unter einem Patent, das in seiner Laufzeit in geographischem oder anderm Umfang begrenzt ist und daher die Erteilung von Rechten an andere unter dem Patent nicht verbietet

licences-réciproques—l'accord réciproque des droits de brevet l'un à l'autre par plusieurs proprietaires de tels droits

cross-license—the reciprocal grant of patent rights to each other by two or more owners of such rights

wechselseitige Lizenz—gegenseitige Bewilligung von Patentrechten, die zwei oder mehr Eigentuemer solcher Rechte einander zugestehen

licencié—une partie à qui on a concédé une licence

licensee—party to whom a license is granted

Lizenztraeger—die Partei, der eine Lizenz erteilt wird

limitation négative—un mot ou une phrase, dans une revendication, qui est vague et indéfinie parce qu'elle récite quelque chose qui n'est pas présent dans la revendication

negative limitation—a word or phrase in a claim that is vague and indefinite because it recites what is not present in the claim

negative Begrenzung—ein Wort oder Satz in einem Anspruch, der verschwommen und unbestimmt ist, da etwas ausgesagt wird, was in dem Anspruch nicht vorhanden ist

litigie—voir litigie des brevets

litigation—see patent litigation

Prozess—vgl. Patentprozess

litigie de brevet—une action civile et légale, présentée dans un tribunal Fédéral par un titulaire de brevet contre un contrefacteur allégué pour enjoindre la contrefaçon continuée du brevet et/ou pour la restitution dûe à cause de la contrefaçon alléguée; une action présentée par le demandeur pour faire déclarer invalide et/ou pas contrefait un brevet

patent litigation—a civil legal action brought in a Federal court by a patent owner against an alleged infringer to enjoin further infringement of the patent and/or for compensation for the alleged infringement; an action brought to have a patent declared invalid and/or not infringed by the claimant

Patent-Prozess—eine zivilrechtliche Klage, die von einem Patentinhaber gegen einen angeblichen Verletzer bei einem Bundesgericht erhoben wird, um von weiterer Patentverletzung abzuhalten und/oder auf Entschaedigung fuer die angebliche Verletzung; eine Klage, die erhoben wird um ein Patent fuer ungueltig und/oder als durch den Klaeger nicht verletzt erklaeren zu lassen

loi de brevets—les statuts au sujet des brevets (trouvés principalement dans Titre 35 du Code des Etats-Unis) et les interprétations juridiques et administratives de tels statuts

patent law—the statutes covering patents (found principally in Title 35 of the US Code) and court and administrative agency interpretations of such statutes

Patent-Gesetz—die Statuten, die auf Patente Bezug nehmen (hauptsaechlich im Titel 35 des US Code) und die Auslegungen dieser Statuten durch Gerichte und Verwaltungsbehoerden

M

machine—une classe de matière brevetable qui couvre une combinaison d'éléments qui coopérent pour accomplir une fonction

machine—a class of patentable subject matter covering a combination of elements that cooperate to perform a function

Vorrichtung (Maschine)—eine Klasse von patentfaehigen Gegenstaenden, die eine Verbindung von Elementen umfassen, die zur Ausfuehrung einer Funktion zusammenarbeiten

Manuel de Classification—un livre qui enregistre toutes les classes et toutes les sous-classes du système des Etats-Unis de classification des brevets, un index de matière, et des renseignements relatifs

Manual of Classification—a book listing all classes and subclasses in the United States patent classification system, a subject matter index, and related information

Klassifizierungs-Handbuch—ein Buch, das alle Gruppen und Untergruppen im Patent-Klassifizierungssystem der Vereinigten Staaten aufzaehlt, ein Sachverzeichnis und verwandte Informationen

Manuel de la Procédure d'Examiner les Brevets—un ouvrage à consulter détaillé, au sujet de la pratique et du procédé d'examiner les brevets, principalement employé par le Corps d'Examinateurs de l'Office des Brevets

Manual of Patent Examining Procedure—a detailed reference work on patent examining practice and procedure, primarily for use by the Examining Corps of the Patent Office

Patentpruefverfahren-Handbuch—ein ausfuehrliches Nachschlagewerk ueber die Praxis und das Verfahren bei Patentpruefungen, hauptsaechlich zum Gebrauch des Prueferstabs des Patentamts

marque de fabrique—un mot ou un signe employé par un marchand pour identifier et distinguer son produit du produit d'autrui; on ne permet pas d'ordinaire l'emploi d'une marque de fabrique pour définir un produit dans une demande de brevet

trademark—a word or symbol used by a merchant to identify and distinguish his product from the product of others; use of a trademark in a patent application to define a product is normally not permitted

Warenzeichen—von einem Kaufmann zur Identifizierung und Unterscheidung seines Erzeugnisses von den Erzeugnissen anderer benutztes Wort oder Zeichen; der Gebrauch eines Warenzeichens zur Definition eines Erzeugnisses ist in einer Patentanmeldung normalerweise nicht gestattet

marquage faux—imitant le nom due breveté, le numéro du brevet ou le mot "brevet", etc., pour faire croire le public que le produit ait été fabriqué ou vendu avec l'accord du breveté; en marquant un produit non-breveté pour faire croire le public que le produit ait été breveté; ou en marquant un produit "brevet demandé", ou "brevet pendant", etc. pour faire croire le public que le brevet soit pendant (Sec. 292)

false marking—imitating the name of the patentee, the patent number or the word "patent" or the like to deceive the public into believing that the article was made or sold with the consent of the patentee; marking an unpatented article to deceive the public into believing the article was patented; or marking an article "patent applied for", or "patent pending" or the like to deceive the public into believing a patent application is pending (Sec. 292)

falsche Bezeichnung—Nachahmung des Namens des Patentinhabers, der Patentnummer, des Wortes "Patent" oder dergleichen um das Publikum zu taeuschen und glauben zu lassen, dass der Artikel mit Zustimmung des Patentinhabers hergestellt oder verkauft wurde; Bezeichnung eines unpatentierten Gegenstandes um das Publikum zu taeuschen und glauben zu lassen der Artikel sei patentiert; oder die Bezeichnung eines Gegenstandes mit "Patent angemeldet" oder "Patentanmeldung anhaengig" oder dergleichen, um das Publikum zu taeuschen und glauben zu lassen, dass eine Patentanmeldung anhaengig ist (Sec. 292)

marquer—mettre le numéro du brevet. Pour réparer les dommages de la contrefaçon, le breveté doit marquer ou l'article ou son paquet du mot "Brevet" (ou "Pat.") et du numéro, ou doit prouver que le contrefacteur continuait à contrefaire après avoir été autrement notifié de la contrefaçon.

marking—applying the patent number. To recover damages for infringement, the patentee must mark the patented article or its package with the word "Patent" (or "Pat.") and the number, or must prove that the infringer continued to infringe after being otherwise notified of the infringement.

kennzeichnen—mit einer Patentnummer versehen. Um Schadenersatz fuer Patentverletzung zu erlangen, muss der Patentinhaber den patentierten Artikel oder dessen Verpackung mit dem Wort "Patent" (oder "Pat.") und der Nummer kennzeichnen, oder er muss beweisen, dass der Patentverletzer die Verletzung fortsetzte nachdem er anderweitig von der Patentverletzung in Kenntnis gesetzt war.

matière essentielle—voir incorporation par renvoi

essential material—see incorporation by reference

wesentliches Material—vgl. Eingliederung durch Hinweis

matière non-essentielle—voir incorporation par renvoi

non-essential material—see incorporation by reference

nicht-wesentliches Material—vgl. Eingliederung durch Hinweis

matière non statutaire—des inventions ou des découvertes qui ne sont pas brevetables sous Sec. 101, tel que le simple arrangement de matière imprimée, une chose qui arrive dans la nature qui est vraiment sans changement, une méthode de faire les affaires, ou une principe scientifique qui est séparée d'aucune structure tangible (MPEP 706.03(a))

non-statutory subject matter—inventions or discoveries that are not patentable under Sec. 101, such as the mere arrangement of printed matter, a thing occurring in nature that is substantially unaltered, a method of doing business, or a scientific principle divorced from any tangible structure (MPEP 706.03(a))

nicht-rechtsverbindliche Gegenstaende—Erfindungen oder Entdeckungen, die unter Sec. 101 nicht patentfaehig sind, wie zum Beispiel, die blosse Anordnung von Gedrucktem, etwas in der Natur Vorkommendes und im Wesentlichen unveraendert Bleibendes, eine Methode der Geschaeftsfuehrung, oder ein von jeder greifbaren Struktur entfernter wissenschaftlicher Grundbegriff (MPEP 706.03(a))

méthode—voir procédé

method—see process

Methode—vgl. Verfahren

mise en pratique d'une invention—la fabrication, l'utilisation ou la vente d'une invention

practising an invention—making, using or selling an invention

Erfindung praktisch ausfuehren—Herstellung, Benutzung oder Verkauf einer Erfindung

modèle—une incarnation structurale de l'invention; pas recu de l'Office des Brevets à moins que le Commissaire le demande spécifiquement (R. 91)

model—a structural embodiment of the invention; not received by the Patent Office unless specifically called for by the Commissioner (R. 91)

Modell—eine strukturelle Darstellung, die dem Patentamt—wenn vom Commissioner nicht besonders angefordert—nicht uebergeben wird (R. 91)

motion—une demande pour obtenir une ordonnance dirgeante une action spécifique. On peut faire des motions dans une "interférence" pour désoudre, pour amender, pour ajouter une autre demande, et pour transférer la charge de la preuve. (R. 231-237)

motion—an application to obtain an order directing a particular action. Motions may be made in interferences to dissolve, to amend, to add another application, and to shift the burden of proof. (R.231-237)

Antrag—ein Gesuch um Erhalt einer Verfuegung, die eine bestimmte Handlung anordnet. Solche Antraege koennen in Interferenz Faellen zur Aufloesung, zur Verbesserung, zur Hinzufuegung einer weiteren Anmeldung und zur Verschiebung der Beweislast gemacht werden. (R. 231-237)

moyen—une force appliquée; une façon d'opérer; un traitement spécifique des objets spécifiques; une partie qui accomplit un résultat mécanique

means—a force applied; a mode of operation; a specific treatment of specific objects; a part accomplishing a mechanical result

Mittel—angewandte Kraft; eine Art der Betriebsmethode; besondere Behandlung besonderer Objekte; ein Teil, der ein mechanisches Ergebnis erzielt

multiplicité de revendications—des revendications qui sont jugées d'être d'un nombre extravagant, en vue de la nature et de l'étendue de l'invention, parce que le nombre de revendications présentées ont la tendance d'obscurcir l'invention

multiplicity of claims—claims that are held to be unreasonable in number, in view of the nature and scope of the invention, because the number of claims presented tend to obscure the invention

Vielheit von Anspruechen—Ansprueche, deren Anzahl im Hinblick auf die Natur und den Umfang der Erfindung fuer uebermaessig gehalten wird, da die Anzahl der vorgebrachten Ansprueche dazu fuehrt die Erfindung unklar erscheinen zu lassen

N

nom employé dans la commerce—un nom qui n'est pas possédé, par lequel un produit industriel est connu dans une technique; on permet l'emploi d'un nom employé en commerce dans une demande de brevet pour définir un produit industriel si sa signification est établie par une définition accompagnante qui est précise et claire, et si la signification est connue et définie dans la littérature aux Etats-Unis

name used in trade—a nonproprietary name by which a product is known in an art; use of a name used in trade in a patent application to define a product is permitted if its meaning is established by an accompanying definition that is precise and definite, and the meaning is known and defined in the literature in the United States

handelsueblicher Name—ein nicht gesetzlich—(patentlich) geschuetzter Name, unter welchem ein Erzeugnis auf einem Fachgebiet bekannt ist; es ist gestattet einen handelsueblichen Namen zur genauen Bezeichnung eines Erzeugnisses zu benutzen, wenn seine Bedeutung durch eine beiliegende, genaue und deutliche Definition festgelegt ist, und die Bedeutung in der Literatur in den Vereinigten Staaten bekannt und genau umrissen ist

notification d'acceptation—conseil de l'Office des Brevets que le demandeur a droit à un brevet, demandant le paiement de la taxe de délivrance dans le délai de trois mois de la date du conseil (R. 311)

notice of allowance—advice by the Patent Office that the applicant is entitled to a patent, calling for the payment of the issue fee within three months from the date of the advice (R. 311)

Zulassungs-Benachrichtigung (Annahme-Nachricht) — Benachrichtigung durch das Patentamt, dass der Anmelder zu einem Patent berechtigt und die Erteilungsgebuehr innerhalb von drei Monaten vom Benachrichtigungsdatum zu entrichten ist (R. 311)

notification de "allowability"—conseil de l'Office des Brevets que le demandeur a droit à un brevet, mais que l'octroi d'un brevet sera remis parce que la demande contient de la matière qu'on ne publiera pas pour protéger la sécurité nationale

notice of allowability—advice by the Patent Office that the applicant is entitled to a patent, but grant of a patent will be postponed because the application contains matter that will not be published to protect national security

Zulaessigkeits-Benachrichtigung—Mitteilung des Patentamts, dass der Anmelder zu einem Patent berechtigt ist, aber die Erteilung des Patents aufgeschoben wird, da die Anmeldung Material enthaelt, das zum Schutz der nationalen Sicherheit nicht veroeffentlicht wird

notification de contrefaçon—un communiqué écrit par le titulaire d'un brevet prétendant qu'on est en train de contrefaire des revendications spécifiees d'un brevet, et demandant qu'on cesse une telle contrefaçon

notice of infringement—written communication from a patent owner asserting that specified claims of a patent are being infringed, and demanding that such infringement cease

Beschwerdeschrift ueber Verletzung—schriftliche Mitteilung eines Patentinhabers mit der Behauptung, dass aufgefuehrte Ansprueche eines Patents verletzt werden und mit der Forderung auf Einstellung solcher Verletzung

notification et raisons d'appel—la notification au Commissaire des raisons d'appel à la "Court of Customs and Patent Appeals", qui doit être déposée dans le délai de soixante jours de la date de la décision appelée, ou dans le délai de trente jours après la date d'une décision de la Commission d'Appel ou la Commission des "Interférences" des Brevets sur un pétition pour une nouvelle considération (R. 302, 304)

notice and reasons of appeal—notice to the Commissioner of the grounds of appeal to the Court of Customs and Patent Appeals, to be filed within sixty days from the date of the decision appealed from, or within thirty days after the date of a decision by the Board of Appeals or the Board of Patent Interferences on a petition for rehearing or reconsideration (R. 302, 304)

Beschwerdeschriftsatz und Berufungsbegruendung—Beschwerdeschrift an den Commissioner ueber die Gruende fuer eine Berufung an den Court of Customs and Patent Appeals, einzureichen innerhalb von sechzig Tagen vom Datum der angefochtenen Entscheidung des Board of Appeals oder des Board of Patent Interferences ueber ein Gesuch zur Wiederverhandlung oder Wiederwaegung (R. 302, 304)

notification judicaire—la reconnaissance par un tribunal de la vérité de certains faits comme connaissance commune, at ainsi ne pas exigeant l'introduction d'évidence pour prouver de tels faits

judicial notice—the recognition by a court of the truth of certain facts as common knowledge, and therefore not requiring the introduction of evidence to prove such facts

gerichtliche Anerkennung—die Anerkennung bestimmter Tatsachen als allgemeine Kenntnis durch ein Gericht, das daher die Einfuehrung von Material zum Beweis dieser Tatsachen nicht verlangt

nouveau—pas présent dans la technique

novel—not present in the art

neuartig—in dem Fachgebiet nicht vorhanden

nouvelle audience—la réconsideration d'un appel, accordée facultativement sur une demande faite dans le délai de trente jours de la date de la décision originale (R. 197 (b))

rehearing—reconsideration of an appeal by the Board of Appeals, granted optionally on a request made within thirty days from the date of the original decision (R. 197(b))

Wiederverhandlung—nochmalige Erwaegung einer Beschwerde durch den Board of Appeals; nach freiem Ermessen, auf ein Ersuchen innerhalb von dreissig Tagen vom Datum der urspruenglichen Entscheidung bewilligt (R. 197(b))

nouvelle matière—une divulgation qui n'est pas présentée dans la spécification, ou dans les dessins, ou dans les revendications de la demande originale. Une addition à la divulgation originale, et ainsi pas admissible par amendement ou par "reissue" demande. (R. 118, Sec. 132, 251)

new matter—a disclosure not set forth in the specification, or drawings or claims of the original application. An addition to the original disclosure, and therefore not admissible by amendment or by reissue application. (R. 118, Sec. 132, 251)

neue Materie—eine Offenbarung, die in der Beschreibung (specification) oder den Zeichnungen oder Anspruechen der urspruenglichen Anmeldung nicht gemacht wurde. Eine Hinzufuegung zu der urspruenglichen Offenbarung und daher durch Berichtigung oder Antrag auf erneute Erteilung nicht zulaessig. (R. 118, Sec. 132, 251)

O

objection—une critique par l'examinateur au sujet de la forme, plutôt que de l'essentiel, de la demande (MPEP 706.01). Pour maîtriser l'examinateur, le demandeur peut pétitionner le Commissaire; une objection n'est pas sujet à appel.

objection—criticism by examiner directed to matters of form, rather than substance, in the application (MPEP 706.01). To overrule the examiner, applicant may petition the Commissioner; an objection is not appealable.

Einwand—Kritik des Pruefers, die auf die Form und nicht den Inhalt der Anmeldung gerichtet ist (MPEP 706.01). Der Anmelder kann beim Commissioner einkommen die Meinung des Pruefers beiseitezusetzen; gegen einen Einwand kann keine Berufung eingelegt werden.

ou—voir expression alternative; revendication "Markush"

or—see alternative expression; Markush claim

oder—vgl. alternative Ausdrucksweise; Markush Anspruch

P

"paper" brevet—un brevet dont on n'a pas pratiqué commercialement l'enseignement

paper patent—a patent whose teaching has not been practised commercially

Papier-Patent—ein Patent, dessen "lehren" nicht handelsmaessig ausgefuehrt worden sind

"parent" demande—la demande originale sur laquelle on base une demande de continuation ou de continuation-en-partie

parent application—the original application on which a continuation or continuation-in-part application is based

Stamm-Anmeldung—die urspruengliche Anmeldung eines Patents, worauf eine Fortfuehrungs- oder Teilfortfuehrungs-Anmeldung begruendet ist

parentheses—les symboles [ ] mis autour d'un mot ou des mots dans une revendication comme une directive à l'examinateur de rayer tel mot ou tels mots de la revendication (R. 121)

brackets—the symbols [ ] placed around a word or words in a claim as a direction to the examiner to delete such word or words from the claim (R. 121)

(eckige) **Klammern**—wenn dieses Zeichen [ ] ein Wort oder Worte in einem Anspruch einklammert, so ist dies als eine Anweisung an den Pruefer solch ein Wort oder Worte von dem Anspruch zu streichen, zu verstehen (R. 121)

pays de pacte (unioniste)—les pays appartenant à l'union instituée par la Convention de Paris, 1883, pour la protection de la propriété industrielle

convention countries—member countries of the Union Convention of Paris, 1883, for the protection of industrial property

Verbandslaender—Mitgliedstaaten der Pariser Union Verbandsuebereinkunft zum Schutze Industriellen Eigentums von 1883

perfectionnement—un avancement inventif d'un degré moins d'une "invention pionnière"

improvement—an inventive advance of a degree less than a "pioneer invention"

Verbesserung—ein erfinderischer Schritt vorwaerts von geringerem Rang als eine "bahnbrechende Erfindung"

période conventionnelle ou unioniste—période d'une année (six mois pour les modèles ou dessins) pendant laquelle on peut revendiquer la date d'une demande antérieure conventionnelle pour une demande déposée sous le bénéfice de la "Union Convention"

convention period—one year period (six months for designs) during which the date of an earlier convention application can be claimed for an application filed under the benefits of the Union Convention

Uebereinkunfts-Frist—Frist eines Jahres (sechs Monate fuer Geschmacksmuster), waehrend welcher Zeit der Stichtag einer Anmeldung unter einem frueheren Abkommen fuer eine Anmeldung, welche unter den Vorrechten der Unionsuebereinkunft eingereicht wurde, beansprucht werden kann

pétition—le paragraphe introductif d'une demande, demandant la délivrance d'un brevet par le Commissaire des Brevets

petition—the introductory paragraph of an application, requesting the grant of a patent by the Commissioner of Patents

Gesuch—der einleitende Abschnitt einer Anmeldung um die Erteilung eines Patents durch den Commissioner of Patents

pétition au Commissaire—la demande pour une revue des objections ou des exigences d'un examinateur au sujet de la forme ou de l'acquiescement aux Règles de la Pratique

petition to Commissioner—request for review of objections or requirements of an examiner as to matters of form or compliance with the Rules of Practice

Eingabe beim Commissioner—Ersuchen um Nachpruefung der Einwaende oder Forderungen eines Pruefers mit Hinsicht auf Form oder Uebereinstimmung mit den Rules of Practice (Ausfuehrungsbestimmungen)

planche de Bristol—le nom commercial d'une planche à dessin à deux ou trois laminae, ayant une surface d'une blanche pure, çalendrée, effaçable et égale, dont on a besoin pour de tels dessins

Bristol board—the commercial name of the two-ply or three-ply drawing board, having a pure white, calendered and smooth erasable surface, that is required for use for drawings

Bristol Board—handelsueblicher Name der zwei-oder dreifachen Zeichenpappe mit reinweisser, glaenzender und glatt-radierbarer Oberflaeche, die fuer den Gebrauch von Zeichnungen verlangt wird

pluralite—dans une revendication pluralité veut dire deux éléments ou plus que deux éléments

plurality—in a claim, "plurality" means two or more elements

Vielheit—in einem Anspruch bedeutet "Vielheit" zwei oder mehr Elemente

plus large que l'invention—des revendications d'une portée qui dépasse les bornes de l'invention définies dans la demande ou dans le brevet

broader than the invention—claim of a scope that exceeds the limits of the invention defined in the application or patent

Umfassender als die Erfindung—Anspruch auf einen die Grenzen der Erfindung—wie sie im Patentantrag festgelegt sind—uebersteigenden Umfang

portée de la revendication—voir largeur de la revendication

scope of claim—see breadth of claim

Umfang des Anspruchs—vgl. Ausmass des Anspruchs

poursuite—les procédés suivis pour obtenir la délivrance d'un brevet

prosecution—the procedures followed to obtain the grant of a patent

Verfolgung—die Massnahmen, die getroffen werden um ein Patent erteilt zu bekommen

pouvoir d'avocat—l'instrument qui autorise une personne d'agir pour une autre personne

power of attorney—the instrument authorizing one person to act for another person

Vollmacht—das Instrument, das eine Person ermaechtigt fuer eine andere Person zu handeln

préférablement—employé pour indiquer que le mot auquel cela rapporte est facultatif et non essentiel, ou n'est pas nécessairement effectif à altérer le résultat à un degré constituant une différence de type

preferably—used to indicate that the word to which it relates is optional and not essential, or not necessarily effective in changing the result to a degree constituting a difference of kind

vorzugsweise—benutzt um anzuzeigen, dass das Wort, worauf es sich bezieht, beliebig gewaehlt und nicht wesentlich ist oder nicht notwendigerweise das Ergebnis in einem Mass, das einen Unterschied in der Art ausmachen wuerde, verandert

présomption de validité—la supposition refutable qu'un brevet délivré soit valide

presumption of validity—the rebuttable assumption that an issued patent is valid

mutmassliche Gueltigkeit—die wiederlegbare Annahme, dass ein erteiltes Patent gueltig ist

priorité d'invention—détermination du premier d'inventer en déterminant le premier de réduire à la pratique et, ou cela importe, la date du commencement de la diligence continuante par l'un qui était le premier de concevoir mais le dernier de réduire à la pratique

priority of invention—determination of the first to invent by determining the first to reduce to practice and, where appropriate, the date of commencement of continuing diligence by one who was first to conceive but last to reduce to practice

Erfindungsprioritaet—Bestimmung des Ersten, der eine Erfindung gemacht hat durch Bestimmung dessen, der sie als Erster in die Praxis umgesetzt hat und—wo es zutrifft—das Datum des Beginns der andauernden Sorgfalt dessen, der zwar die Erfindung als Erster gedanklich erfasst, aber sie als Letzter in die Praxis umgesetzt hat

procédé—une classe de matière brevetable au sujet d'une série cohérente de démarches ou d'opération pour accomplir un résultat physique

process—a class of patentable subject matter covering a connected series of steps or operations for accomplishing a physical result

Verfahren—eine Klasse von patentfaehigen Gegenstaenden, die sich ueber eine zusammenhaengende Reihe von Stufen oder Vorgaengen erstreckt um ein greifbares Ergebnis zu erzielen

procédé ex parte—un procédé entre un demandeur et l'Office des Brevets, sans aucune troisième partie opposante

ex parte proceeding—a proceeding between an applicant and the Patent Office, with no third and opposing party

einseitiges Verfahren—Verfahren zwischen einem Anmelder und dem Patentamt ohne eine dritte und Gegenpartei

procédé inter partes—un procédé comprenant plusieurs demandeurs ou inventeurs opposés

inter partes proceeding—a proceeding involving two or more opposing applicants or inventors

inter partes Verfahren—ein Verfahren, bei dem es sich um zwei oder mehr "einsprechende" Anmelder oder Erfinder handelt

procédé spécial d'examiner—l'examen accélére d'une nouvelle demande basé sur une pétition écrit de rendre spéciale la demande, la concession de limiter la demande à dix revendications au moins, et la soumission d'une recherche faite avant l'examen et la différenciation des revendications des renvois de cette recherche. Une première action complète sera faite avant toutes les autres demandes sauf celles qui sont en condition pour action de l'examinateur; on donnera au demandeur trois mois pour y répondre; après une entrevue facultative, on doit limiter la réponse aux rejets, objections et exigences faits; le jugement final sera fait par l'examinateur dans le délai d'un mois de la réponse. (R. 102, MPEP 708.01 et 708.02)

special examining procedure—accelerated examination of a new application based upon a written petition to make special, agreement to keep the application limited to ten claims or less, and submission of a pre-examination search and differentiation of the claims from the references of that search. A complete first action will be made prior to all applications except those in condition for allowance or under a fixed time limit for action by the Examiner; applicant will be given three months to respond; after an optional interview, the response must be limited to the rejections, objections and requirements made; final disposition will be made by the Examiner within one month of the response. (R. 102, MPEP 708.01 and 708.02)

Sonderpruefverfahren—beschleunigte Pruefung einer neuen Anmeldung auf einem schriftlichen Gesuch um Sonderbehandlung beruhend, Uebereinkommen die Anmeldung auf zehn oder weniger Ansprueche beschraenkt zu halten, und Vorlage einer Vorpruefungs-Untersuchung und Differenzierung der Ansprueche von dem Hinweisen in dieser Untersuchung. Eine vollstaendige erste Behandlung wird vor allen Anmeldungen unternommen, mit Ausnahme derjenigen, die in der Zulassung begriffen sind oder mit einem festgesetzten Termin dem Pruefer zur Behandlung vorliegen; der Anmelder hat drei Monate Zeit zur Erwiderung; nach einem in Belieben der Beteiligten stehenden Interview muss die Erwiderung auf die gemachten Zurueckweisungen, Einwaende und Forderungen begrenzt sein; der Pruefer trifft innerhalb eines Monats nach der Erwinderung seine endgueltige Anordnung. (R. 102, MPEP 708.01 and 708.02)

procédés de l'utilisation publique—basé sur un pétition soutenu d'attestations, l'audience et l'enregistrement d'évidence concernant la question de savoir si l'invention avait été à l'utilisation publique ou en vente un an avant le dépôt de la demande, ou avant la date alléguée, dans une déclaration préliminaire ou avant la date d'invention établie par une partie (R. 292)

public use proceedings—based upon a petition supported by affidavits, the hearing and the taking of testimony on the question of whether an invention had been in public use or on sale one year before the filing of the application, or before the date alleged in a preliminary statement or before the date of invention established by a party (R. 292)

Verfahren ueber offenkundige Benutzung—diese Verfahren beruhen auf einem durch beschworene schriftliche Erklaerungen gestuetzten Gesuch; die Verhandlung und das Aufnehmen von Zeugenaussagen ueber die Frage, ob eine Erfindung ein Jahr vor dem Einreichungsdatum der Anmeldung, oder vor dem in einer Vorerklaerung angegebenen Datum, oder vor dem von einer Partei festgesetzten Erfindungsdatum in offenkundigem Gebrauch oder verkaeuflich war (R. 292)

proces civil—action dans le District Court of the District of Columbia pour revoir une décision de la Commission d'Appel (Sec. 145) ou pour revoir une décision de la Commission des "Interférences" des Brevets (Sec. 146)

civil suit—action in the District Court for the District of Columbia to review a decision of the Board of Appeals (Sec. 145) or to review a decision of the Board of Patent Interferences (Sec. 146)

Zivilklage—Klage beim Distriktgericht fuer den Distrikt von Columbia (Washington, D. C.) um einen Entscheid des Board of Appeals (Sec. 145) oder des Board of Patent Interferences (Sec· 146) nachzupruefen

produit industriel—voir fabrication

article of manufacture—see manufacture

Gegenstand, der hergestellt wird—vgl. herstellen

prolixité—réciter des détails insignifiants d'une telle façon qu'on cache ou obscurcit l'invention (MPEP 706.03 (g))

prolixity—reciting unimportant details in such a manner as to hide or obscure the invention (MPEP 706.03(g))

Weitschweifigkeit—unwichtige Einzelheiten so vortragen, dass dadurch die Erfindung verborgen oder unverstaendlich gemacht wird (MPEP 706.03 (g))

protestation—l'opposition à la délivrance d'un brevet, soumise par un membre du public. L'Office des Brevets reconnaît simplement et dépose de tels documents après les avoir révélés à l'examinateur pour sa propre référence. (R. 291)

protest—opposition to the grant of a patent, submitted by a member of the public. The Patent Office merely acknowledges and files such papers after referral to the examiner for his information. (R.291)

Protest—Widerspruch gegen die Erteilung eines Patents aus der Oeffentlichkeit. Nachdem die Pruefer zu seiner Information darauf hingewiesen wurde, bestaetigt das Patentamt nur den Eingang eines solchen Schriftstuecks und laesst es zu den Akten legen. (R. 291)

publication—voir publication imprimée

publication—see printed publication

Veroeffentlichung—vgl. gedruckte Veroeffentlichung

publication défensive—abandon du droit à un brevet en déposant une demande, un abandon des droits de brevet, le consentement à une publication de l'Office des Brevets d'un abstraction de la divulgation, une autorisation d'ouvrir la démande à l'examen public, et une déclaration d'abandon. Le demandeur retient les droits à une "interférence" pendant cinq années de la date d'effet de dépô la plus ancienne des Etats-Unis. (R. 139)

defensive publication—conditional waiver of right to a patent by filing an application, a waiver of patent rights, consent to a publication by the Patent Office of an abstract of the disclosure, an authorization to open the application to public inspection, and a declaration of abandonment. Applicant retains rights to an interference for five years from the earliest effective United States filing date, and is entitled to the benefit of the filing date of the defensively published application by filing a continuing application within thirty months of the earliest effective United States filing date. (R. 139)

Einspruchs-Bekanntmachung—bedingter Verzicht auf das Recht zu einem Patent durch Einreichung einer Anmeldung, eines Verzichts auf Patentenrechte, Zustimmung zu einer Veroeffentlichung des Auszugs aus der Offenbarung durch das Patentamt, einer Ermaechtigung zur oeffentlichen Einsichtnahme der Anmeldung und einer Aufgaberklaerung. Der Anmelder behaelt fuenf Jahre vom fruehest wirksamen United States Einreichungsdatum das Recht zu einer Interferenz; er ist durch Einreichung einer Fortfuehrungs-Anmeldung innerhalb von dreissig Monaten vom fruehest wirksamen United States Einreichungsdatum zu dem aus dem Einreichungsdatum der Bekanntmachung der Einspruchsanmeldung erwachsenden Vorteil berechtigt. (R. 139)

publication imprimée—un document qui est imprimé et rendu disponible au public, présumant que les personnes intéressées à la technique en sachent

printed publication—a document that is printed and is made accessible to the public, raising a presumption that the public concerned with the art would know of it

gedruckte Veroeffentlichung—ein Dokument, das gedruckt und der Allgemeinheit zugaenglich gemacht worden ist, und daher zu der Annahme berrechtigt, dass das fachlich interessierte Publikum davon weiss

R

recherche—une revue des brevets et d'autres publications pour déterminer ce que sait le public au sujet d'une invention alléguée, ainsi ramassant les renseignements pour soutenir une opinion au sujet de la brevetabilité de l'invention, ou de la validité d'un brevet sur l'invention, ou de l'état de la technique

search—a review of patents and other publications to determine what is known to the public in relation to an alleged invention, thus collecting the information to support an opinion on the patentability of the invention or on the validity of a patent on the invention, or on the state of the art

Untersuchung—Nachpruefung von Patenten und andern Veroeffentlichungen um festzustellen, was der Oeffentlichkeit in Bezug auf eine angebliche Erfindung bekannt ist; dadurch wird die Information zur Unterstuetzung eines Gutachtens ueber die Patentfaehigkeit der Erfindung, oder ueber die Gueltigkeit eines Patents an der Erfindung, oder am Stand der Technik gesammelt

recherche de brevetabilité—voir recherche

patentability search—see search

Patentfaehigkeits-Untersuchung—vgl. Untersuchung

recherche de la nouveauté—voir recherche

novelty search—see search

Untersuchung auf Neuheit—vgl. Untersuchung

recherche de validité—voir recherche

validity search—see search

Gueltigkeits-Untersuchung—vgl. Untersuchung

recherche préliminaire—un examen des brevets, fait d'ordinaire à l'Office des Brevets par un chercheur privé au dépens de l'inventeur, pour déterminer si l'invention est antériorisée par une technique antérieure

preliminary search—an examination of patents, usually made in the Patent Office by a private searcher at the expense of the inventor, to determine whether the invention is anticipated by prior art

Voruntersuchung—eine Ueberpruefung von Patenten, gewoehnlich im Patentamt durch eine Privatperson auf Kosten des Erfinders vorgenommen, um festzustellen, ob die Erfindung durch den Stand der Technik vorweggenommen ist

redevances—paiement pour l'utilisation d'une invention

royalty—payment for use of an invention

Lizenzgebuehr—Bezahlung fuer die Benutzung einer Erfindung

réduction actuelle à la pratique—la construction de l'invention ou du mécanisme, ou travaillant de procédé de l'invention

actual reduction to practice—construction of the device or carrying out the process of the invention

Tatsaechliche Umsetzung in die Praxis—Konstruktion des Geraetes oder Ausfuehrung des Erfindungsvorgangs

réduction à la pratique—un procédé est réduit à la pratique quand il est exécuté avec succès; une machine, est réduite à la pratique quand elle est assemblée et employée; une fabrication est réduite à la pratique quand elle est complètement fabriquée; une composition est réduite à la pratique quand elle est complètement composée

reduction to practice—a process is reduced to practice when it is successfully performed; a machine is reduced to practice when it is assembled and used; a manufacture is reduced to practice when it is completely manufactured; a composition is reduced to practice when it is completely composed

Umsetzen in die Praxis—ein Verfahren ist in die Praxis umgesetzt, wenn es erfolgreich ausgefuehrt wird; eine Vorrichtung ist in die Praxis umgesetzt, wenn sie zusammengesetzt und benutzt wird; ein Herstellungsverfahren ist in die Praxis umgesetzt, wenn es vollstaendig hergestellt ist; eine Zusammensetzung ist in die Praxis umgesetzt, wenn sie vollstaendig zusammengesetzt ist

réduction constructive à la pratique—déposant une demande pour un brevet (MPEP 715.07)

constructive reduction to practice—the equivalent of actual reduction to practice, effected by filling an application for patent (MPEP 715.07)

konstruktive Umsetzen in die Praxis—gleichbedeutend mit dem tatsaechlichen Umsetzen in die Praxis, zur Ausfuehrung gebracht durch das Einreichen einer Patentenanmeldung (MPEP 715.07)

Règles de Pratique—les règlements établis du Commissaire des Brevets qui gouvernent la conduite des procédés à l'Office des Brevets (Sec. 6, 11)

Rules of Practice—the regulations established by the Commissioner of Patents governing the conduct of proceedings in the Patent Office (Sec. 6, 11)

Ausfuehrungsbestimmungen (Rules of Practice)—die vom Commissioner of Patents festgesetzten Vorschriften, die das Verhalten bei Verfahren im Patentamt bestimmen (Sec. 6, 11)

"reissue"—la délivrance d'un brevet substitut pour le reste du terme du brevet original, faite quand le brevet originalement délivré, par erreur et sans intention déceptive, est découvert d'être entièrement ou partiellement inopératif (R. 171–179)

reissue—the grant of a substitute patent for the remainder of the term of the original patent, made when the patent granted originally, through error and without deceptive intent, is found to be wholly or partly inoperative (R.171–179)

erneute Erteilung—die Erteilung eines Ersatzpatents fuer die verbleibende Laufzeit des Stammpatents; dies wird getan, wenn das urspruenglich erteilte Patent durch Irrtum und ohne Taeuschungsabsicht ganz oder teilweise unwirksam befunden wird (R. 171–179)

"reissue" série de brevets—la distincte série de numéros des brevets "reissue" précédée de "Re." (MPEP 901.04)

reissue patent series—the separate series of numbers for reissue patents preceded by "Re". (MPEP 901.04)

Serie fuer erneut erteilte Patente—die separate Reihenfolge von Nummern fuer erneut erteilte Patente mit dem Vorsatz "Re." (MPEP 901.04)

rejet—action de l'office des Brevets niant la brevetabilité et y inclus la notification des causes de l'action accompagnée des renseignements et des renvois sur lesquels a été basés le rejet (Sec. 132)

rejection—action of the Patent Office denying patentability, and including notice of the reasons for the action together with the information and references on which the rejection was based (Sec. 132)

Zurueckweisung—eine Handlung des Patentamts, welche die Patentfaehigkeit in Abrede stellt, einschliesslich einer Mitteilung ueber die Beweggruende der Handlung, zusammen mit Auskuenften und Hinweisen auf denen die Zurueckweisung begruendet war (Sec. 132)

rejet final—une action de l'examinateur qui termine le procédé devant l'examinateur, limitant le demandeur à un appel devant la Commission d'Appel, un pétition au Commissaire des objections ou des exigences qui n'entrent pas dans le rejet d'une revendication, un amendement rendant la demande recevable ou, à la discrétion de l'examinateur, un amendement rendant la demande d'une meilleure forme un appel (R. 116)

final rejection—an action by the examiner that concludes prosecution before the examiner, limiting applicant to appeal to the Board of Appeals, petition to the Commissioner from objections or requirements not involved in the rejection of a claim, amendment placing the application in condition for allowance or, at the discretion of the examiner, amendment placing the application in better form for appeal (R. 116)

endgueltige Zurueckweisung—eine Handlung des Pruefers, die die Verfolgung (der Patentanmeldung) vor dem Pruefer beendet, den Anmelder darauf beschraenkend beim Board of Appeals Beschwerde einzulegen, den Commissioner mit Entgegenhaltungen und Anforderungen, welche nicht in die Ablehnung eines Anspruchs einbezogen waren zu ersuchen, eine Verbesserung, die die Zulassung der Anmeldung ermoeglicht, oder, im Ermessen des Pruefers, eine Verbesserung, welche die Anmeldung in eine bessere Form fuer Berufung bringt (R. 116)

renonciation—une déclaration écrite de l'abandon d'une revendication invalide qu'on a déposée sans intention déceptive. La renonciation doit être enregistrée dans l'Office des Brevets. (Sec. 253, R. 231)

disclaimer—written statement of abandonment of an invalid claim that had been filed without deceptive intent. The disclaimer must be recorded in the Patent Office. (Sec. 253, R. 321)

Widerruf—schriftliche Erklaerung, durch die ein ungueltiger Patentanspruch, der ohne Taeuschungsabsicht gemacht war, aufgegeben wird. Der Widerruf muss beim Patentamt aktenmaessig beurkundet sein. (Sec. 253, R. 321)

renonciation terminale—rendre une invention revendiquée disponible à l'utilisation libre pendant une partie terminale de la période du brevet (Sec. 253)

terminal disclaimer—making a claimed invention available for free use for a terminal part of the period of the patent (Sec. 253)

Verzicht auf den Restteil—eine beanspruchte Erfindung fuer den Restteil ihrer Patentlaufzeit dem freien Gebrauch zugaenglich machen (Sec. 253)

renouvellement—rendre la viabilité d'une demande abandonnée par pétition au Commissaire avec une preuve vérifiée d'un délai inévitable en poursuivant la demande abandonnée, accompagné de la réponse offerte et la taxe de pétition de $15. (R. 137)

revival—restoring the pendency of an abandoned application by petition to the Commissioner with a verified showing of unavoidable delay in prosecuting the abandoned application, together with the proposed response and the petition fee of $15.00 (R.137)

Wiederinkraftsetzung—Wiederherstellung der Anhaegigkeit einer fallengelassenen Anmeldung durch Gesuch beim Commissioner mit einem beglaubigten Nachweis unvermeidlichen Verzugs in der Verfolgung der fallengelassenen Anmeldung, zusammen mit der vorgeschlagenen Entgegnung und der Antragsgebuehr von $15. (R. 137)

renvoi—une technique entérieure dont dépend l'examinateur en rejetant une revendication comme non brevetable. La convenance du renvoi, si elle n'est pas évidente, doit être expliquée et chaque revendication rejetée doit être spécifiée.

reference—prior art relied upon by the examiner in rejecting a claim as unpatentable. The pertinence of the reference, if not obvious, must be clearly explained and each rejected claim must be specified.

Hinweis—Stand der Technik, worauf sich der Pruefer bei der Zurueckweisung eines Anspruchs als nicht patentfaehig beruft. Sofern der Hinweis nicht offensichtlich zutrifft, muss er deutlich erklaert und jeder zurueckgeweisene Anspruch einzeln beschrieben werden.

réponse—réplique à un rejet

response—reply to a rejection

Erwiderung—Antwort auf eine Ablehnung

réponse de l'examinateur—réponse d'un examinateur primaire au dossier du demandeur à la Commission d'Appel, une telle réponse comprenante aucune explication nécessaire de l'invention revendiquée et des raisons de rejet (R. 193)

examiner's answer—response by primary examiner to brief of appellant to Board of Appeals, such answer including any necessary explanation of the invention claimed and of the references and grounds of rejection (R. 193)

Pruefers Antwort—Erwiderung des Vorpruefers auf den Schriftsatz des Berufungsklaegers beim Board of Appeals, mit einem Bescheid, der alle notwendigen Erklaerungen fuer die beanspruchte Erfindung und die Belege und Gruende der Ablehnung enthaelt (R. 193)

représentant légal—une entité qu'on a désignée pour demander un brevet au nom d'un inventeur légalement incapacité (mort, incompétent, etc.)

legal representative—an entity that has been designated to apply for a patent on behalf of a legally incapacitated (dead, incompetent, etc.) inventor

gesetzlicher Vertreter—eine juristische Person, die ernannt worden ist im Namen eines gesetzlich in der Verfuegung beschraenkten (tot, inkompetent, usw.) Erfinders ein Patent anzumelden

res adjudicata—un verdict que la question identique a été décidée antérieurement finalement contre la même partie (MPEP 706.03 (w))

res adjudicata—a finding that the identical issue was previously decided finally against the same party (MPEP 706.03(w))

res adjudicata—der Befund, dass dieselbe Streitfrage gegen die gleiche Partei schon frueher endgueltig entschieden wurde (MPEP 706.03 (w))

restriction—limitant les revendications à une seule invention. Après une exigence de restriction (autrefois appelé division) parce qu'on revendique plusieurs inventions dans une seule demande, une demande restreinte peut se concerner seulement d'une des inventions mentionnées. Si on le dépose avant d'être breveté, l'abandon ou la terminaison des procédés sur la demande originale, le nouveau cas a droit au bénéfice de la date de dépôt de la demande originale, et on ne peut employer comme référence l'un contre l'autre ni le cas original ni le nouveau cas. (Sec. 121, R. 147)

restriction—directing claims to a single invention. After a requirement for restriction (formerly called division) because two or more independent inventions are claimed in a single application, a restricted application may be directed solely to one of said inventions. If filed before the patenting, abandonment or termination of proceedings on the original application, the new case is entitled to the benefit of the filing date of the original application, and neither the original nor the restricted applications or patents can be used as references against each other. (Sec. 121, R.147)

Beschraenkung—Ansprueche auf nur eine Erfindung ausrichten. Nach einer Forderung zur Beschraenkung (frueher Ausscheidung genannt), da zwei oder mehr unabhaengige Erfindungen in einer einzigen Anmeldung beansprucht wurden, kann eine beschraenkte Anmeldung allein nur auf eine der beiden erwaehnten Erfindungen ausgerichtet werden. Wird der neue Fall vor der Patentierung, dem Fallenlassen, oder der Beendigung des Verfahrens gegen die Erstanmeldung eingereicht, so steht ihm das Einreichungsdatum der urspruenglichen Anmeldung zu; weder die urspruenglichen noch die beschraenkten Anmeldungen oder Patente koennen als Belege gegeneinander verwendet werden (Sec. 121, R. 147).

revendication fonctionnelle—une revendication qui ne conforme pas à S. 112 parce qu'au moins un élément ou procédé est défini entièrement ou partiellement en termes de sa conduite ou en termes des résultats qui proviennent de sa conduite, et une telle définition rend la revendication trop large ou indéfinie

functional claim—a claim that fails to comply with S. 112 because at least one element or step is defined in whole or in part in terms of its behavior or in terms of the results that follow from its behavior, and such definition makes the claim too broad or indefinite

funktioneller Anspruch—ein Anspruch, welcher nicht Sec. 112 entspricht, da mindestens ein Element oder eine Stufe im Ganzen oder teilweise in der Terminologie seines Verhaltens definiert ist, oder in der Terminologie der Resultate, die aus seinem Verhalten hervorgehen; und diese Definition macht den Anspruch zu breit oder unbestimmt

revendication générique—une revendication qui comprend dans son étendue plusieurs variantes de l'invention

generic claim—a claim that includes within its scope two or more disclosed embodiments (species) of the invention

Gattungen umfassender Anspruch—ein Anspruch, der in seinen Bereich zwei oder mehr offenbarte Ausfuehrungsformen (Gattungen) der Erfindung einschliesst

revendication Jepson—une espéce de revendication où la matière connue est récitée dans un préambule, ainsi présentant l'environnement, et le perfectionnement est présenté dans la portion restante de la revendication

Jepson claim—a form of claim in which the known matter is recited in a preamble, thus setting forth the environment, and the improvement is set forth in the remaining portion of the claim

Jepson Anspruch—eine Art von Anspruch, wobei die bekannte Materie in einer Einleitung vorgetragen—damit die Umwelt darlegend—und die Verbesserung im restlichen Teil des Anspruchs dargelegt wird

revendication liante—une revendication qui est inséparable des revendications à plusieurs inventions convenablement divisibles, comme une revendication générique qui lie des revendications des variantes

linking claim—a claim that is inseparable from claims to two or more properly divisible inventions, such as a genus claim linking species claims

verkettender Anspruch—ein Anspruch, der untrennbar von Anspruechen auf zwei oder mehr richtig teilbare Erfindungen ist, wie zum Beispiel ein Art-(genus) Anspruch, der Gattungs-Ansprueche zusammenkettet

revendication Markush—une revendication de la forme ". . en quoi________est un matérial choisi du groupe qui consiste de________, ________et________", or ". . en quoi ________est________, ________ou________", employé comme une expression générique couvrant un groupe de plusieurs matériels où il n'y a pas de nom générique pour le groupe, permis où les matériels appartiennent à une classe physique, chimique, ou technique reconnue, ou possèdent en commun au moins une qualité qui est principalement responsible de leur fonction dans la relation revendiquée

Markush claim—a claim of the form ". . wherein________is a material selected from the group consisting of________, ________and________" or ". . wherein________is________, ________or________", used as a generic expression covering a group of two or more materials where there is no generic name for the group, permitted where the materials belong to a recognized physical, chemical or art-recognized class, or possess at least one property in common that is mainly responsible for their function in the claimed relationship

Markush Anspruch—ein Anspruch in der Art ". . worin ________ist ein Stoff ausgewaehlt aus der Gruppe bestehen aus________, ________und________"oder ". . worin ________ist________, ________oder________", als Gattungen umfassender Ausdruck benutzt fuer eine Gruppe von zwei oder mehr Stoffen, fuer die es keinen Gattungen umfassenden Gruppenamen gibt; dies est erlaubt, sofern die Stoffe zu einer anerkannten physikalischen, chemischen, oder einer technisch anerkannten Klasse gehoeren, oder wenigstens eine gemeinsame Eigenschaft haben, die hauptsaechlich fuer ihre Funktion in dem mit Anspruch belegten Verhaeltnis verantwortlich ist

revendication multiple dépendante—une revendication qui fait référence à n'importe quelle revendication antérieure, indépendante ou dépendante, dans l'alternatif. (MPEP Change Notice 17-2 du 4 juin 1968) Discontinuer—cf. 864 O. G. 323, 8 July 1969.

multiple dependent claim—a claim that refers back to any of the preceding independent or dependent claims in the alternative. (MPEP Change Notice 17-2 of 4 June 1968) Discontinued—cf. 864 O. G. 323, 8 July 1969.

mehrfacher Unteranspruch—ein Anspruch, der auf die vorhergehenden unabhaengigen oder abhaengigen Ansprueche in der Alternative zurueckverweist. (MPEP Change Notice 17-2 of 4 June 1968). Unterbrechen—864 O. G. 323, 8 July 1969.

revendication subordonnée—une revendication qui fait allusion à, et limite, une revendication précédante. Plusieurs séries de revendications subordonnées peuvent paraître dans une demande unique, mais toutes les revendications dans chaque série doivent être en ordre exact et consécutif, ou aussi près qu'il soit physiquement possible à un tel ordre. (R. 75)

dependent claim—a claim that refers back to and restricts a single preceding claim. Several series of dependent claims may appear in a single application, but all claims in each series must be in immediate consecutive order or as close to such order as physically possible. (R. 75)

Unteranspruch—ein Anspruch, der auf einen einzelnen vorhergegangenen Anspruch zurueckverweist und diesen begrenzt. Mehrere Serien von Unteranspruechen koennen in einer einzigen Anmeldung erscheinen, aber alle Ansprueche in jeded Serie muessen in unmittelbar aufeinanderfolgender Ordnung oder so dicht wie moeglich zusammenstehen. (R. 75)

revendication synoptique—une revendication dans laquelle les plusieurs clauses ou sous-paragraphes sont mis intérieurement dans la marge pour pourvoir le récit en colonne des éléments et des sous-éléments de la revendication

tabular claim—a claim in which the several clauses or subparagraphs are indented from the margin to provide columnar recital of the elements and sub-elements of the claim

tabellarischer Anspruch—ein Anspruch, wobei die verschiedenen Klauseln oder Unterabschnitte vom Rand eingerueckt sind, um die Aufreihung der Elemente und Unterelemente des Anspruchs in Kolonnen anzuordnen

revendications—la partie finale d'une spécification signalant et nettement proposant la matière de l'invention (Sec. 112; R. 71, 75)

claims—the concluding part of a specification particularly pointing out and distinctly setting forth the subject matter of the invention (Sec. 112; R. 71, 75)

Ansprueche—der abschliessende Teil einer Beschreibung (specification), welcher den Gegenstand der Erfindung besonders hervorhebt und eindeutig darlegt (Sec. 112, R. 71, 75)

revendications de variantes—une incarnation unique, spécifiquement différente, d'une invention (MPEP 806.04(e)). On peut revendiquer cinq variantes dans une demande. (R. 141)

species claim—a single specifically different embodiment of an invention (MPEP 806.04(e)). Five species may be claimed in one application. (R. 141)

Gattungs-Anspruch—eine einzelne im besondern differenzierte Ausfuehrung einer Erfindung (MPEP 806.04(e)). Fuenf Gattungen koennen in einer Anmeldung beansprucht werden. (R. 141)

révocation—décision d'un tribunal qui annule la délivrance du brevet

revocation—ruling of a court cancelling the patent grant

Widerrufung—Gerichtsentscheid, der eine Patenterteilung fuer nichtig erklaert

S

salle d'archives—voir Salle Publique de Recherche

record room—see Public Search Room

Aktenzimmer—vgl. oeffentlicher Nachschlage-Saal

Salle Publique de Recherche—une salle à l'Office des Brevets, ouverte au public, où sont déposées selon la classification de l'Office des Brevets, des copies de tous les brevets des Etats-Unis. Une Bibliothèque Scientifique adjointe, ouverte au public, contient des livres et des périodiques scientifiques et techniques en langues diverses, les journaux officiels des offices étrangers des brevets, et des copies des brevets étrangers, organisées en ordre numérique et selon la classiffication du pays d'origine du brevet. Une salle d'archives adjointe, ouverte au public, contient les archives et les dossiers des brevets délivrés, les brevets des Etats-Unis organisés en ordre numérique, et un ensemble de la Gazette Officielle.

Public Search Room—a room in the Patent Office, open to the public, in which copies of all United States patents are filed according to the Patent Office classification. An adjunct Scientific Library, open to the public, contains scientific and technical books and periodicals in various languages, the official journals of foreign patent offices, and copies of foreign patents arranged in numerical order and according to the classification of the country of origin of the patent. An adjunct record room, open to the public, contains the records and files of issued patents, United States patents arranged in numerical order, and a set of the Official Gazette.

oeffentlicher Nachschlag-Saal—ein der Oeffentlichkeit zugaenglicher Raum im Patentamt, wo Kopien aller Patente der Vereinigten Staaten nach ihrer patentamtlichen Klassifizierung eingeordnet sind. Eine zusaetzliche auch der Allgemeinheit zugaengliche wissenschaftliche Bibliothek enthaelt wissenschaftliche und technische Buecher und Zeitschriften in verschiedenen Sprachen, die officiellen Veroeffentlichungen auslaendischer Patentamter und Kopien auslaendischer Patente in zahlenmaessiger Anordnung und gemaess den Klassifizierungen des Ursprungslandes des Patents. Ein zusaetzliches, ebenfalls der Oeffentlichkeit zugaengliches Aktenzimmer enthaelt die Protokolle und Akten von erteilten Patenten, mit den Patenten der Vereinigten Staaten in zahlenmaessiger Ordnung und eine Ausgabe des Amtsblatts.

savoir-faire—les renseignements ou les connaissances pratiques qui permettent la pratique d'une technologie

know-how—practical information or knowledge permitting practice of a technology

know-how (gewusst wie . .)—Informationen und Sachkenntnis, die die Ausuebung technischen Koennens in der Praxis erlauben

secret—quand la publication des données pourrait affecter la sécurité nationale, on rend la demande disponible pour l'inspection de l'agence convenable du Gouvernement. Si l'agence trouve que la publication de l'invention serait nuisible à la sécurité nationale, le Commissaire ordonnera qu'on garde secrète l'invention; pendant cette période, la poursuite continuera, mais on n'établira aucune audience d'appel et on ne délivrera pas le brevet jusqu'à ce que la décision de mise au secret soit ôtét. (Sec. 181)

secrecy—when the publication of data in a patent application might affect national security, the application is made available for inspection by an appropriate agency of the Government. If the agency finds that publication of the invention would be detrimental to the national security, the Commissioner shall order the invention kept secret; during this period, prosecution will proceed, but no appeal hearing will be set nor will the patent issue until the secrecy order is removed. (Sec. 181)

Geheimhaltung—Koennte die Veroeffentlichung von Angaben in einer Patentanmeldung die nationale Sicherheit beeintraechtigen, so wird die Anmeldung einer zustaendigen Dienststelle zur Einsichtnahme zugaenglich gemacht. Befindet die Dienststelle, dass Veroeffentlichung der Erfindung von Nachteil fuer die nationale Sicherheit waere, dann soll der Commissioner die Geheimhaltung der Erfindung anordnen; waehrend dieser Zeitspanne wird die Weiterverfolgung aufrechterhalten, aber keine Berfungsverhandlung anberaumt, noch wird das Patent erteilt bis die Geheimhaltungsanordnung entfernt ist. (Sec. 181)

senior party—dans une "interférence", la partie qui a la date d'effet de dépôt plus ancienne

senior party—in an interference, the party having the earlier established effective filing date

aeltere Partei (Senior Party)—die Partei in einer Interferenz, die der ersten festgesetzen Termin fuer das Inkrafttreten des Einreichungsdatums hat

série de brevets de plantes—la serie distincte de numéros pour les brevets de plantes précédée des lettres "P.P." (MPEP 901.04)

plant patent series—the separate series of numbers for plant patents preceded by the letters "P.P." (MPEP 901.04)

Pflanzen-Patentserie—die besondere Serie von Nummern fuer Pflanzen-Patente, der die Buchstaben "P.P." voranstehen (MPEP 901.04)

serie de dessin ou modèle déposé—la distincte série de numéros pour des dessin ou modèles déposés, précédée par la lettre D (MPEP 901.04)

design patent series—the separate series of numbers for design patents preceded by the letter D (MPEP 901.04)

Geschmacksmuster-Patentserie—die besondere Serie von Nummern fuer Geschmacksmusterpatente, der der Buchstabe D voransteht (MPEP 901.04)

serment—une déclaration jurée ou affirmée du demandeur qu'il a accédé aux stipulations de Sec. 101 et Sec. 102 (R. 65)

oath—sworn or affirmed statement of the applicant that he has complied with the provisions of Sec. 101 and Sec. 102 (R. 65)

Eid—beschworene oder bekraeftigte Erklaerung des Patentanmelders, dass er die Bedingungen unter Sec. 101 und Sec. 102 erfuellt hat (R. 65)

serment ou déclaration supplémentaire—un serment ou une déclaration déposée, au choix, à l'appui de nouvelles revendications pour la matière originalement décrite mais pas revendiquée (R. 67)

supplemental oath or declaration—an oath or declaration filed, optionally, in support of new claims for subject matter originally described but not claimed (R. 67)

Ergaenzungs-Eid oder eidesstattliche Erklaerung—ein nach freiem Ermessen geleisteter Eid oder eidesstattliche Erklaerung zur Unterstuetzung neuer Ansprueche fuer urspruenglich beschriebene, aber nicht beanspruchte Anmeldungsgegenstaende (R. 67)

"shifting ground"—changer de position quant à ce que comprend l'invention, ou quant à ce que sont les différences entre les renvois et l'invention

shifting ground—changing position as to what the invention comprises, or as to what the differences are between the references and the invention

Veraenderung des Standpunkts—Aenderung der Einstellung im Hinblick auf das, was die Erfindung in sich fasst oder was die Unterschiede zwischen den Hinweisen und der Erfindung sind

"shop right"—le droit pour un employeur d'utiliser dans son entreprise l'invention d'un employé, lorsque celui-ci l'a faite avec l'équipement de l'employeur ou durant les heures de travail

shop right—the right of an employer to use in his shop the invention made by an employee with the employer's equipment or time

shop right—Recht eines Arbeitgebers, die von einem Arbeitnehmer mit den Einrichtungen oder in der Zeit des Arbeitgebers gemachte Erfindung in seinem Betrieb zu benutzen

signature—le complet prénom sans abréviation, l'initiale ou le nom intermédiaire, s'il y en ą, et le complet surnom du demandeur, qu'on doit endosser sur la demande (R. 57)

signature—the full first name without abbreviation, middle initial or name, if any, and full surname of the applicant, which must be endorsed on the application (R. 57)

Unterschrift—der vollstaendige, unabgekuerzte Vorname, der Anfangsbuchstabe oder volle Mittelname—wenn vorhanden—und der vollstaendige Nachname des Anmelders, der auf der Anmeldung gegengezeichnet sein muss (R. 57)

"soft copy"—une copie de la spécification des revendications et des dessins d'un brevet délivré d'utilité ou de dessin

soft copy—a copy of the specification, claims and drawing of an issued utility or design patent

inoffizielle Abschrift—eine Abschrift der Beschreibung (specification), Ansprueche und Zeichnungen eines Gebrauchs- oder Geschmacksmusterpatents

soliciter—la préparation et la poursuite des demandes de brevet

soliciting—the preparation and prosecution of patent applications

Bewerbung—die Vorbereitung und Verfolgung von Patentanmeldungen

sommaire de l'invention—une déclaration en termes généraux du progrès de la technique, les avantages fournis et produits par l'invention, et une brève description fonctionnelle et généralisée de comment le concept inventif achève des résultats supérieurs, incluse dans la spécification après la declaration du fond de l'invention

summary of the invention—statement in general terms of the advance in the art, the advantages provided by the invention, and a brief, generalized functional description as to how the inventive concept attains the superior results, included in the specification after the statement of the background of the invention

Zusammenfassung der Erfindung—eine allgemein gehaltene Darstellung des technischen Fortschritts, der Vorteile, welche die Erfindung mit sich bringt und eine kurze, verallgemeinerte, funktionelle Schilderung, wie die erfinderische Idee ueberragende Ergebnisse erzielt; enthalten in der Beschreibung (specification), nach der Darstellung des Hintergrundes der Erfindung

souligner—une ligne horizontale mise sous un mot ou plusieurs mots dans une revendication, comme une directive à l'examinateur d'ajouter tel mot ou tels mots à la revendication (R. 121)

underlining—a horizontal line placed under a word or words in a claim as a direction to the examiner to add such word or words to the claim (R. 121)

unterstreichen—eine waagrechte Linie unter einem Wort oder Worten in einem Anspruch ist eine Anweisung an den Pruefer solch ein Wort oder Worte dem Anspruch hinzuzufuegen (R. 121)

soumission—requête de l'appelant que la Commission d'Appel considère l'appel sur le dossier écrit, la requête résulte de la manque de l'appelant de demander une audience orale

submission—request by appellant that the Board of Appeals consider the appeal on the written record, the request being effected by failure of appellant to request oral hearing

Vorlage—Antrag des Berufungsklaegers, der Board of Appeals moege die Berufung auf Grund von schriftlichen Unterlagen erwaegen; der Antrag ist durch die Unterlassung des Berufungsklaegers um eine muendliche Verhandlung nachzusuchen veranlasst

sous-classe—la designation numérique de l'Office des Brevets de la division de matière d'un brevet ou d'une publication, dans une particularisation plus grande de la classification de telle matière

subclass—the Patent Office numerical designation of the subject matter division of a patent or publication, in further particularization of a classification of such subject matter

Unterklasse—die nummerische Bestimmung der Unterteilung der Gegenstaende eines Patents oder einer Veroeffentlichung durch das Patentamt zur weiteren Detailierung der Klassifizierung solcher Gegenstaende

spécification—une description précise d'une incarnation préférée de l'invention, distinguant l'invention de ce qui est vieille. La spécification doit être complète, nette, concise et exacte, afin qu'une personne adroite dans la technique puisse employer l'invention; elle comprend, en ordre, un titre, une abstraction de la divulgation, un renvoi à aucune invention relative, le fond de l'invention, un bref sommaire de l'invention, une brève description des vues des dessins, une description détaillée, les revendications et une signature. (R. 77)

specification—a precise description of a preferred embodiment of an invention, distinguishing the invention from what is old. The specification must be full, clear, concise and exact, so that a person skilled in the art can make and use the invention; it comprises, in order, a title, an abstract of the disclosure, cross-reference to any related application, the background of the invention, a brief summary of the invention, a brief description of the views of the drawing, a detailed description, claims, and a signature. (R. 77)

Beschreibung (specification)—eine genaue Schilderung einer bevorzugten Ausfuehrungsform einer Erfindung, die diese von allem schon Dagewesenen unterscheidet. Die Beschreibung (specification) muss so vollstaendig, klar, knapp und exakt sein, dass ein Fachmann auf dem Gebiet sie ausfuehren und benutzen kann; gemaess nachstehender Reihenfolge umfasst sie einen Titel, einen Auszug aus der Offenbarung, Hinweise auf all verwandten Anmeldungen, den Hintergrund der Erfindung, eine kurze Zusammenfassung der Erfindung, eine kurze Schilderung der Ansichten der Zeichnung, eine ausfuehrliche Beschreibung, Ansprueche und eine Unterschrift. (R. 77)

statutaire—établi par un acte du Congrès proprement rendu une loi

statutory—established by act of Congress duly enacted into law

rechtsverbindlich—durch Congress-Beschluss festgesetzt und ordnungsgemaess zum Gesetz erhoben

"streamlined continuation" demande—une demande où les dessins et la spécification sont identiques avec ceux d'une demande pendante du même demandeur, les revendications concernent la même invention que celles poursuivies dans la demande pendante, et on a suivi les procédés pour céder les dessins et la spécification de la demande pendante à la nouvelle demande (Notification 824 O.G. 1)

streamlined continuation application — an application in which the drawings and specification are identical with those of a pending application of the same applicant, and the claims are directed to the same invention as that prosecuted in the pending application, and procedures for transferring the drawings and specification from the pending application to the new application have been followed (Notice 824 O.G. 1)

"streamlined" Fortfuehrungs-Anmeldung—eine Anmeldung in der die Zeichnungen und Beschreibung (specification) mit einer anhaengigen Anmeldung desselben Anmelders identisch sind; die Ansprueche beziehen sich auf dieselbe Erfindung, die in der anhaengigen Anmeldung verfolgt wurden, und die Durchfuehrungsvorschriften zur Uebertragung von Zeichnungen und Beschreibung (specification) von der anhaengigen Anmeldung zur neuen Anmeldung sind befolgt worden (Notice 824 O. G. 1)

"substantially"—dans les revendications, une qualification qui a une signification qu'on devrait soutenir par illustration ou par example dans la spécification

substantially—in claims, a qualification having a meaning that should be supported by illustration in the specification

im Wesentlichen—in Anspruechen eine Einschraenkung, deren Bedeutung durch Illustration in der Beschreibung (specification) unterstuetzt werden sollte

succès commercial—acceptation significative des consommateurs d'un produit ou d'un procès tendant à soutenir l'argument que le produit ou le procès est un avancement remarquable dans la technique

commercial success—significant consumer acceptance of a product or process, tending to support the argument that the product or process is a notable advance in the art

geschaeftlicher Erfolg—bedeutende Verbraucherannahme eines Produktes oder Herstellungsverfahrens, welche die Auffassung, das Produkt oder Verfahren sei ein beachtenswerter Fortschritt in der Technik, unterstuetzt

suspension d'action—tenir en suspens une action pour une bonne raison, à la requête du demandeur ou de l'Office des Brevets, pendant un temps raisonnable et spécifié (R. 103)

suspension of action—postponement of action by the Patent Office for good cause, at the request of applicant or at the instance of the Patent Office, for a reasonable specified time (R. 103)

Aussetzung der Behandlung—angemessen befristeter Aufschub der Behandlung durch das Patentamt aus guten Gruenden, entweder auf Ansuchen des Anmelders oder auf Veranlassung des Patentamts (R. 103)

"swearing back of reference"—exposé sous serment démontrant la complétion aux Etats-Unis d'une invention à une date antérieure à la date d'effet du renvoi (R. 131)

swearing back of reference—making an oath showing completion of the invention of the application in the United States before the effective date of the reference (R. 131)

"swearing back of reference"—einen Eid leisten, mit dem die Vollendung der in der Anmeldung genannten Erfindung in den Vereinigten Staaten, vor dem Datum des Inkrafttretens des Hinweises beschworen wird (R. 131)

T

taxe—les frais statutaires ou administratifs pour les services de l'Office des Brevets (R. 21-26)

fee—the statutory or administrative charges for Patent Office services (R. 21-26)

Gebuehr—die gesetzlichen oder Verwaltungskosten fuer Dienstleistungen des Patentamts (R. 21-26)

taxe de dépôt—la taxe pour la déposition d'une demande; la taxe de dépôt pour un brevet original est $65., $10. de plus pour chaque revendication indépendante en excès d'une, $2. de plus pour chaque revendication en excès de dix; la taxe de dépôt pour un brevet de dessin est $20.; la taxe de dépôt pour un brevet "reissue" est $65. plus $10. pour chaque revendication en excès du nombre de revendications indépendantes dans le brevet original plus $2. pour chaque revendication en excès de dix et aussi en excès du nombre de revendications dans le brevet original (Sec. 41)

filing fee—the fee for filing an application; the filing fee for an original patent is $65. plus $10. for each independent claim in excess of one plus $2. for each claim in excess of ten; the filing fee for a design patent is $20.; the filing fee for a reissue patent is $65. plus $10. for each independent claim in excess of the number of independent claims in the original patent plus $2. for each claim in excess of ten and also in excess of the number of claims in the original patent (Sec. 41)

Anmeldegebuehr—die Gebuehr fuer die Anmeldung eines Patents; die Gebuehr fuer ein Hauptpatent ist $65., plus $10. fuer jeden weiteren Anspruch ausser einem, und $2. fuer jeden Anspruch nach den ersten zehn; die Anmeldegebuehr fuer ein Geschmacksmuster ist $20.; die Gebuehr fuer Wiedererteilung eines Patents ist $65., plus $10. fuer jeden unabhaengigen Anspruch, der ueber die Anzahl der unabhaengigen Ansprueche im Hauptpatent hinausgeht, plus $2. fuer jeden weiteren Anspruch nach den ersten zehn, und der auch ueber die Anzahl der Ansprueche im Hauptpatent hinausgeht (Sec. 41)

taxe finale—la taxe pour la délivrance d'un brevet original ou "reissue", $100. plus $10. pour chaque page de spécification imprimée plus $2. pour chaque feuille de dessin; en cas des dessins, la taxe finale est $10. pour une durée de trois ans et demi, $20. pour une durée de sept ans et $30. pour une durée de quatorze ans (Sec. 41)

final fee—the fee for issue of an original or reissue patent, $100. plus $10. for each page of printed specification plus $2. for each sheet of drawing; in design cases, the final fee is $10. for a term of three and one half years, $20. for seven years and $30. for fourteen years (Sec. 41)

Schlussgebuehr—die Gebuehr fuer die Erteilung eines Hauptpatents oder die Wiederausgabe eines Patents, $100., plus $10. fuer jede Seite mit gedruckter Beschreibung, plus $2. fuer jeden Bogen mit Zeichnungen; im Falle von Geschmacksmustern ist die Schlussgebuehr $10. fuer eine Frist von dreieinhalb Jahren, $20. fuer sieben Jahre und $30. fuer vierzehn Jahre (Sec. 41)

taxe minimale de délivrance—la somme dûe du demandeur, son concessionnaire, son avocat, ou une partie d'intérêt enregistrée, payable dans le délai de trois mois après la date de la notification d'acceptation, consistante de $100. plus $10 pou la première page de spécification imprimée plus $2. pour chaque feuille de dessin. Tout solde de la taxe de délivrance dûe, comme paiement pour des pages additionnelles de spécification imprimée, est attachée à l'octroi du brevet, et on doit le payer dans le délai de trois mois de la date du brevet pour éviter la déchéance du brevet. (860 OG 2)

minimum issue fee—sum due from applicant, his assignee, attorney, or a party of record interest, payable within three months after the date of notice of allowance, consisting of $100. plus $10. for the first page of printed specification plus $2. for each sheet of drawing. Any balance of the issue fee due, in payment for any additional pages of printed specification, is billed by attachment to the patent grant, and must be paid within three months of the date of the patent to avoid lapse of the patent. (860 OG 2)

Minimum-Erteilungsgebuehr—Summe, die vom Anmelder, seinem Rechtsnachfolger, Anwalt, oder einer Partei, deren Interesse aktenkundig ist, faellig ist; zahlbar innerhalb von drei Monaten vom Datum der Zulassungs-Benachrichtigung, bestehend aus $100. plus $10. fuer die erste Seite gedruckter Beschreibung (specification) plus $2. fuer jeden Bogen mit Zeichnungen. Jede faellige Restsumme der Erteilungsgebuehr—zur Bezahlung von zusaetzlichen Seiten gedruckter Beschreibung (specification)—wird auf einer Beilage zur Patenterteilung berechnet, und ist innerhalb von drei Monaten vom Datum des Patents zu zahlen, um Verfallen des Patents zu vermeiden. (860 O. G. 2)

technique—les données techniques de n'importe quelle forme

art—technical data of any form

Technik—technische Daten aller Art

technique analogue—un renvoi divulguant la même fonction ou la même utilité dans un domaine technologiquement relatif

analogous art—a reference disclosing the same function or the same utility, in a technologically related field

analoge Technik—ein Hinweis, welcher dieselbe Funktion oder den gleichen Gebrauch auf einem technisch verwandten Gebiet enthuellt

technique serrée—une technologie dans la quelle il y avait des progrès nombreux pendant une période de temps relativement courte

crowded art—a technology in which there have been numerous advances over a relatively short period of time

Ueberfuelltes Fach (gebiet)—ein technisches Gebiet, auf dem in verhaeltnismaessig kurzer Zeit zahlreiche Fortschritte gemacht wurden

terme du brevet—la période pour laquelle on a délivré les droits de brevet. La période des brevets d'utilité et de plantes est 17 ans de la date de délivrance; la période des brevets de dessin est 3½ ans, 7 ans ou 14 ans de la date de délivrance, au choix du demandeur.

term of patent—period for which patent rights are granted. The period of utility patents and plant patents is 17 years from the date of grant; the period of design patents is 3½, 7 or 14 years from the date of grant, at the option of applicant.

Laufzeit des Patents—Zeitspanne fuer die Patentrechte erteilt werden. Die Dauer von Gebrauchsmuster- und Pflanzen-Patenten ist siebzehn Jahre vom Erteilungsdatum; die Dauer von Geschmacksmuster-Patenten ist 3½, 7 oder 14 Jahre vom Verleihungsdatum, nach Belieben des Anmelders.

titre—l'en-tête de la première page de la spécification; une courte description qui est généralement représentative du perfectionnement revendiqué

title—the heading on the first page of the specification; a short description that is representative generally of the claimed improvement

Titel—die Ueberschrift auf der ersten Seite der Beschreibung (specification); eine kurze Darstellung, die allgemein bezeichnend fuer die beanspruchte Verbesserung ist

"traverse"—argument qu'une action n'était pas juste

traverse—argument that an action was not proper

Rechtseinwand—das Argument, dass eine Klage nicht korrekt war

U

un—dans l'interprétation des revendications, "un" veut dire "au moins un"

one—in claim interpretation, "one" is read to mean "at least one"

a—in claim interpretation, "a" is read to mean "at least a"

ein(e)—bei der Auslegung eines Patentanspruchs ist "ein(e)" als mindestens "ein(e)" aufzufassen

"unobviousness"—les différences entres la matière qu'on veut rendre brevetée et la technique antérieure, d'une telle nature que la matière entière n'aurait pas été évidente à une personne qui a une habileté moyenne dans la technique à l'heure où on a créé l'invention (Sec. 103)

unobviousness—differences between the subject matter sought to be patented and the prior art of such a nature that the subject matter as a whole would not have been obvious at the time the invention was made to a person having ordinary skill in the art involved (Sec. 103)

Nicht-Selbstverstaendlichkeit—Unterschiede zwischen dem zu patentierended Erfindungsgegenstand und dem Stand der Technik, die solcher Art sind, dass der Erfindungsgegenstand als Ganzes zu der Zeit, als die Erfindung gemacht wurde, einem auf dem Gebiet des Erfindungsgegenstandes Sachverstaendigen nicht selbstverstaendlich gewesen waere (Sec. 103)

utilisation—mettre en pratique une invention

use—to put into practice

Benutzung—in die Praxis umsetzen

utilisation à titre expérimental–l'utilisation d'une invention par un inventeur pour essayer son "operability"

experimental use–use of an invention by an inventor to test its operability

experimentelle Benutzung–von einem Erfinder zur Pruefung ihrer Wirksamkeit benutzte Erfindung

utilité–opératif et pas frivole, frauduleux ou contre la politique publique (MPEP 706.3(p))

utility–operative and not frivolous, fraudulent or against public policy (MPEP 706.3(p))

Nuetzlichkeit–wirksam und nicht frivol, betreugerisch oder gegen das Wohl der Oeffentlichkeit (MPEP 706.03(p))

V

vague et indéfini—manquant un degré raisonnable de particularité et de clarité

vague and indefinite—lacking a reasonable degree of particularity and distinctness

verschwommen und bestimmt—einen angemessenen Grad von Genauigkeit und Klarheit vermissen lassend

violation de droits d'auteur—reproduction, représentation ou diffusion d'une oeuvre protégée au titre des droits d'auteur sans autorisation de l'auteur

copyright infringement—reproduction, performance or distribution of a copyrighted work without the permission of the author

Copyright Verletzung—Reproduktion, Auffuehrung, oder Verteilung eines unter copyright-Schutz stehenden Werkes ohne Erlaubnis des Urhebers

vue éclatée—un dessin où les parties distinctes d'une figure, renfermées des parenthèses, sont illustrées pour montrer le rapport ou l'ordre d'assemblage des parties diverses (R. 84(i))

exploded view—a drawing in which the separated parts of a figure, embraced by a bracket, are illustrated to show the relationship or order of assembly of various parts (R. 84(i))

Aufriss—eine Zeichnung, auf der die einzelnen Teile einer Abbildung dargestellt sind, von einer Klammer zusammengehalten, um die Beziehung zueinander oder die Reihenfolge der Zusammensetzung der verschiedenen Teile zu zeigen (R. 84(i))

W

"whereby" clause—une clause facultative dans une revendication, d'ordinaire la clause finale, qui présente la fonction de la combinaison ou du procédé revendiqué

whereby clause—an optional clause in a claim, usually the ultimate clause, setting forth the function of the claimed combination or process

"whereby clause"—eine im Belieben des Anmelders stehende Klausel in einem Anspruch—gewoehnlich die allerletzte Klausel—welche die Funktion der beanspruchten Zusammensetzung oder des Verfahrens darlegt

SECTION III

GERMAN

ENGLISH

FRENCH

SPEZIALWOERTERBUCH UEBER DIE HANDHABUNG VON PATENTEN IN DEN VEREINIGTEN STAATEN

ABKUERZUNGEN

Sec. ——— Der angegebene Paragraph von Title 35, U.S. Code

R. ——— Die angegebene Vorschrift des U. S. Patent Office Rules of Practice

MPEP ——— Der angegebene Abschnitt des U. S. Patentamt Handbuchs zu Patentpruefungsverfahren, 3. Ausgabe

vgl. ——— vergleiche

A

Abfindung—Rueckerstattung fuer einen Verlust

compensation—restitution for a loss

compensation—la restitution d'une perte

abgelaufenes Patent—die Bezeichnung eines Patents nach Beendigung der Laufzeit, fuer die as erteilt war

expired patent—the denotation of a patent after the end of the term for which it was granted

brevet expiré—la désignation d'un brevet après la fin de la durée pour laquelle il a été délivré

Abschrift eines Anspruchs—eine Anmeldung dahingehend zu berichtigen, dass der Anspruch eines anderen zum Zwecke einer Interferenz Erklaerung eingeschlossen wird, um festzustellen, wer der erste Erfinder dessen ist, was in der Abschrift des Anspruchs beschrieben wird

copying a claim—amending an application to include a claim of another for the purpose of the declaring of an interference, to determine who is the first inventor of what the copied claim describes

copiant une revendication—faisant des amendements à une demande pour y inclure une revendication faite à un autre, dans le but de décider ce lui qui est le premier inventeur de ce que décrit la revendication copiée

aeltere Partei (Senior Party)—die Partei in einer Interferenz, die der ersten festgesetzen Termin fuer das Inkrafttreten des Einreichungsdatums hat

senior party—in an interference, the party having the earlier established effective filing date

senior party—dans une "interférence", la partie qui a la date d'effet de dépôt plus ancienne

Akte—die gesamten schriftlichen Aufzeichnungen ueber eine Anmeldung im Archiv des Patentamts

file wrapper—the total written record in the Patent Office file of an application

histoire du brevet—tous les archives écrits dans le dépôt d'une demande à l'Office des Brevets

Akten-Nachfrage (Status-Brief)—Anfrage an den Pruefer den gegenwaertigen Stand einer Anmeldung betreffend. Es ist ratsam diesen Brief zu senden, wenn eine ungewoehnlich lange Zeit vergangen ist, seit das Patentamt zuletzt etwas in dem Fall unternommen hat.

status letter—inquiry to the examiner about the present status of an application. Sent, advisably, when an unduly long time has elapsed since the Patent Office last acted on the case.

lettre de condition—une requête à l'examinateur au sujet de la condition présente d'une demande. Envoyée, judicieusement, quand il est passé une période de temps excessivement longue depuis que l'Office des Brevets a agi sur le cas.

Aktenzimmer—vgl. oeffentlicher Nachschlage-Saal

record room—see Public Search Room

salle d'archives—voir Salle Publique de Recherche

alleiniger Erfinder—eine Person, die allein eine Erfindung gemacht hat

sole inventor—a person who singly made an invention

inventeur unique—une personne qui seule a créé une invention

Alleinunterschrifts-Formblatt—eine Kombination von Gesuch, Eid oder eidesstattlicher Erklaerung und gesetzlicher Vollmacht, als letzte Seite der Beschreibung (specification) zur Ausfuehrung durch den Erfinder angehaftet

single signature form—a combined petition, oath or declaration, and power of attorney attached to the specification as the last page, for execution by the inventor

forme avec une signature—une pétition, serment ou déclaration, et le pouvoir d'avocat combinés attaché à la spécification comme la dernière page, pour la signature par l'inventeur

alternative Ausdrucksweise—Definition **eines** Elements in einem Patentanspruch durch mehr als **ein** Wort oder **einen** Ausdruck (MPEP 706.03 (d))

alternative expression—definition of one element, in a claim, by more than one word or phrase (MPEP 706.03(d))

expression alternative—la définition d'un élément dans une revendication par plusieurs mots ou par une phrase (MPEP 706.03(d))

Amtsblatt—woechentliche, amtliche Veroeffentlichung des Patentamts mit einem Auszug aus der Offenbarung jeden, an diesem Tag erteilten Patents; mit Information ueber Patente, Warenzeichen, Geschmacksmuster- und Pflanzenpatente; mit Verfuegungen, Amtsbescheiden, eingereichten Klagen und ausgewaehlten Gerichtsentscheiden auf dem Patent- und Warenzeichengebiet

Official Gazette—the official weekly publication of the Patent Office that contains an abstract of the disclosure of each patent issued that day; information on patents, trademarks, designs and plant patents; and orders, notices, suits filed and selected court decisions in the patent and trademark fields

Gazette Officielle—la publication officielle hebdomadaire de l'Office des Brevets qui contient une abstraction de la divulgation de chaque brevet délivré ce jour-là; des renseignements au sujet des brevets, marques de fabrique, brevets de dessin et de plante; et des ordonnances, des notifications, des litigies déposées et des décisions choisies du tribunal dans le domaine des brevets et des marques de fabrique

analoge Technik—ein Hinweis, welcher dieselbe Funktion oder den gleichen Gebrauch auf einem technisch verwandten Gebiet enthuellt

analogous art—a reference disclosing the same function or the same utility, in a technologically related field

technique analogue—un renvoi divulguant la même fonction ou la même utilité dans un domaine technologiquement relatif

Aneinanderreihung—die Abwesenheit einer zusammenwirkenden Beziehung zwischen einem Element eines Patentanspruches und mindestens einem zweiten (MPEP 706.03 (i))

aggregation—the absence of a cooperative relation between an element of a claim and at least one other element of the claim (MPEP 706.03(i))

"aggregation"—l'absence d'une relation coopérative entre un élément d'une revendication et au moins un autre élément de la revendication (MPEP 706.03(i))

Anfuehrung von Autoritaeten—Hinweis auf Gesetze, Gerichtsfaelle order Veroeffentlichungen um eine im Klagefall eingenommene Position zu stuetzen

citation of authorities—laws, court cases or publications referred to in an action to support a position taken

citation des sources—les lois, les affaires de tribunal, ou les publications auxquelles on fait allusion dans une action pour soutenir une position prise

Anmeldedatum—vgl. Einreichungsdatum

application date—see filing date

date de demande—voir date de dépôt

Anmeldegebuehr—die Gebuehr fuer die Anmeldung eines Patents; die Gebuehr fuer ein Hauptpatent ist $65., plus $10. fuer jeden weiteren Anspruch ausser einem, und $2. fuer jeden Anspruch nach den ersten zehn; die Anmeldegebuehr fuer ein Geschmacksmuster ist $20.; die Gebuehr fuer Wiedererteilung eines Patents ist $65., plus $10. fuer jeden unabhaengigen Anspruch, der ueber die Anzahl der unabhaengigen Ansprueche im Hauptpatent hinausgeht, plus $2. fuer jeden weiteren Anspruch nach den ersten zehn, und der auch ueber die Anzahl der Ansprueche im Hauptpatent hinausgeht (Sec. 41)

filing fee—the fee for filing an application; the filing fee for an original patent is $65. plus $10. for each independent claim in excess of one plus $2. for each claim in excess of ten; the filing fee for a design patent is $20.; the filing fee for a reissue patent is $65. plus $10. for each independent claim in excess of the number of independent claims in the original patent plus $2. for each claim in excess of ten and also in excess of the number of claims in the original patent (Sec. 41)

taxe de dépôt—la taxe pour la déposition d'une demande; la taxe de dépôt pour un brevet original est $65., $10. de plus pour chaque revendication indépendante en excès d'une, $2. de plus pour chaque revendication en excès de dix; la taxe de dépôt pour un brevet de dessin est $20.; la taxe de dépôt pour un brevet "reissue" est $65. plus $10. pour chaque revendication en excès du nombre de revendications indépendantes dans le brevet original plus $2. pour chaque revendication en excès de dix et aussi en excès du nombre de revendications dans le brevet original (Sec. 41)

Anmelder—der Erfinder oder die Erfindergemeinschaft, die ein Patent eingereicht haben; oder der gesetzliche Vertreter (R. 42, 43), oder der Miterfinder (R. 47(a)), oder der rechtliche Eigentuemer (R. 47(b)) der an Stelle des Erfinders ein Patent zur Anmeldung eingereicht hat

applicant—the inventor or the joint inventors who have applied for a patent; or the legal representative (R. 42, 43) or joint inventor (R. 47(a)) or proprietary interest (R. 47(b)) who has applied for a patent in place of the inventor

demandeur–l'inventeur ou les co-inventeurs qui ont demandé un brevet; ou le représentant légal (R. 42, 43) ou le co-inventeur (R. 47 (a)) ou l'intérêt propriétaire (R. 47(b)) qui a demandé un brevet au lieu de l'inventeur

Ansprueche–der abschliessende Teil einer Beschreibung (specification), welcher den Gegenstand der Erfindung besonders hervorhebt und eindeutig darlegt (Sec. 112, R. 71, 75)

claims–the concluding part of a specification particularly pointing out and distinctly setting forth the subject matter of the invention (Sec. 112; R. 71, 75)

revendications–la partie finale d'une spécification signalant et nettement proposant la matière de l'invention (Sec. 112; R. 71, 75)

Antrag–ein Gesuch um Erhalt einer Verfuegung, die eine bestimmte Handlung anordnet. Solche Antraege koennen in Interferenz Faellen zur Aufloesung, zur Verbesserung, zur Hinzufuegung einer weiteren Anmeldung und zur Verschiebung der Beweislast gemacht werden. (R. 231-237)

motion–an application to obtain an order directing a particular action. Motions may be made in interferences to dissolve, to amend, to add another application, and to shift the burden of proof. (R.231-237)

motion–une demande pour obtenir une ordonnance dirgeante une action spécifique. On peut faire des motions dans une "interférence" pour désoudre, pour amender, pour ajouter une autre demande, et pour transférer la charge de la preuve. (R. 231-237)

Anwalt–vgl. Patentanwalt

attorney–see patent attorney

avocat–voir avocat de brevets

Art (genus)—ein Klasse, die umfangreicher ist und mehr als eine Gattung umfasst

genus—a class that is broader than or includes more than one species

genre—une classe qui est plus large que, ou comprend plus d'une variante

Aufgabe des Wettstreits—Zugestaendnis der Prioritaet oder Fallenlassen der Erfindung durch eine Partei in einer Interferenz. Hat eine Patent uebertragung stattgefunden, so ist die schriftliche Zustimmung des Rechtsnachfolgers erforderlich.

abandonment of contest—concession of priority or abandonment of the invention by a party in an interference. The written consent of the assignee is required when an assignment was made.

abandon de contestation—la concession de la priorité ou l'abandon de l'invention par une partie de la "interférence". On a besoin de l'accord écrit du cessionnaire de propriété.

Aufriss—eine Zeichnung, auf der die einzelnen Teile einer Abbildung dargestellt sind, von einer Klammer zusammengehalten, um die Beziehung zueinander oder die Reihenfolge der Zusammensetzung der verschiedenen Teile zu zeigen (R. 84(i))

exploded view—a drawing in which the separated parts of a figure, embraced by a bracket, are illustrated to show the relationship or order of assembly of various parts (R. 84(i))

vue éclatée—un dessin où les parties distinctes d'une figure, renfermées des parenthèses, sont illustrées pour montrer le rapport ou l'ordre d'assemblage des parties diverses (R. 84(i))

ausdruecklicher Einschluss von Elementen—Aufzaehlung mittels eines ausdruecklichen Wortes oder Satzes jeder Eigenschaft in einem Anspruch, von der die Patentfaehigkeit des Anspruche abhaengt

positive inclusion of elements—recital in a claim, in a positive word or phrase, of every feature on which the claim depends for patentability

inclusion positive d'éléments—le récit dans une revendication, dans un mot ou une phrase positive, de chaque trait dont dépend la revendication pour être brevetable

Ausfertigung der Anmeldung—Leistung der Anmeldungsunterschrift vor einem Notar oder einer andern dazu befugten Person in den Vereinigten Staaten. Eine Anmeldung, die im Ausland vor einem Notar oder einer andern dazu befugten Person ausgefertigt wurde, muss durch einen Konsulats-oder Botschaftsbeamten der Vereinigten Staaten beglaubigt werden. Andern Falls kann auch eine eidesstattliche Erklaerung (R. 68) an Stelle der Unterschrift vor einem Notar oder einer anderen dazu befugten Person abgegeben werden.

execution of application—signature of an application before a notary or other authorized person in the United States. An application executed abroad before a notary or other authorized person must be legalized by a United States consular or diplomatic officer. Alternatively, a declaration (R. 68) may be made instead of signature before a notary or other authorized person.

exécution de demande—signature d'une demande devant un notaire, ou une autre personne autorisée aux Etats-Unis. Une demande exécutée à l'étranger devant un notaire ou une autre personne autorisée doit être légalisée par un consulat ou par un officier diplomatique des Etats-Unis. Alternativement, on peut faire une déclaration (R. 68) au lieu d'une signature devant un notaire ou une autre personne autorisée.

Ausfuehrungsbestimmungen (Rules of Practice)—die vom Commissioner of Patents festgesetzten Vorschriften, die das Verhalten bei Verfahren im Patentamt bestimmen (Sec. 6, 11)

Rules of Practice—the regulations established by the Commissioner of Patents governing the conduct of proceedings in the Patent Office (Sec. 6, 11)

Règles de Pratique—les règlements établis du Commissaire des Brevets qui gouvernent la conduite des procédés à l'Office des Brevets (Sec. 6, 11)

Ausgabe—die Erteilung eines Patents

issue—the grant of a patent

délivrance—l'octroi d'un brevet

Ausgeschiedene Anmeldung—eine Anmeldung, die eine von einer andern unabhaengige und verschiedene Erfindung darlegt, die in einer Anmeldung eingeschlossen war, welche eine andere unabhaengige und verschiedene Erfindung darlegt

divisional application—an application setting forth an independent and distinct invention that had been included in an application setting forth another independent and distinct invention

demande divisionnaire—une demande présentant une invention indépendante et distincte qu'on a incluse dans une demande présentant une autre invention indépendante et distincte

ausgeschoepfte Verbindung—eine Verbindung von Elementen, die sich durch den Stand der Technik als vorweggenommen erweist

exhausted combination—a combination of elements shown by the prior art to be anticipated

"exhausted combination"—une combinaison d'éléments démontrée d'être antériorisée par la technique antérieure

Ausmass des Anspruchs—der Umfang in welchem ein Anspruch ueber eine Technik vorherrscht

breadth of claim—the extent to which a claim dominates an art

largeur de la revendication—l'étendue à laquelle une revendication domine une technique

Ausscheidung—vgl. ausgeschiedene Anmeldung

division—see divisional application

division—voir demande divisionnaire

ausschliessliche Lizenz—vgl. Lizenz

exclusive license—see license

licence exclusive—voir licence

Ausschliessung—vgl. Untersagung

estop—see estoppel

estop—voir estoppel

Aussetzung der Behandlung—angemessen befristeter Aufschub der Behandlung durch das Patentamt aus guten Gruenden, entweder auf Ansuchen des Anmelders oder auf Veranlassung des Patentamts (R. 103)

suspension of action—postponement of action by the Patent Office for good cause, at the request of applicant or at the instance of the Patent Office, for a reasonable specified time (R. 103)

suspension d'action—tenir en suspens une action pour une bonne raison, à la requête du demandeur ou de l'Office des Brevets, pendant un temps raisonnable et spécifié (R. 103)

Auszug aus dem Titel–Patentamt-Eintragung ueber das Eigentumsrecht an einem Patent

abstract of title–Patent Office record of ownership of a patent

abstraction de titre–les archives de l'Office des Brevets qui indiquent le propriétaire d'un brevet

Auszug aus der Offenbarung–eine knappe nichtjuristische technische Darstellung des Inhalts der Offenbarung, unmittelbar nach dem Titel in der Beschreibung (specification) als Untersuchungs und Pruefwerkzeug enthalten; eine auf ungefaehr hundert Worte begrenzte Darlegung, die ausfuehrliche mechanische und Muster Einzelheiten auslaesst, aber die Organisation und den Betrieb einer Maschine oder eines Apparates, oder die Methode zur Herstellung eines Artikels, oder die Identitaet und den Gebrauch einer chemischen Verbindung, oder die Bestandteile einer Mischung, oder die Stufen eines Vorgangs einschliesst (R. 72(b))

abstract of the disclosure–a concise, non-legal technical statement of the contents of the disclosure, included in the specification as a searching-scanning tool immediately after the title; a statement limited to about 100 words, omitting extensive mechanical and design details but including the organization and operation of a machine or apparatus, or the method of making an article, or the identity and use of a chemical compound, or the ingredients of a mixture, or the steps of a process (R. 72(b))

abstraction de la divulgation–une déclaration technique, qui est concise et non-légal, du contenu de la divulgation, incluse dans la spécification comme un instrument "cherchant-scrutant" immédiatement après le titre; une déclaration limitèe à environs cent mots, omettant de vastes détails mécaniques et désignatifs, mais comprenant l'organisation et l'opération d'une machine ou d'un appareil, ou la méthode de fabriquer une chose, ou l'identité et l'utilisation d'un composé chimique, ou les ingrédients d'une mixture, ou bien les démarches d'un procédé (R. 72(b))

B

bedingte Uebertragung—eine Uebertragung, welche auf Grund der Ausfuehrung einer Handlung oder eines Ereignisses in Kraft tritt; falls schriftlich niedergelegt, werden solche Uebertragungen fuer die Zwecke des Patentamts als definitive Uebertragungen betrachtet (R. 333)

conditional assignment—an assignment provided to be effective on the performance of an act or event; if recorded, such assignments are regarded as absolute assignments for Patent Office purposes (R. 333)

cession conditionelle—une cession qui deviendra effective après l'accomplissement d'un acte ou événement; si elles sont enregistrées, de telles cessions sont regardées comme des cessions absolues selon les intentions de l'Office des Brevets (R. 333)

beglaubigte Abschrift—eine Abschrift mit der Bestaetigung des Patentamts, dass es sich um eine wortgetreue Kopie handelt, wie sie in Prioritaetsfaellen (Sec. 119) oder zu anderen Zwecken verlangt wird

certified copy—a copy bearing the attestation of the Patent Office that it is a true copy, as may be required in priority cases (Sec. 119) or for other purposes

copie certifiée—une copie portant l'attestation de l'Office des Brevets qu'elle est une vraie copie, qu'on peut exiger dans des affaires de priorité (Sec. 119) ou pour des autres intentions

Behandlung—vgl. Behandlung durch das (Patent)amt

action—see Office action

action—voir action d'Office

Behandlung durch das Amt—ein Schriftsatz des Pruefers mit der Stellungnahme des Patentamts zu der Anmeldung, unter Aufzaehlung von Zurueckweisungen und/oder Einwaenden

office action—a paper from the examiner setting forth the Patent Office position on the application, enumerating rejections and/or objections

action d'office—un document de l'examinateur déclarant l'attitude de l'Office des Brevets au sujet de la demande, énumérant les rejets et/ou les objections

Beihilfe zur Patentverletzung—die Veranlassung zur Ausfuehrung einer beanspruchten Erfindung durch Unbefugte; oder der Verkauf eines Teiles einer patentierten Erfindung, oder eines Stoffes, oder Apparates, die der Ausuebung eines patentierten Verfahrens dienen, wohlwissend, dass sie eigens zur Benutzung bei der Verletzung eines solchen Patents hergestellt oder dazu besonders angepasst wurden, sofern der Teil keine zu wesentlicher nicht-patent-verletzender Benutzung geeignete Stapelware ist (Sec. 271)

contributory infringement—inducing the practice of a claimed invention by an unauthorized person, or selling a component of a patented invention or a material or apparatus used in practising a patented process while knowing it was specially made and adapted for use in an infringement of such patent, unless the component is a staple article suitable for substantial non-infringing use (Sec. 271)

contribuant à la contrefaçon—encourageant l'utilisation d'une invention revendiquée par une personne sans autorisation, ou vendant une partie constituante d'une invention brevetée ou d'un matériel ou d'un appareil employé dans la partique d'un procédé breveté, tout en sachant qu'il était fabriqué et adapté spécialement pour l'employer dans un contrefaçon d'un tel brevet, à moins que la partie constituante soit un article régulaire ou établi à un grand emploi non-contrefaisant (Sec. 271)

Benutzung—in die Praxis umsetzen

use—to put into practice

utilisation—mettre en pratique une invention

Berichtigung—Anweisung an das Patentamt dem Antrag etwas zuzufuegen oder von dem Antrag etwas zu streichen (R. 21(k), 33, 67, 85, 111, 115-119, 121-127, 135, 173, 174, 196, 203-206, 212, 222, 231, 312)

amendment—instruction to the Patent Office to add and/or delete matter from the application (R. 21(k), 33, 67, 85, 111, 115-119, 121-127, 135, 173, 174, 196, 203-206, 212, 222, 231, 312)

amendement—directive à l'Office des Brevets d'ajouter et/ou de rayer quelque chose de la demande (R. 21(k), 33, 67, 85, 111, 115-119, 121-127, 135, 173, 174, 196, 203-206, 212, 222, 231, 312)

Berufung an den Board of Appeals (Berufungsinstanz)—vgl. Board of Appeals

appeal to Board of Appeals—see Board of Appeals

Appel à la Commission d'Appel—voir la Commission d'Appel

Berufung an den Court of Appeals (Berufungsgericht)—vgl. Court of Appeals

appeal to Court of Appeals—see Court of Appeals

appel à la Cour de Cassation—voir Cour de Cassation

Berufung an den Court of Claims—vgl. Court of Claims

appeal to Court of Claims—see Court of Claims

appel à la Cour de Réclamation—voir la Cour de Réclamation

Berufung an den Court of Customs and Patent Appeals—vgl. Court of Customs and Patent Appeals

appeal to Court of Customs and Patent Appeals—see Court of Customs and Patent Appeals

appel à la "Court of Customs and Patent Appeals"—voir Court of Customs and Patent Appeals

Berufungsgericht (Court of Appeals)—ein Gericht, welches in seinem Gebiet fuer die Einlegung von Berufung gegen endgueltige Entscheidungen des U. S. District Courts zustaendig ist

Court of Appeals—a court having jurisdiction in its area over appeals from final decisions of U. S. District Courts

Court of Appeals (cour de cassation)—un tribunal qui a la jurisdiction dans son domaine sur des appels des décisions finales des United States District Courts

Beschraenkung—Ansprueche auf nur eine Erfindung ausrichten. Nach einer Forderung zur Beschraenkung (frueher Ausscheidung genannt), da zwei oder mehr unabhaengige Erfindungen in einer einzigen Anmeldung beansprucht wurden, kann eine beschraenkte Anmeldung allein nur auf eine der beiden erwaehnten Erfindungen ausgerichtet werden. Wird der neue Fall vor der Patentierung, dem Fallenlassen, oder der Beendigung des Verfahrens gegen die Erstanmeldung eingereicht, so steht ihm das Einreichungsdatum der urspruenglichen Anmeldung zu; weder die urspruenglichen noch die beschraenkten Anmeldungen oder Patente koennen als Belege gegeneinander verwendet werden (Sec. 121, R. 147).

restriction—directing claims to a single invention. After a requirement for restriction (formerly called division) because two or more independent inventions are claimed in a single application, a restricted application may be directed solely to one of said inventions. If filed before the patenting, abandonment or termination of proceedings on the original application, the new case is entitled to the benefit of the filing date of the original application, and neither the original nor the restricted applications or patents can be used as references against each other. (Sec. 121, R.147)

restriction—limitant les revendications à une seule invention. Après une exigence de restriction (autrefois appelé division) parce qu'on revendique plusieurs inventions dans une seule demande, une demande restreinte peut se concerner seulement d'une des inventions mentionnées. Si on le dépose avant d'être breveté, l'abandon ou la terminaison des procédés sur la demande originale, le nouveau cas a droit au bénéfice de la date de dépôt de la demande originale, et on ne peut employer comme référence l'un contre l'autre ni le cas original ni le nouveau cas. (Sec. 121, R. 147)

Beschreibung (specification)—eine genaue Schilderung einer bevorzugten Ausfuehrungsform einer Erfindung, die diese von allem schon Dagewesenen unterscheidet. Die Beschreibung (specification) muss so vollstaendig, klar, knapp und exakt sein, dass ein Fachmann auf dem Gebiet sie ausfuehren und benutzen kann; gemaess nachstehender Reihenfolge umfasst sie einen Titel, einen Auszug aus der Offenbarung, Hinweise auf all verwandten Anmeldungen, den Hintergrund der Erfindung, eine kurze Zusammenfassung der Erfindung, eine kurze Schilderung der Ansichten der Zeichnung, eine ausfuehrliche Beschreibung, Ansprueche und eine Unterschrift. (R. 77)

specification—a precise description of a preferred embodiment of an invention, distinguishing the invention from what is old. The specification must be full, clear, concise and exact, so that a person skilled in the art can make and use the invention; it comprises, in order, a title, an abstract of the disclosure, cross-reference to any related application, the background of the invention, a brief summary of the invention, a brief description of the views of the drawing, a detailed description, claims, and a signature. (R. 77)

spécification—une description précise d'une incarnation préférée de l'invention, distinguant l'invention de ce qui est vieille. La spécification doit être complète, nette, concise et exacte, afin qu'une personne adroite dans la technique puisse employer l'invention; elle comprend, en ordre, un titre, une abstraction de la divulgation, un renvoi à aucune invention relative, le fond de l'invention, un bref sommaire de l'invention, une brève description des vues des dessins, une description détaillée, les revendications et une signature. (R. 77)

Beschwerdeschrift ueber Verletzung—schriftliche Mitteilung eines Patentinhabers mit der Behauptung, dass aufgefuehrte Ansprueche eines Patents verletzt werden und mit der Forderung auf Einstellung solcher Verletzung

notice of infringement—written communication from a patent owner asserting that specified claims of a patent are being infringed, and demanding that such infringement cease

notification de contrefaçon—un communiqué écrit par le titulaire d'un brevet prétendant qu'on est en train de contrefaire des revendications spécifiees d'un brevet, et demandant qu'on cesse une telle contrefaçon

Beschwerdeschriftsatz und Berufungsbegruendung—Beschwerdeschrift an den Commissioner ueber die Gruende fuer eine Berufung an den Court of Customs and Patent Appeals, einzureichen innerhalb von sechzig Tagen vom Datum der angefochtenen Entscheidung des Board of Appeals oder des Board of Patent Interferences ueber ein Gesuch zur Wiederverhandlung oder Wiederwaegung (R. 302, 304)

notice and reasons of appeal—notice to the Commissioner of the grounds of appeal to the Court of Customs and Patent Appeals, to be filed within sixty days from the date of the decision appealed from, or within thirty days after the date of a decision by the Board of Appeals or the Board of Patent Interferences on a petition for rehearing or reconsideration (R. 302, 304)

notification et raisons d'appel—la notification au Commissaire des raisons d'appel à la "Court of Customs and Patent Appeals", qui doit être déposée dans le délai de soixante jours de la date de la décision appelée, ou dans le délai de trente jours après la date d'une décision de la Commission d'Appel ou la Commission des "Interférences" des Brevets sur un pétition pour une nouvelle considération (R. 302, 304)

beschworene schriftliche Erklaerung—Darlegung von Tatsachen unter Eid um ein angefuehrtes Patent oder eine Veroeffentlichung ausser Kraft zu setzen (R. 131), einen Grund zur Ablehnung zu ueberbruecken (R. 132), zur Unterstuetzung einer Anmeldung zur Wiedererteilung (R. 175), vor einer Interferenz Erklaerung (R. 202, 204), oder nach einer Berufung (R. 195)

affidavit—statement of facts under oath to overcome a cited patent or publication (R. 131), to traverse a ground of rejection (R. 132), in support of an application for reissue (R. 175), before a declaration of interference (R. 202, 204), or after appeal (R. 195)

déclaration sour serment—la declaration des faits sous serment pour surmonter un brevet cité ou une publication (R. 131), pour nier une raison de rejet (R. 132), pour soutenir une demande pour "reissue" (R. 175), avant une déclaration de "interférence" (R. 202, 204), ou après un appel (R. 195)

Bestaetigung—Beweismaterial zur Bezeugung der Darlegung eines Erfinders

corroboration of an inventor—evidence to prove statements made by an inventor

corroboration d'un inventeur—la preuve des déclarations faites du part d'un inventeur

bestehend aus—eine Einschraenkung, welche einen Anspruch vom Einschluss von Materialien ausser den genannten ausschliesst, mit Ausnahme von Unreinheiten, welche im Allgemeinen mit den genannten Materielien verbunden sind. Wird "wesentlich" zu "bestehend aus" hinzugefuegt, so wird damit der Anspruch Bestandteilen geoeffnet, die die grundlegenden und neuartigen Eigentuemlichkeiten der Zusammensetzung nicht wesentlich beeintrachtigen.

consisting of—a qualification that closes a claim to the inclusion of materials other than those recited, except for impurities ordinarily associated with the recited materials. Adding "essentially" to "consisting of" opens the claim to ingredients that do not materially affect the basic and novel characteristics of the composition.

"consisting of"—une qualification qui ferme une revendication à l'inclusion des substances ou des matériels hors de ceux qui sont énumérés, sauf les impuretés associées ordinairement avec les substances ou matériels énumérés. En ajoutant "essentiellement" à "consisting of" on ouvre la revendication aux ingrédients, qui n'influencent pas matériellement les caractéristiques fondamentales et nouvelles de la composition.

Bevorzugung einer Anmeldung—die vorzeitige Pruefung einer Anmeldung, ausserhalb der zeitlichen Reihenfolge, aus Alters-oder Gesundheitsgruenden des Anmelders, oder wegen Gefaehrdung der kommerziellen Ansprueche des Anmelders

advancement of application—examination of an application in advance of its chronological turn, made on a showing of age or infirmity of applicant or jeopardy of commercial rights of the applicant

avancement d'une demande—l'examen d'une demande avant son tour chronologique, fait à preuve de l'âge ou de l'infirmité du demandeur, ou de l'hasard aux droits commerciaux du demandeur

Bewerbung—die Vorbereitung und Verfolgung von Patentanmeldungen

soliciting—the preparation and prosecution of patent applications

soliciter—la préparation et la poursuite des demandes de brevet

Board of Appeals—die Instanz innerhalb des Patentamts, welche bei einer Berufung des Anmelders zustaendig ist, die Entscheidung eines Pruefers nachzupruefen. Diese Instanz besteht aus drei aus der Gruppe des Commissioner, der Assistant Commissioners, und der Hauptpruefer ausgewaehlten Mitgliedern.

Board of Appeals—the court in the Patent Office having jurisdiction to review the decision of an examiner on appeal by an applicant. The court consists of three members selected from the group of Commissioner, Assistant Commissioners and Examiners-in-Chief.

Commission d'Appel—le tribunal dans l'Office des Brevets qui a la juridiction de revoir la décision d'un examinateur sur l'appel d'un demandeur. Le tribunal consiste de trois membres choisis du groupe du Commissaire, des Commissaires Adjoints, et des Examinateurs-en-chef.

Board of Patent Interferences—die Instanz im Patentamt, der die Rechtsprechung in Interferenz Faellen obliegt

Board of Patent Interferences—the court in the Patent Office having jurisdiction to decide interference issues

Commission des "Interférences" des Brevets—le tribunal dans l'Office des Brevets qui a la juridiction de décider les questions de "interférence"

Bristol Board—handelsueblicher Name der zwei-oder dreifachen Zeichenpappe mit reinweisser, glaenzender und glatt-radierbarer Oberflaeche, die fuer den Gebrauch von Zeichnungen verlangt wird

Bristol board—the commercial name of the two-ply or three-ply drawing board, having a pure white, calendered and smooth erasable surface, that is required for use for drawings

planche de Bristol—le nom commercial d'une planche à dessin à deux ou trois laminae, ayant une surface d'une blanche pure, calendrée, effaçable et égale, dont on a besoin pour de tels dessins

C

c. i. p.—vgl. Teilfortfuehrung

c. i. p.—see continuation-in-part

c. i. p.—voir continuation-en-partie

Commissioner of Patents—der Chef des Patentamts, vom Praesidenten mit der Zustimmung des Senats auf unbefristete Zeit als Verwaltungsbeamter ernannt

Commissioner of Patents—the head of the Patent Office, designated by the President with the consent of the Senate, to serve for an indefinite term as administrator of the Patent Office

Commissaire des Brevets—le chef de l'Office des Brevets, désigné par le Président avec l'accord du Sénat, pour servir pendant un nombre d'années indéfinies comme administrateur de l'Office des Brevets

Copyright (Urheberrecht)—ein Reservatsrecht des Urhebers oder seines Interessen-Nachfolgers ein literarisches oder kuenstlerisches Werk zu reproduzieren; dieses Reservatsrecht ist durch Erfuellung der Bestimmungen der Copyright Statuten und der Ausfuehrungsbestimmungen geschuetzt

copyright—a reservation to the originator, or to his successor in interest, of the right to reproduce a literary or artistic work, such reservation being protected by compliance with the provisions of the copyright statutes and supporting administrative regulations

copyright (droit d'auteur)—une restriction à l'initiateur ou à son successeur en intérêt, du droit de reproduire une oeuvre littéraire ou artistique, telle restriction étant protégée par conformité des stipulations des statuts des droits d'auteur et soutenant les règlements administratifs

Copyright Verletzung—Reproduktion, Auffuehrung, oder Verteilung eines unter copyright-Schutz stehenden Werkes ohne Erlaubnis des Urhebers

copyright infringement—reproduction, performance or distribution of a copyrighted work without the permission of the author

violation de droits d'auteur—reproduction, représentation ou diffusion d'une oeuvre protégée au titre des droits d'auteur sans autorisation de l'auteur

Court of Claims—ein Gerichtshof, in dem Klagen gegen die Regierung der Vereinigten Staaten zur Verhandlung kommen; in Patentangelegenheiten koennte dies eine Schadenersatzklage wegen unbefugter Benutzung eines Patents durch die Regierung der Vereinigten Staaten sein

Court of Claims—a court that hears cases against the Government of the United States; in patent matters, such a case could be a claim for compensation for unauthorized use of a patent by the Government of the United States

Court of Claims (cour des réclamation)—un tribunal qui entend des plaintes contre le Gouvernement des Etats-Unis; en matières des brevets, une telle plainte pourrait être une réclamation pour restitution, à cause d'un emploi sans autorisation d'un brevet par le Gouvernement des Etats-Unis

Court of Customs and Patent Appeals—ein Gerichtshof in Washington, D. C., in dem Berufungen gegen die Entscheidungen des Board of Appeals und des Board of Interference Examiners zur Verhandlung kommen, auf Grund von Beweismaterial, das vor dem Patentamt erbracht wurde (Sec. 141)

Court of Customs and Patent Appeals—a court in Washington, D. C. that hears appeals from decisions of the Board of Appeals and the Board of Interference Examiners, on the evidence produced before the Patent Office (Sec. 141)

Court of Customs and Patent Appeals—un tribunal à Washington, D. C. qui entend des appels des décisions de la Commission d'Appel et de la Commission des Examineteurs d'Interférence par le témoignage produit devant l'Office des Brevets (Sec. 141)

D

Datum der Patenterteilung—vgl. Erteilungsdatum

grant date—see date of grant

date de délivrance—voir date de délivrance

Datum der Verbands-Prioritaet—Prioritaetsdatum einer Anmeldung und des darauffolgenden Patents, eingereicht gemaess den Bestimmungen der Pariser Union Verbandsuebereinkunft

convention date—priority date of an application, and of the patent thereon, filed under the provisions of the Union Convention of Paris

date de priorité conventionnelle ou unioniste—la date de priorité d'une demande, et du brevet y inclus, déposée sous le bénéfice de la Convention d'Union de Paris

Datum des Inkrafttretens einer Anmeldung—das Einreichungsdatum einer Stamm-Anmeldung oder einer Anmeldung, die von derselben Person fuer diesselbe Erfindung in einem auslaendischen Verbandsstaat eingereicht wurde und die Vorschriften unter Sec. 119 erfuellt

effective date of application—the date of filing of a parent application, or of an application filed by the same person for the same invention in a foreign convention country and complying with the provisions of Sec. 119

date d'effet de demande—la date de dépôt d'une "parent" demande, ou d'une demande déposée de la même personne pour la même invention dans un pays étranger unioniste et accédant aux conditions de Sec. 119

District Court—ein Bundesgerichtshof (Federal Court), der die Gerichtsbarkeit in Zivilklagen mit Bezug auf Patente hat. Patentverletzungsklagen koennen im Wohnbezirk des Angeklagten angestrengt werden oder dort, wo er das Patent verletzt hat oder ein eingefuehrtes Geschaeft besitzt. (28 USC 1338, 1400)

District Court—a Federal court having jurisdiction of an action relating to patents. Infringement suit can be brought in the district where the defendant resides, or has committed acts of infringement and has an established business. (28 USC 1338, 1400)

District Court—un tribunal Fédéral qui a la juridiction d'une action relative aux brevets. On peut présenter les procès de contrefaçon dans le district où demeure le défendeur, ou dans le district, où il a commis des actes de contrefaçon et où il a établi ses affaires. (28 USC 1338, 1400)

District Court for District of Columbia—ein Bundesgerichtshof (Federal Court), der die Gerichtsbarkeit in Berufungen gegen Entscheidungen des Board of Appeals und des Board of Patent Interferences hat, wenn die Gegenparteien in verschiedenen Gerichtsbezirken, nicht innerhalb desselben Bundesstaates, oder im Ausland wohnhaft sind und, wenn beim Court of Customs and Patent Appeals keine Berufung eingelegt wurde (Sec. 145, 146)

District Court for District of Columbia—a Federal court having jurisdiction of appeals from decisions of the Board of Appeals and the Board of Patent Interferences, when adverse parties reside in different judicial districts not within one state or in a foreign country, and when the appeal is not filed with the Court of Customs and Patent Appeals (Sec. 145, 146)

District Court for District of Columbia—un tribunal Fédéral qui a la juridiction des appel d'une décision de la Commision d'Appel et de la Commission des "Interférences" des Brevets, quant des parties opposées habitent des districts judiciaux différents, pas dedans un état ou habitent un pays étranger, et quand l'appel n'est pas déposé avec la Court of Customs and Patent Appeals (Sec. 145, 146)

Doppelpatentierung–zwei oder mehr Anmeldung und/oder Patente haben diesselbe erfinderische Einheit und eine beanspruchte Erfindung ist diesselbe, oder patentmaessig nicht verschieden, von der Erfindung im andern Fall (MPEP 804)

double patenting–where two or more applications and/or patents have the same inventive entity and an invention claimed in one case is the same as, or not patentably distinct from, an invention in the other case (MPEP 804)

breveter double–où plusieurs demandes et/ou brevets ont la même entité inventive et une invention revendiquée dans un cas est la même que, ou n'est pas brevetablement distincte de, une invention dans l'autre cas (MPEP 804)

E

Eid—beschworene oder bekraeftigte Erklaerung des Patentanmelders, dass er die Bedingungen unter Sec. 101 und Sec. 102 erfuellt hat (R. 65)

oath—sworn or affirmed statement of the applicant that he has complied with the provisions of Sec. 101 and Sec. 102 (R. 65)

serment—une déclaration jurée ou affirmée du demandeur qu'il a accédé aux stipulations de Sec. 101 et Sec. 102 (R. 65)

eidesstattliche Erklaerung—Mitteilung des Anmelders, dass er die Vorschriften unter Sec. 101 und Sec. 102 erfuellt hat, angenommen an Eides statt, sofern diese die Versicherung enthaelt, dass die aus eigener Kenntnis gemachten Behauptungen wahr sind und, dass Behauptungen begruendet auf Auskuenften und Glauben fuer wahr gehalten werden. Auch ist die Benachrichtigung, dass absichtlich gemachte falsche Aussagen mit Geldstrafe und/oder Gefangenschaft strafbar sind enthalten (18 USC 1001) und die Gueltigkeit der Anmeldung oder eines auf der Erklaerung begruendeten Patents gefaehrden. Eine eidesstattliche Erklaerung kann auch dann benuetzt werden, wenn ein Anspruch auf urspruenglich nicht beanspruchte Materie geltend gemacht wird (R. 67), beim Anmelden eines Wiedererteilungs-Patents (R. 171, -172), beim Anmelden eines Geschmacksmusters (R. 151, 153), beim Anmelden eines Pflanzenpatents (R. 161, 162), und beim Einreichen einer vom 42 USC 2182 oder 2457 (c) verlangten Aufstellung (mit Hinsicht auf Erfindungen, die unter die Vorschriften der Atomic Energy Commission oder des National Space Program fallen).

declaration—statement of the applicant that he has complied with the provisions of Sec. 101 and Sec. 102, accepted in lieu of oath if it includes the averments that statements made of his own knowledge are true, that statements made on information and belief are believed to be true, and there is included the notice that willful false statements are punishable by fine and/or imprisonment (18 USC 1001) and may jeopardize the validity of the application or any patent issuing on such declaration. Declaration can also be used when presenting a claim for matter not claimed originally (R. 67), when applying for a reissue patent (R. 171, 172), when applying for a design patent (R. 151, 153), when applying for a plant patent (R. 161, 162) and when filing a statement required by 42 USC 2182 or 2457(c) (as to inventions under Atomic Energy Commission or National Space Program regulations).

déclaration—déclaration du demandeur qu'il a accédé aux stipulations de Sec. 101 et Sec. 102, acceptée au lieu d'un serment si elle comprend les affirmations que les déclarations faites de sa propre connaissance sont vraies, que les déclarations faites des renseignements et de la croyance sont crues d'être vraies, et qu'on punira les déclarations fausses faites volontairement par amende et/ou incarcération (18 USC 1001) et que telles déclarations peuvent nasarder la validité de la déclaration ou d'aucun brevet qui est délivré d'une telle déclaration. On peut aussi employer la déclaration quand on présente une revendication pour la matière qui n'était pas originalement revendiquée (R. 67), quand on demande un brevet "reissue" (R. 171, 172), quand on demande un brevet de dessein (R. 151, 153), quand on demande un brevet de plante (R. 161, 162), et quand on dépose une déclaration exigée de 42 USC 2182 ou 2457 (c) (comme les inventions sous les règlements de la Commission d'Energie Atomique ou le Programme de l'Espace Nationale).

eidliche Aussage—Protokoll des muendlichen Verhoers eines Zeugen in einer Interferenz unter den Bestimmungen von R. 272 et seq.

deposition—the record of the oral examination of a witness in an interference under the provisions of R. 272 et seq.

dépôt—la transcription des épreuves orales d'un temoin dans une "interférence" sous les conditions de R. 272 et seq.

ein (eine, eins)—bei der Auslegung von Patentanspruechen ist "ein (eine, eins)" als "mindestens ein (eine, eins)" aufzufassen

a—in claim interpretation, "a" is read to mean "at least a"

an—in claim interpretation, "an" is read to mean "at least an"

one—in claim interpretation, "one" is read to mean "at least one"

un—dans l'interprétation des revendications, "un" veut dire "au moins un"

Eingabe beim Commissioner—Ersuchen um Nachpruefung der Einwaende oder Forderungen eines Pruefers mit Hinsicht auf Form oder Uebereinstimmung mit den Rules of Practice (Ausfuehrungsbestimmungen)

petition to Commissioner—request for review of objections or requirements of an examiner as to matters of form or compliance with the Rules of Practice

pétition au Commissaire—la demande pour une revue des objections ou des exigences d'un examinateur au sujet de la forme ou de l'acquiescement aux Règles de la Pratique

eingetragen—zu einem permanenten Teil der Akte gemacht (MPEP 717)

entered—made a permanent part of the file wrapper (MPEP 717)

entré—fait une partie permanente de l'histoire du brevet (MPEP 717)

Eingliederung durch Hinweis—Einschluss von Daten in einer Anmeldung mittels einer Zusammenfassung, welche die Information in genuegender Einzelheit identifiziert, um sie wieder auffinden zu koennen; ausgenommen von der Materie, die durch Hinweis eingegliedert werden kann, sind geheime oder privilegierte Materialien, wie einige fallengelassene Anmeldungen, und Material, das der Oeffentlichkeit oder dem Patentamt nicht ohne Weiteres zugaenglich ist, wie unveroeffentlichte Schriften, wenig bekannte auslaendische Veroeffentlichungen und Veroeffentlichungen, von denen keine englischen Uebersetzungen vorhanden sind. Wesentliches Material (Gegenstaende, die zur Unterstuetzung der Ansprueche oder ausreichender Offenbarung der Erfindung notwendig sind) duerfen durch Hinweis auf ein amerikanisches Patent oder eine angenommene amerikanische Anmeldung eingegliedert werden. Nicht-wesentliches Material darf durch Hinweis auf amerikanische oder auslaendische Patente, auf früher eingereichte amerikanische Anmeldungen in gemeinsamen Besitz und auf nicht-Patent-Veroeffentlichungen eingeordnet werden, um den Hintergrund der Erfindung oder den Stand der Technik anzudeuten. (MPEP 608.01 (p))

incorporation by reference—including data in an application by means of a summary statement identifying the information in such detail that it can be retrieved; excluded from matter that can be incorporated by reference are secret or privileged materials such as some abandoned applications, and material not easily available to the public or the Patent Office such as unpublished papers, obscure foreign publications, and publications on which there are no available English translations. Essential material (subject matter that is necessary to support the claims or for adequate disclosure of the invention) may be incorporated by reference to a United States patent or an allowed United States application. Non-essential material may be incorporated by reference to United States or foreign patents, prior filed commonly owned United States applications and non-patent publications to indicate the background of the invention or the state of the art. (MPEP 608.01(p))

incorporation par renvoi—inclure dans une demande des données au moyen d'une déclaration sommaire identifiant les renseignements d'une facon si détaillée qu'on peut l'obtenir; exclues de la matière qu'on peut incorporer par renvoi sont les matières secrètes ou privilégiées, comme des demandes abandonnées, et de la matière qui n'est pas facilement disponible au public, tel que des études inédites, des publications étrangères et obscures, des publications auxquelles il n'y a pas de traductions disponibles en anglais. La matière essentielle (matière qui est nécessaire pour soutenir les revendications ou pour une divulgation suffisante de l'invention) peut être incorporée par renvoi à un brevet des Etats-Unis, ou une demande acceptée des Etats-Unis. La matière qui n'est pas essentielle peut être incorporée par renvoi aux brevets étrangers ou des Etats-Unis, des demandes des Etats-Unis antrieurement déposées, du même propriétaire, et des publications qui ne sont pas brevetées pour indiquer le fond de l'invention ou l'état de la technique. (MPEP 608.01))

einseitiges Verfahren—Verfahren zwischen einem Anmelder und dem Patentamt ohne eine dritte und Gegenpartei

ex parte proceeding—a proceeding between an applicant and the Patent Office, with no third and opposing party

procédé ex parte—un procédé entre un demandeur et l'Office des Brevets, sans aucune troisième partie opposante

Einspruchs-Bekanntmachung—bedingter Verzicht auf das Recht zu einem Patent durch Einreichung einer Anmeldung, eines Verzichts auf Patentenrechte, Zustimmung zu einer Veroeffentlichung des Auszugs aus der Offenbarung durch das Patentamt, einer Ermaechtigung zur oeffentlichen Einsichtnahme der Anmeldung und einer Aufgaberklaerung. Der Anmelder behaelt fuenf Jahre vom fruehest wirksamen United States Einreichungsdatum das Recht zu einer Interferenz; er ist durch Einreichung einer Fortfuehrungs-Anmeldung innerhalb von dreissig Monaten vom fruehest wirksamen United States Einreichungsdatum zu dem aus dem Einreichungsdatum der Bekanntmachung der Einspruchsanmeldung erwachsenden Vorteil berechtigt. (R. 139)

defensive publication—conditional waiver of right to a patent by filing an application, a waiver of patent rights, consent to a publication by the Patent Office of an abstract of the disclosure, an authorization to open the application to public inspection, and a declaration of abandonment. Applicant retains rights to an interference for five years from the earliest effective United States filing date, and is entitled to the benefit of the filing date of the defensively published application by filing a continuing application within thirty months of the earliest effective United States filing date. (R. 139)

publication défensive—abandon du droit à un brevet en déposant une demande, un abandon des droits de brevet, le consentement à une publication de l'Office des Brevets d'un abstraction de la divulgation, une autorisation d'ouvrir la démande à l'examen public, et une déclaration d'abandon. Le demandeur retient les droits à une "interférence" pendant cinq années de la date d'effet de dépô la plus ancienne des Etats-Unis, et il a droit au bénéfice de la date de dépôt de la demande défensivement publiée en déposent une demande continuante dans un délai de trente mois de la date d'effet de dépôt la plus ancienne des Etats-Unis. (R. 139)

einstweilige Verfuegung—eine gerichtliche Verhinderungs-Verfuegung, die von einer prozessierenden Partei verlangt von der Ausfuehrung bestimmter Handlungen Abstand zu nehmen, bis das Gericht Beweismaterial aufnehmen und bestimmen kann, ob die Partei das Recht hat solche Handlungen auszufuehren

preliminary injunction—a restraining order issued by a court, requiring a litigant to desist from performing specified acts until the court can hear evidence and determine whether he has the right to perform such acts

injonction préliminaire—ordonnance conservatoire délivrée par un tribunal, exigeant qu'un litigant cesse d'exécuter des actes spécifiés jusqu'à ce que le tribunal puisse entendre les preuves et déterminer s'il a droit à exécuter de tels actes

Einwand—Kritik des Pruefers, die auf die Form und nicht den Inhalt der Anmeldung gerichtet ist (MPEP 706.01). Der Anmelder kann beim Commissioner einkommen die Meinung des Pruefers beiseitezusetzen; gegen einen Einwand kann keine Berufung eingelegt werden.

objection—criticism by examiner directed to matters of form, rather than substance, in the application (MPEP 706.01). To overrule the examiner, applicant may petition the Commissioner; an objection is not appealable.

objection—une critique par l'examinateur au sujet de la forme, plutôt que de l'essentiel, de la demande (MPEP 706.01). Pour maîtriser l'examinateur, le demandeur peut pétitionner le Commissaire; une objection n'est pas sujet à appel.

endgueltige Zurueckweisung—eine Handlung des Pruefers, die die Verfolgung (der Patentanmeldung) vor dem Pruefer beendet, den Anmelder darauf beschraenkend beim Board of Appeals Beschwerde einzulegen, den Commissioner mit Entgegenhaltungen und Anforderungen, welche nicht in die Ablehnung eines Anspruchs einbezogen waren zu ersuchen, eine Verbesserung, die die Zulassung der Anmeldung ermoeglicht, oder, im Ermessen des Pruefers, eine Verbesserung, welche die Anmeldung in eine bessere Form fuer Berufung bringt (R. 116)

final rejection—an action by the examiner that concludes prosecution before the examiner, limiting applicant to appeal to the Board of Appeals, petition to the Commissioner from objections or requirements not involved in the rejection of a claim, amendment placing the application in condition for allowance or, at the discretion of the examiner, amendment placing the application in better form for appeal (R. 116)

rejet final—une action de l'examinateur qui termine le procédé devant l'examinateur, limitant le demandeur à un appel devant la Commission d'Appel, un pétition au Commissaire des objections ou des exigences qui n'entrent pas dans le rejet d'une revendication, un amendement rendant la demande recevable ou, à la discrétion de l'examinateur, un amendement rendant la demande d'une meilleure forme un appel (R. 116)

Entgegenhaltung—fruehere Technik, die vom Pruefer als vorwegnehmend oder einschlaegig angefuehrt wird

citation—prior art listed by the examiner as anticipatory or pertinent

citation—état de la technique enregistré par l'examinateur comme antériorisé ou pertinent

Erfindung—vgl. patentfaehige Erfindung

invention—see patentable invention

invention—voir invention brevetable

Erfindung praktisch ausfuehren—Herstellung, Benutzung oder Verkauf einer Erfindung

practising an invention—making, using or selling an invention

mise en pratique d'une invention—la fabrication, l'utilisation ou la vente d'une invention

Erfindungsprioritaet—Bestimmung des Ersten, der eine Erfindung gemacht hat durch Bestimmung dessen, der sie als Erster in die Praxis umgesetzt hat und—wo es zutrifft—das Datum des Beginns der andauernden Sorgfalt dessen, der zwar die Erfindung als Erster gedanklich erfasst, aber sie als Letzter in die Praxis umgesetzt hat

priority of invention—determination of the first to invent by determining the first to reduce to practice and, where appropriate, the date of commencement of continuing diligence by one who was first to conceive but last to reduce to practice

priorité d'invention—détermination du premier d'inventer en déterminant le premier de réduire à la pratique et, ou cela importe, la date du commencement de la diligence continuante par l'un qui était le premier de concevoir mais le dernier de réduire à la pratique

Ergaenzungs-Eid oder eidesstattliche Erklaerung—ein nach freiem Ermessen geleisteter Eid oder eidesstattliche Erklaerung zur Unterstuetzung neuer Ansprueche fuer urspruenglich beschriebene, aber nicht beanspruchte Anmeldungsgegenstaende (R. 67)

supplemental oath or declaration—an oath or declaration filed, optionally, in support of new claims for subject matter originally described but not claimed (R. 67)

serment ou déclaration supplémentaire—un serment ou une déclaration déposée, au choix, à l'appui de nouvelles revendications pour la matière originalement décrite mais pas revendiquée (R. 67)

erneute Erteilung—die Erteilung eines Ersatzpatents fuer die verbleibende Laufzeit des Stammpatents; dies wird getan, wenn das urspruenglich erteilte Patent durch Irrtum und ohne Taeuschungsabsicht ganz oder teilweise unwirksam befunden wird (R. 171–179)

reissue—the grant of a substitute patent for the remainder of the term of the original patent, made when the patent granted originally, through error and without deceptive intent, is found to be wholly or partly inoperative (R.171–179)

"reissue"—la délivrance d'un brevet substitut pour le reste du terme du brevet original, faite quand le brevet originalement délivré, par erreur et sans intention déceptive, est découvert d'être entièrement ou partiellement inopératif (R. 171–179)

Ersatz-Anmeldung—ein Duplikat einer Anmeldung von demselben Anmelder, die vor dem Einreichen des spaeteren Falles fallengelassen worden ist (MPEP 201.09)

substitute application—a duplicate of an application by the same applicant that was abandoned before the filing of the later case (MPEP 201.09)

demande substitute—un double d'une demande du même demandeur qui a été abandonnée avant le dépôt de la demande postérieure (MPEP 201.09)

erster Pruefer—vgl. Hauptpruefer

principal examiner—see primary examiner

examinateur principal—voir examinateur primaire

Erteilungsdatum—Datum der Patentverleihung

date of grant—date of issue of a patent

date de délivrance—la date de la délivrance d'un brevet

Erwiderung—Antwort auf eine Ablehnung

response—reply to a rejection

réponse—réplique à un rejet

Erwiderungs-Schriftsatz—Entgegnung auf neue Argumente, die durch die Antwort des Pruefers hervorgerufen wurden; sie ist innerhalb von zwanzig Tagen vom Datum dieser Antwort einzureichen (R. 193)

reply brief—response to new points of argument raised by the examiner's answer, to be filed within twenty days from the date of such answer (R.193)

dossier de réplique—réponse aux nouveaux points d'argument posés par la réponse de l'examinateur, qui doit être déposée dans le délai de vingt jours de la date de telle réponse (R. 193)

experimentelle Benutzung—von einem Erfinder zur Pruefung ihrer Wirksamkeit benutzte Erfindung

experimental use—use of an invention by an inventor to test its operability

utilisation à titre expérimental—l'utilisation d'une invention par un inventeur pour essayer son "operability"

F

Faelligkeitstermin—der letzte Tag der Frist, innerhalb welcher der Anmelder auf eine Klage des Patentamts antworten muss

due date—the last day of the time period in which applicant must answer an action by the Patent Office

date due—le dernier jour de la période de temps dans laquelle le demandeur doit répondre à une action de l'Office des Brevets

Fallengelassene Anmeldung—ein Fall, den der Anmelder innerhalb der festgesetzten Frist zu verfolgen versaeumt hat; oder ein Fall, der nach ausdruecklicher Erklaerung des Anmelders nicht weiter verfolgt wird (R. 135)

abandoned application—a case that applicant has failed to prosecute within the time fixed, or a case that applicant has declared expressly will not be further prosecuted (R. 135)

demande abandonnée—une plainte que le demandeur n'a pas poursuivie pendant le temps détérminé, ou une plainte que le demandeur a declarée, d'une manière expressive, ne sera pas revendiquée (R. 135)

Fallenlassen der Erfindung—ausdrueckliche oder stillschweigend verstandene Erklaerung des Patentanmelders, dass er kein Eigentumsrecht auf die Erfindung geltend machen wird (Sec. 102)

abandonment of invention—express or implied declaration by applicant that he will not assert a property right in the invention (Sec. 102)

abandon d'invention—une déclaration explicite ou tacite du demandeur qu'il ne prétendra pas un droit de propriété industrielle dans l'invention (Sec. 102)

falsche Bezeichnung–Nachahmung des Namens des Patentinhabers, der Patentnummer, des Wortes "Patent" oder dergleichen um das Publikum zu taeuschen und glauben zu lassen, dass der Artikel mit Zustimmung des Patentinhabers hergestellt oder verkauft wurde; Bezeichnung eines unpatentierten Gegenstandes um das Publikum zu taeuschen und glauben zu lassen der Artikel sei patentiert; oder die Bezeichnung eines Gegenstandes mit "Patent angemeldet" oder "Patentanmeldung anhaengig" oder dergleichen, um das Publikum zu taeuschen und glauben zu lassen, dass eine Patentanmeldung anhaengig ist (Sec. 292)

false marking–imitating the name of the patentee, the patent number or the word "patent" or the like to deceive the public into believing that the article was made or sold with the consent of the patentee; marking an unpatented article to deceive the public into believing the article was patented; or marking an article "patent applied for", or "patent pending" or the like to deceive the public into believing a patent application is pending (Sec. 292)

marquage faux–imitant le nom due breveté, le numéro du brevet ou le mot "brevet", etc., pour faire croire le public que le produit ait été fabriqué ou vendu avec l'accord du breveté; en marquant un produit non-breveté pour faire croire le public que le produit ait été breveté; ou en marquant un produit "brevet demandé", ou "brevet pendant", etc. pour faire croire le public que le brevet soit pendant (Sec. 292)

Feiertag–ein amtlicher Nicht-Arbeitstag im District of Columbia: der Neujahrstag am 1. Januar; Washington's Geburtstag am 22. Februar; Memorial Day am 30. Mai; Unabhaengigkeitstag am 4. Juli; Labor Day am ersten Montag im September; Tag der Veteranen am 11. November; Weihnachten am 25. Dezember; und alle vier Jahre der 20. Januar, die Amtseinsetzung des Praesidenten; faellt der Feiertag auf einen Samstag, ist der vorhergehende Freitag ein Feiertag

holiday—an official non-work day in the District of Columbia: New Year's Day, January 1; Washington's Birthday, February 22; Memorial Day, May 30; Independence Day, July 4; Labor Day, first Monday in September; Veterans Day, November 11; Thanksgiving Day, fourth Thursday in November; Christmas Day, December 25; and Inauguration Day, January 20 every four years; when the holiday falls on a Saturday, the preceding Friday is observed as a holiday

congé—un jour officiel où on ne travaille pas dans le District of Columbia: le Jour de l'An, le 1er janvier; l'anniversaire de Washington, le 22 février; le Jour Commémoratif, le 30 mai; le Jour d'Indépendance, le 4 juillet; le Jour de Travail, le premier lundi de septembre; le Jour des Anciens Combattants, de 11 novembre; le Jour des Actions de Grâce, le quatrième jeudi de novembre; le Jour de Noël, le 25 décembre; et le Jour de l'Inauguration, le 20 janvier, tous les quatre ans. Quand le congé est le samedi, on observe le vendredi précédant comme jour de congé.

Feststellungs-Urteil—ein Gerichtsentscheid ueber Patentgueltigkeit oder Patentverletzung in einer Klage, die von einer mit Patentverletzung bedrohten Partei angestrengt wurde

declaratory judgment—a decision by a court, in an action started by a party threatened with infringement suit, as to whether the patent is valid and/or infringed

jugement déclaratif—une décision par un tribunal, dans une action commencée par une partie menacée d'un procès de contrefaçon, au sujet de la validité ou de la contrefaçon d'un brevet

Fortfuehrung—eine zweite Anmeldung fuer die gleiche, in einer frueheren Anmeldung beanspruchte und offenbarte Erfindung, bei der die zweite Anmeldung von demselben Anmelder eingereicht wurde, ehe die Erst-Anmeldung aufgegeben war, und kein neues Material eingefuehrt wird. Eine Fortfuehrung kann dazu benutzt werden, eine neue Serie von Anspruechen—nach der endgueltigen Ablehnung des Vorpruefers—zur weiteren Pruefung einzureichen (MPEP 201.07); die Fortfuehrung berechtigt von dem Einreichungstermin der Erst-Anmeldung zu profitieren. (MPEP 201.11)

continuation—a second application for the same invention claimed or disclosed in a prior application, where the second application is filed, before the original application is abandoned, by the same applicant, and no new matter is introduced. A continuation may be used to introduce a new set of claims after final rejection for further examination by the Primary Examiner (MPEP 201.07) and is entitled to the benefit of the filing date of the original application. (MPEP 201.11)

continuation—une deuxième demande pour la même invention revendiquée ou divulguée dans une demande antérieure, où la deuxiéme demande est déposée avant que la demande originale soit abandonnée, par le même demandeur, et il n'y introduit aucune matière nouvelle. On peut employer une continuation pour introduire un nouvel ensemble de revendications après le rejet final pour un autre examen par l'examinateur Primaire (MPEP 201.07) at a droit à la date de dépôt de la demande originale. (MPEP 201.11)

fruehere Kenntnis oder Benutzung—vgl. Vorwegnahme

prior knowledge or use—see anticipation

connaissance ou usage antérieur—voir antériorité

funktioneller Anspruch—ein Anspruch, welcher nicht Sec. 112 entspricht, da mindestens ein Element oder eine Stufe im Ganzen oder teilweise in der Terminologie seines Verhaltens definiert ist, oder in der Terminologie der Resultate, die aus seinem Verhalten hervorgehen; und diese Definition macht den Anspruch zu breit oder unbestimmt

functional claim—a claim that fails to comply with S. 112 because at least one element or step is defined in whole or in part in terms of its behavior or in terms of the results that follow from its behavior, and such definition makes the claim too broad or indefinite

revendication functionnelle—une revendication qui ne conforme pas à S. 112 parce qu'au moins un élément ou procédé est défini entièrement ou partiellement en termes de sa conduite ou en termes des résultats qui proviennent de sa conduite, et une telle définition rend la revendication trop large ou indéfinie

G

Gattungen umfassender Anspruch—ein Anspruch, der in seinen Bereich zwei oder mehr offenbarte Ausfuehrungsformen (Gattungen) der Erfindung einschliesst

generic claim—a claim that includes within its scope two or more disclosed embodiments (species) of the invention

revendication générique—une revendication qui comprend dans son étendue plusieurs variantes de l'invention

Gattungs-Anspruch—eine einzelne im besondern differenzierte Ausfuehrung einer Erfindung (MPEP 806.04(e)). Fuenf Gattungen koennen in einer Anmeldung beansprucht werden. (R. 141)

species claim—a single specifically different embodiment of an invention (MPEP 806.04(e)). Five species may be claimed in one application. (R. 141)

revendications de variantes—une incarnation unique, specifiquement différente, d'une invention (MPEP 806.04(e)). On peut revendiquer cinq variantes dans une demande. (R. 141)

Gebiet der Erfindung—vgl. Hintergrund der Erfindung

field of the invention—see background of the invention

domaine de l'invention—voir fond de l'invention

Gebuehr—die gesetzlichen oder Verwaltungskosten fuer Dienstleistungen des Patentamts (R. 21-26)

fee—the statutory or administrative charges for Patent Office services (R. 21-26)

taxe—les frais statutaires ou administratifs pour les services de l'Office des Brevets (R. 21-26)

gedankliche Erfassung–der geistige Teil des Erfindungsprozesses der vollendet ist, wenn eine wirksame Ausfuehrungsform der Erfindung anerkannt ist. Die gedankliche Erfassung muss z. B. durch Zeichnungen oder Offenbarung einem anderen gegenueber beweisfaehig sein um sich darauf stuezen zu koennen. (MPEP 715.07)

conception–the mental part of the inventive act, which is completed when an operative embodiment of the invention is recognized. Conception must be capable of proof, such as by drawings or disclosure to another person, if it is to be relied upon. (MPEP 715.07)

conception–la partie mentale de l'acte inventif, qui est accompli quand on reconnaît une incarnation active de l'invention. On doit pouvoir prouver la conception, au moyen des dessins ou de la communication faite à une autre personne, si on peut y compter. (MPEP 715.07)

gedruckte Veroeffentlichung–ein Dokument, das gedruckt und der Allgemeinheit zugaenglich gemacht worden ist, und daher zu der Annahme berrechtigt, dass das fachlich interessierte Publikum davon weiss

printed publication–a document that is printed and is made accessible to the public, raising a presumption that the public concerned with the art would know of it

publication imprimée–un document qui est imprimé et rendu disponible au public, présumant que les personnes intéressées à la technique en sachent

Gegenstand, der hergestellt wird–vgl. herstellen

article of manufacture–see manufacture

produit industriel–voir fabrication

Geheimhaltung—Koennte die Veroeffentlichung von Angaben in einer Patentanmeldung die nationale Sicherheit beeintraechtigen, so wird die Anmeldung einer zustaendigen Dienststelle zur Einsichtnahme zugaenglich gemacht. Befindet die Dienststelle, dass Veroeffentlichung der Erfindung von Nachteil fuer die nationale Sicherheit waere, dann soll der Commissioner die Geheimhaltung der Erfindung anordnen; waehrend dieser Zeitspanne wird die Weiterverfolgung aufrechterhalten, aber keine Berfungsverhandlung anberaumt, noch wird das Patent erteilt bis die Geheimhaltungsanordnung entfernt ist. (Sec. 181)

secrecy—when the publication of data in a patent application might affect national security, the application is made available for inspection by an appropriate agency of the Government. If the agency finds that publication of the invention would be detrimental to the national security, the Commissioner shall order the invention kept secret; during this period, prosecution will proceed, but no appeal hearing will be set nor will the patent issue until the secrecy order is removed. (Sec. 181)

secret—quand la publication des données pourrait affecter la sécurité nationale, on rend la demande disponible pour l'inspection de l'agence convenable du Gouvernement. Si l'agence trouve que la publication de l'invention serait nuisible à la sécurité nationale, le Commissaire ordonnera qu'on garde secrète l'invention; pendant cette période, la poursuite continuera, mais on n'établira aucune audience d'appel et on ne délivrera pas le brevet jusqu'à ce que la décision de mise au secret soit ôtét. (Sec. 181)

geistige Schritte—Schritte in einem Vorgang, die im menschlichen Verstand geleistet werden koennen, wie zum Beispiel, rechnen, vergleichen, bestimmen, zaehlen, beobachten, registrieren und auswerten

mental steps—steps in a process that can be performed in the human mind, such as calculating, comparing, determining, counting, observing, recording and computing

démarches mentales—les démarches dans un procédé qu'on peut exécuter dans l'esprit humain, tel que calculer, comparer, déterminer, compter, observer, enregistrer et supputer

Genehmigung ein Patent im Ausland anzumelden—Erlaubnis vom Commissioner of Patents ein Patent weniger als sechs Monate nach seiner Anmeldung in den Vereinigten Staaten im Ausland anzumelden. Die Genehmigung eine unter Geheimhaltungs-Befehl stehende Anmeldung im Ausland einzureichen wird nicht erteilt werden, wenn eine Anmeldung im Ausland versehentlich ohne Genehmigung eingereicht worden war. (Sec. 184)

foreign filing authorization—permission by the Commissioner of Patents to file an application in a foreign country in less than six months after the filing of such application in the United States. License to file abroad will not be granted for an application under a secrecy order, but may be granted retroactively in other cases where an application has been filed abroad inadvertently without such license. (Sec. 184)

autorisation étrangere de dépôt—permission du Commissaire des Brevets déposêr une demande dans un pays étranger dans moins de six mois après avoir déposé la même demande aux Etats-Unis. On ne concédera pas une licence pour déposer a l'étranger une demande frappée d'une decision de mise au secret, mais on peut la concéder rétroactivement dans les autres instances où on a déposé par inadvertance une demande à l'ètranger sans une telle licence. (Sec. 184)

gerichtliche Anerkennung—die Anerkennung bestimmter Tatsachen als allgemeine Kenntnis durch ein Gericht, das daher die Einfuehrung von Material zum Beweis dieser Tatsachen nicht verlangt

judicial notice—the recognition by a court of the truth of certain facts as common knowledge, and therefore not requiring the introduction of evidence to prove such facts

notification judicaire—la reconnaissance par un tribunal de la vérité de certains faits comme connaissance commune, at ainsi ne pas exigeant l'introduction d'évidence pour prouver de tels faits

geschaeftlicher Erfolg—bedeutende Verbraucherannahme eines Produktes oder Herstellungsverfahrens, welche die Auffassung, das Produkt oder Verfahren sei ein beachtenswerter Fortschritt in der Technik, unterstuetzt

commercial success—significant consumer acceptance of a product or process, tending to support the argument that the product or process is a notable advance in the art

succès commercial—acceptation significative des consommateurs d'un produit ou d'un procès tendant à soutenir l'argument que le produit ou le procès est un avancement remarquable dans la technique

Geschmacksmusterpatent—Patent fuer ein neues, eigenartiges und ornamentales Muster fuer einen gewerblichen Artikel, das fuer eine Zeitspanne von dreieinhalb, sieben oder vierzehn Jahren erteilt wird; die Dauer der Laufzeit liegt beim Anmelder (R. 151-155)

design patent—patent on a new, original and ornamental design for an article of manufacture, granted for a period of three and one-half, seven or fourteen years, the term being at the option of applicant (R. 151-155)

dessin ou modèle déposé—un brevet sur un dessin nouveau, original et ornémental, conçu pour un produit industriel, délivré pour une période de trois et demie, sept ou quatorze ans, la durée est au choix du demandeur (R. 151-155)

Geschmacksmuster-Patentserie—die besondere Serie von Nummern fuer Geschmacksmusterpatente, der der Buchstabe D voransteht (MPEP 901.04)

design patent series—the separate series of numbers for design patents preceded by the letter D (MPEP 901.04)

serie de dessin ou modèle déposé—la distincte série de numéros pour des dessin ou modèles déposés, précédée par la lettre D (MPEP 901.04)

gesetzlicher Hinderungsgrund—vgl. Hinderungsgrund zur Patenterteilung

statutory bar—see bar to patent grant

interdiction statutaire—voir interdiction à la délivrance d'un brevet

gesetzlicher Vertreter—eine juristische Person, die ernannt worden ist im Namen eines gesetzlich in der Verfuegung beschraenkten (tot, inkompetent, usw.) Erfinders ein Patent anzumelden

legal representative—an entity that has been designated to apply for a patent on behalf of a legally incapacitated (dead, incompetent, etc.) inventor

représentant légal—une entité qu'on a désignée pour demander un brevet au nom d'un inventeur légalement incapacité (mort, incompétent, etc.)

Gesuch—der einleitende Abschnitt einer Anmeldung um die Erteilung eines Patents durch den Commissioner of Patents

petition—the introductory paragraph of an application, requesting the grant of a patent by the Commissioner of Patents

pétition—le paragraphe introductif d'une demande, demandant la délivrance d'un brevet par le Commissaire des Brevets

gleichwertig—durch den zutreffenden Stand der Technig gelehrtes technisches Koennen

equivalent—functionally duplicate technology taught by the pertinent prior art

équivalent—technologie enseignée par la technique antérieure et pertinente

gleichzeitig anhaengig—Anmeldungen, die zur gleichen Zeit in den Akten vorhanden und aktiv sind

copending—applications that are on file and active in the Patent Office at the same time

co-pendant—des demandes viables qui sont simultanément à l'Office des Brevets

Grund-Patent—ein Patent, das ueber viele spaetere Patente vorherrscht, so dass die Benutzung der spaeteren Patente eine Verletzun des Grund-Patentes ausmachen wuerded. Vgl. Pionier-Patent.

basic patent—a patent that dominates many later patents, so that use of the later patents would constitute infringement of the basic patent. See pioneer patent.

brevet de base—un brevet qui domine plusieurs brevets postérieurs, de sorte que l'emploi des brevets postérieurs constituent la contrefaçon du brevet de base. Voir brevet de pionnier.

gueltiges Patent—ein ordnungsgemaess erteiltes Patent, das die Bedingungen zur Patentfaehigkeit unter Sec. 102 und 103 erfuellt

valid patent—a duly granted patent that complies with the conditions for patentability of Sec. 102 and 103

brevet valide—un brevet proprement délivré qui se conforme aux conditions de brevetabilité de Sec. 102 et 103

Gueltigkeits-Untersuchung—vgl. Untersuchung

validity search—see search

recherche de validité—voir recherche

H

handelsueblicher Name—ein nicht gesetzlich—(patentlich) geschuetzter Name, unter welchem ein Erzeugnis auf einem Fachgebiet bekannt ist; es ist gestattet einen handelsueblichen Namen zur genauen Bezeichnung eines Erzeugnisses zu benutzen, wenn seine Bedeutung durch eine beiliegende, genaue und deutliche Definition festgelegt ist, und die Bedeutung in der Literatur in den Vereinigten Staaten bekannt und genau umrissen ist

name used in trade—a nonproprietary name by which a product is known in an art; use of a name used in trade in a patent application to define a product is permitted if its meaning is established by an accompanying definition that is precise and definite, and the meaning is known and defined in the literature in the United States

nom employé dans la commerce—un nom qui n'est pas possédé, par lequel un produit industriel est connu dans une technique; on permet l'emploi d'un nom employé en commerce dans une demande de brevet pour définir un produit industriel si sa signification est établie par une définition accompagnante qui est précise et claire, et si la signification est connue et définie dans la littérature aux Etats-Unis

Haupt-Pruefer—"Oberpatentpruefer" (dienstaeltere Pruefer), die zusammen mit dem Commissioner of Patents und den Assistant Commissioners den Board of Appeals bilden

examiners-in-chief—senior patent examiners who, with the Commissioner of Patents and the Assistant Commissioners, constitute the Board of Appeals

examinateurs-en-chef—"senior" examinateurs des brevets qui, avec le Commissaire des Brevets et les Commissaires Auxiliaires, constituent la Commission d'Appel

Hauptpruefer—der Chef einer Pruefungsgruppe im Patentamt

primary examiner—the chief of an examining group in the Patent Office

examinateur primaire—le chef d'un groupe d'examinateurs à l'Office des Brevets

Herstellungsweise—eine Klasse von patentfaehigen Gegenstaenden, die ein koerperlich greifbares Objekt liefern

manufacture—a class of patentable subject matter providing a physical tangible thing

fabrication—une classe de matière brevetable rendant une chose physìque et tangible

Hinderungsgrund zur Patentverleihung—ein die Patentverleihung verbietender Umstand; Umstaende, die in Sec. 102 (Neuheit und Verlust des Rechts auf ein Patent) oder in S. 103 (nicht-selbstverstaendlicher Erfindungsgegenstand) dargelegt sind

bar to patent grant—a condition that prohibits the grant of a patent; a condition set forth in Sec. 102 (novelty and loss of right to patent) or in Sec. 103 (non-obvious subject matter)

interdiction à la délivrance d'un brevet—une condition qui défend la délivrance d'un brevet; une condition établie dans la Sec. 102 (nouveauté et perte du droit d'un brevet) ou dans la Sec. 103 (de la matière non-évidente)

Hintergrund der Erfindung—eine allgemeine Darstellung der Technik, auf deren Gebiet die Erfindung liegt, des bestimmten Zweiges dieser Technik mit einer Charakterisierung der Erfindung, einer kurzen Beschreibung der bisherigen Technik und der besonderen Nachteile derselben; diese Darstellung ist in der Beschreibung (specification) eingeschlossen und folgt unmittelbar einem Hinweis auf alle verwandten Anmeldungen

background of the invention—a general statement of the art in which the invention lies, of the specific branch of that art with a characterization of the invention, a brief description of the prior art, and the specific disadvantages of the prior art, included in the specification immediately after a cross-reference to any related application

fond de l'invention—une déclaration générale de la technique dans laquelle se trouve l'invention, de la branche (partie) spécifique de cette technique avec une caractérisation de l'invention, une brève description de la technique antérieure, et les désavantages spécifiques de la technique antérieure, incluse dans la spécification immédiatement après un renvoi à aucune demande relative

Hinterlegungs–Konto—eine Summe von mindestens $50., die ein Anwalt oder gesetzlicher Vertreter zur Deckung von Anmelde–und Schluss–gebuehren, Berufungs–und Eingebegebuehren, sowie Kosten fuer Dienstleistungen des Patentamts, wie Gesuche um Abschriften einer Akte und Zeichnungs–Korrekturen, beim Patentamt unterhaelt (R. 25)

deposit account—a sum, maintained at a minimum of $50.00, kept on deposit with the Patent Office by an attorney or agent to be charged to cover filing, final, appeal and petition fees, and cost of Patent Office services such as requests for copies of records, file histories, and correction of drawings (R. 25)

compte de dépôt—une somme, maintenue à un minimum de $50.00, gardée sur dépôt avec l'Office des Brevets par un avocat ou un agent, chargée pour couvrir les taxes de délivrance, les taxes finales, les taxes d'appel et de pétition, et la coûte des services de l'Office des Brevets, tel que des requêtes des copies des archives, des histoires du brevet, et la correction des dessins (R. 25)

Hinweis—Stand der Technik, worauf sich der Pruefer bei der Zurueckweisung eines Anspruchs als nicht patentfaehig beruft. Sofern der Hinweis nicht offensichtlich zutrifft, muss er deutlich erklaert und jeder zurueckgeweisene Anspruch einzeln beschrieben werden.

reference—prior art relied upon by the examiner in rejecting a claim as unpatentable. The pertinence of the reference, if not obvious, must be clearly explained and each rejected claim must be specified.

renvoi—une technique entérieure dont dépend l'examinateur en rejetant une revendication comme non brevetable. La convenance du renvoi, si elle n'est pas évidente, doit être expliquée et chaque revendication rejetée doit être spécifiée.

Hinweis auf eine verwandte Anmeldung—die Angabe in einer Beschreibung (specification) sofort nach dem Auszug aus der Offenbarung, welche eine frueher eingerichte, gleichzeitig schwebende Anmeldung des gleichen Anmelders fuer die gleiche Erfindung mit laufender Nummer, Einreichungsdatum und Beziehung identifiziert, um in die Nutzniessung des Einreichungsdatums der frueheren Anmeldung zu gelangen

cross-reference to a related application—the statement in a specification, immediately after the abstract of the disclosure, identifying an earlier filed co-pending application of the same applicant for the same invention by serial number, filing date and relationship, for the purpose of getting the benefit of the filing date of the prior application

cross-reference—renvoi à une demande relative—la déclaration dans une spécification, suivant immédiatement l'abstraction de la divulgation, identifiant une demande copendante, antérieurement déposée par le même demandeur pour la même invention par nombre successif, le date de dépôt et relation, dans le but d'obtenir l'avantage de la date de dépôt de la demande antérieure

I

inbegriffen—eine Qualifikation, welche einen Anspruch auf Einschluss sicht-spezifizierter Bestandteile selbst in groesseren Mengen offen laesst. "Im wesentlichen inbegriffen" bedeutet dasselbe.

comprising—a qualification that leaves a claim open for the inclusion of unspecified ingredients, even in major amounts. "Comprising essentially" has the same meaning.

"comprising"—une qualification qui laisse ouverte une revendication pour y inclure des ingrédients non-spécifiés, même dans des quantités majeures. "Comprising essentially" a la même signification.

inoffizielle Abschrift—eine Abschrift der Beschreibung (specification), Ansprueche und Zeichnungen eines Gebrauchs- oder Geschmacksmusterpatents

soft copy—a copy of the specification, claims and drawing of an issued utility or design patent

"soft copy"—une copie de la spécification des revendications et des dessins d'un brevet délivré d'utilité ou de dessin

Inspektion—das Recht der Oeffentlichkeit ein erteiltes Patent einzusehen, sowie Kopien desselben und seiner Beschreibungs- (specification) Zeichnungen und aller zu den Akten genommenen Schriftstuecke zu erhalten—soweit sie sich auf den Fall beziehen; die Akte einzusehen und Kopien zu erhalten von einer beendeten Interferenz, bei der es sich um ein Patent oder um eine Anmeldung, zu der ein Patent erteilt wurde, behandelt (R. 11, 15)

inspection—the right of the public to inspect and obtain copies of an issued patent and its specification, drawings and all papers of record relating to the case, and to inspect and obtain copies of the file of a terminated interference involving a patent or an application on which a patent issued (R. 11, 15)

inspection—le droit du public d'examiner et d'obtenir des copies d'un brevet délivré et ses dessin de spécification et tous les histoires du brevet de la demande, et d'examiner et d'obtenir des copies des archives d'une "interférence" terminée entraînant un brevet ou une demande sur laquelle on a délivrée un brevet (R. 11, 15)

inter partes Verfahren—ein Verfahren, bei dem es sich um zwei oder mehr "einsprechende" Anmelder oder Erfinder handelt

inter partes proceeding—a proceeding involving two or more opposing applicants or inventors

procédé inter partes—un procédé comprenant plusieurs demandeurs ou inventeurs opposés

Interferenz—ein Verfahren, das dazu dient zu bestimmen, welcher von zwei oder mehr Patentanmeldern der Erst-Erfinder ist. Es kann sich bei der Interferenz um eine Anmeldung und ein Patent handeln, vorausgesetzt der Anspruch in der Anmeldung ist mehr als ein Jahr vor dem Datum der Patenterteilung gemacht. (Sec. 135)

interference—a proceeding to determine which of two or more applicants for a patent is the first inventor. The interference may involve an application and a patent, provided the claim is made in the application prior to one year from the date on which the patent issued. (Sec. 135)

"interférence"—une procédure tendant à déterminer lequel des plusieurs demandeurs de brevet est le premier inventeur. "Interférence" peut s'agir d'une demande et d'un brevet, pourvu que la revendication soit faite dans la demande avant une année de la date sur laquelle le brevet a été délivré. (Sec. 135)

Internationale Uebereinkunft zum Schutz gewerblichen Eigentums—eine Vereinbarung ueber Patente und Warenzeichen, die Anmeldern in einem Mitgliedsland dasselbe Einreichungsdatum als Termin des Inkrafttretens, wie in anderen Uebereinkunftslaendern, fuer eine innerhalb eines Jahres vom ersten Einreichungsdatum eingereichte Anmeldung, zugesteht. Die Anmeldung muss den Patentgesetzen des Landes, in dem um die Einreichung nachgesucht wird, genuegen.

International Convention for Protection of Industrial Property—an agreement respecting patents and trademarks giving an applicant in one member country the same effective filing date in other Convention Countries for an application filed within a year of the first filing date. The application must comply with the patent laws of the country in which filing is sought.

Convention Internationale pour la Protection de la Propriété Industrielle—un acord au suject des brevets et des marques de fabrique, concédant à un demandeur d'un pays unioniste la même date d'effet de dépôt dans d'autres pays unionistes pour une demande déposée dans le délai d'une année de la première date de dépôt. La demande doit acceder aux lois des brevets du pays où on veut le déposer.

Interview—muendliche Eroerterung der Einwaende und Zurueckweisungen mit dem Pruefer im Patentamt—gewoehnlich auf Wunsch des Pruefers—um die Loesung von Streitfragen zu beschleunigen (R. 133)

interview—oral discussion of objections and rejections with the examiner in the Patent Office, usually at the request of the examiner, to expedite resolution of issues (R. 133)

entrevue—discussion orale des objections et des rejets, avec l'examinateur à l'Office des Brevets, d'ordinaire à la requête de l'examinateur, pour expédier la résolution des questions (R. 133)

J

Jepson Anspruch—eine Art von Anspruch, wobei die bekannte Materie in einer Einleitung vorgetragen—damit die Umwelt darlegend—und die Verbesserung im restlichen Teil des Anspruchs dargelegt wird

Jepson claim—a form of claim in which the known matter is recited in a preamble, thus setting forth the environment, and the improvement is set forth in the remaining portion of the claim

revendication Jepson—une espèce de revendication où la matière connue est récitée dans un préambule, ainsi présentant l'environnement, et le perfectionnement est présenté dans la portion restante de la revendication

juengere Partei (Junior Partei)—in einer Interferenz der Ansmelder, der den spaeter festgesetzten Termin fuer das Inkrafttreten des Einreichungsdatums hat

junior party—in an interference, the applicant having the later established effective filing date

"junior party"—dans une "interférence", le demandeur qui a la date d'effet de dépôt la plus postérieure

K

kennzeichnen—mit einer Patentnummer versehen. Um Schadenersatz fuer Patentverletzung zu erlangen, muss der Patentinhaber den patentierten Artikel oder dessen Verpackung mit dem Wort "Patent" (oder "Pat.") und der Nummer kennzeichnen, oder er muss beweisen, dass der Patentverletzer die Verletzung fortsetzte nachdem er anderweitig von der Patentverletzung in Kenntnis gesetzt war.

marking—applying the patent number. To recover damages for infringement, the patentee must mark the patented article or its package with the word "Patent" (or "Pat.") and the number, or must prove that the infringer continued to infringe after being otherwise notified of the infringement.

marquer—mettre le numéro du brevet. Pour réparer les dommages de la contrefaçon, le breveté doit marquer ou l'article ou son paquet du mot "Brevet" (ou "Pat.") et du numéro, ou doit prouver que le contrefacteur continuait à contrefaire après avoir été autrement notifié de la contrefaçon.

Klagepunkt—in Interferenz Praxis, ein kollidierender Anspruch (ein von den Parteien in einer Interferenz gemachter Anspruch)

count—in interference practice, an interfering claim (a claim made by the parties to an interference)

"count"—dans la practique d'interférence une revendication qui intervient (une réclamation faite des parties d'une "interference")

(eckige) **Klammern**—wenn dieses Zeichen [ ] ein Wort oder Worte in einem Anspruch einklammert, so ist dies als eine Anweisung an den Pruefer solch ein Wort oder Worte von dem Anspruch zu streichen, zu verstehen (R. 121)

brackets—the symbols [ ] placed around a word or words in a claim as a direction to the examiner to delete such word or words from the claim (R. 121)

parentheses—les symboles [ ] mis autour d'un mot ou des mots dans une revendication comme une directive à l'examinateur de rayer tel mot ou tels mots de la revendication (R. 121)

Klassifizierung—die vom Patentamt bestimmte zahlenmaessige Einordnung eines Patentgegenstands oder einer Veroeffentlichung in die verschiedenen Sparten der Technik. Die Klassifizierung wird in einem Klassifizierungshandbuch und in Klassifizierungsbekanntmachungen veroeffentlicht.

classification—the Patent Office numerical designation of the subject matter division of a patent or publication in the various arts. Classification is published in the Manual of Classification and in Classification Bulletins.

classification—la désignation numérique de l'Office des Brevets de la catégorie de la matière d'un brevet ou d'une publication das les diverses techniques. La classification est publiée dans le Manuel de Classification et dans les Bulletins de Classification.

Klassifizierungs-Handbuch—ein Buch, das alle Gruppen und Untergruppen im Patent-Klassifizierungssystem der Vereinigten Staaten aufzaehlt, ein Sachverzeichnis und verwandte Informationen

Manual of Classification—a book listing all classes and subclasses in the United States patent classification system, a subject matter index, and related information

Manuel de Classification—un livre qui enregistre toutes les classes et toutes les sous-classes du système des Etats-Unis de classification des brevets, un index de matière, et des renseignements relatifs

know-how (gewusst wie . .)—Informationen und Sachkenntnis, die die Ausuebung technischen Koennens in der Praxis erlauben; Fachkenntnis

know-how—practical information or knowledge permitting practice of a technology

savoir-faire—les renseignements ou les connaissances pratiques qui permettent la pratique d'une technologie

konstruktive Umsetzen in die Praxis—gleichbedeutend mit dem tatsaechlichen Umsetzen in die Praxis, zur Ausfuehrung gebracht durch das Einreichen einer Patentenanmeldung (MPEP 715.07)

constructive reduction to practice—the equivalent of actual reduction to practice, effected by filling an application for patent (MPEP 715.07)

réduction constructive à la pratique—déposant une demande pour un brevet (MPEP 715.07)

Korrektur-Beschernigung—Erklärung des Patentamts zwecks Korrektur eines sachlichen Irrtums in einem verliehenen Patent, wenn die Schuld an dem unterlaufenen Fehler beim Patentamt liegt, oder ein entschuldbarer Fehler des Patentanmelders vorliegt

certificate of correction—statement by the Patent Office correcting a material error in an issued patent where the error is due to the fault of the Patent Office or is due to the excusable fault of the applicant

certificat de correction—la déclaration de l'Office des Brevets qui corrige une erreur matérielle dans un brevet délivré où l'erreur est par suite de la faute de l'Office des Brevets ou est par suite d'une faute pardonnable du demandeur

Kupon—ein vom Patentamt einzeln oder in Heften mit Werten von 20 und 50 cents verkaufter Bezugschein zur Benutzung beim Erwerb von Patentabschriften, Geschmacksmuster und Pflanzen Patenten, sowie Registrierung von Warenzeichen (R. 24)

coupon—a voucher sold by the Patent Office individually or in books in denominations of twenty cents and fifty cents for use in purchasing copies of patents, design and plant patents, and trademark registrations (R.24)

coupon—an garant vendu, par l'Office des Brevets, individuellement ou dans les livrets en dénominations de vingt ou cinquante cents, emploé pour l'achat des copies de brevets, des brevets de dessein et de plante, et des dépôts de marque de fabrique (R. 24)

L

Last der Beweisfuehrung—die Verpflichtung Beweise zur Aufrechterhaltung eines eingenommenen Standpunkts zu erbringen. In Interferenz Faellen faellt die Last der Beweisfuehrung der Juniorpartei (mit dem spaeteren Anmeldetermin) zu; bei Patentverletzungsklagen muss der Klaeger den Beweis der Patentverletzung erbringen; wo die Gueltigkeit in Frage steht, muss der Angeklagte die Ungueltigkeit beweisen.

burden of proof—the obligation to introduce evidence to sustain a position taken on an issue. In interferences, the burden of proof is on the junior party; in infringement suits, the burden of proof of infringement is on the plaintiff; where validity is an issue, the burden of proof of invalidity is on the defendant.

charge de la preuve—le devoir d'introduire de la preuve pour soutenir une position prise au sujet d'une question. Dans les "interférences", la charge de la preuve reste avec le "junior party"; dans le litigies de contrefaçon, la charge de la preuve de contrefaçon reste avec le plaignant; où il s'agit de la validité d'une question, la charge de la preuve d'invalidité reste avec le défendeur.

Laufzeit des Patents—Zeitspanne fuer die Patentrechte erteilt werden. Die Dauer von Gebrauchsmuster- und Pflanzen-Patenten ist siebzehn Jahre vom Erteilungsdatum; die Dauer von Geschmacksmuster-Patenten ist 3½, 7 oder 14 Jahre vom Verleihungsdatum, nach Belieben des Anmelders.

term of patent—period for which patent rights are granted. The period of utility patents and plant patents is 17 years from the date of grant; the period of design patents is 3½, 7 or 14 years from the date of grant, at the option of applicant.

terme du brevet—la période pour laquelle on a délivré les droits de brevet. La période des brevets d'utilité et de plantes est 17 ans de la date de délivrance; la période des brevets de dessin est 3½ ans, 7 ans ou 14 ans de la date de délivrance, au choix du demandeur.

Lizenz—die Erteilung eines Rechts eine Erfindung zu bestimmten Bedingungen praktisch auszufuehren

license—the grant of a right to practice an invention on terms specified

licence—la cession d'un droit d'utiliser une invention aux conditions spécifiées

Lizenz zur Einreichung im Ausland—vgl. Genehmigung ein Patent im Ausland anzumelden

license for foreign filing—see foreign filing authorization

licence de déposer à l'étranger—voir autorisation de déposer à l'étranger

Lizenzgeber—Anmelder oder Patentinhaber, der eine Lizenz erteilt

licensor—applicant or patentee who grants a license

concédant—un demandeur ou un breveté qui accorde la licence

Lizenzgebuehr—Bezahlung fuer die Benutzung einer Erfindung

royalty—payment for use of an invention

redevances—paiement pour l'utilisation d'une invention

Lizenztraeger—die Partei, der eine Lizenz erteilt wird

licensee—party to whom a license is granted

licencié—une partie à qui on a concédé une licence

M

Markush Anspruch—ein Anspruch in der Art ". . worin ________ ist ein Stoff ausgewaehlt aus der Gruppe bestehen aus ________, ________ und ________" oder ". . worin ________ ist ________, ________ oder ________", als Gattungen umfassender Ausdruck benutzt fuer eine Gruppe von zwei oder mehr Stoffen, fuer die es keinen Gattungen umfassenden Gruppenamen gibt; dies est erlaubt, sofern die Stoffe zu einer anerkannten physikalischen, chemischen, oder einer technisch anerkannten Klasse gehoeren, oder wenigstens eine gemeinsame Eigenschaft haben, die hauptsaechlich fuer ihre Funktion in dem mit Anspruch belegten Verhaeltnis verantwortlich ist

Markush claim—a claim of the form ". . wherein ________ is a material selected from the group consisting of ________, ________ and ________" or ". . wherein ________ is ________, ________ or ________", used as a generic expression covering a group of two or more materials where there is no generic name for the group, permitted where the materials belong to a recognized physical, chemical or art-recognized class, or possess at least one property in common that is mainly responsible for their function in the claimed relationship

revendication Markush—une revendication de la forme ". . en quoi ________ est un matérial choisi du groupe qui consiste de ________, ________ et ________", or ". . en quoi ________ est ________, ________ ou ________", employé comme une expression générique couvrant un groupe de plusieurs matériels où il n'y a pas de nom générique pour le groupe, permis où les matériels appartiennent à une classe physique, chimique, ou technique reconnue, ou possèdent en commun au moins une qualité qui est principalement responsible de leur fonction dans la relation revendiquée

mehrfacher Unteranspruch—ein Anspruch, der auf die vorhergehenden unabhaengigen oder abhaengigen Ansprueche in der Alternative zurueckverweist. (MPEP Change Notice 17-2 of 4 June 1968). Unterbrechen—864 O. G. 323, 8 July 1969.

multiple dependent claim—a claim that refers back to any of the preceding independent or dependent claims in the alternative. (MPEP Change Notice 17-2 of 4 June 1968) Discontinued—cf. 864 O. G. 323, 8 July 1969.

revendication multiple dépendante—une revendication qui fait référence à n'importe quelle revendication antérieure, indépendante ou dépendante, dans l'alternatif. (MPEP Change Notice 17-2 du 4 juin 1968) Discontinuer—cf. 864 O. G. 323, 8 July 1969.

Methode—vgl. Verfahren

method—see process

méthode—voir procédé

Minimum-Erteilungsgebuehr—Summe, die vom Anmelder, seinem Rechtsnachfolger, Anwalt, oder einer Partei, deren Interesse aktenkundig ist, faellig ist; zahlbar innerhalb von drei Monaten vom Datum der Zulassungs-Benachrichtigung, bestehend aus $100. plus $10. fuer die erste Seite gedruckter Beschreibung (specification) plus $2. fuer jeden Bogen mit Zeichnungen. Jede faellige Restsumme der Erteilungsgebuehr—zur Bezahlung von zusaetzlichen Seiten gedruckter Beschreibung (specification)—wird auf einer Beilage zur Patenterteilung berechnet, und ist innerhalb von drei Monaten vom Datum des Patents zu zahlen, um Verfallen des Patents zu vermeiden. (860 O. G. 2)

minimum issue fee—sum due from applicant, his assignee, attorney, or a party of record interest, payable within three months after the date of notice of allowance, consisting of $100. plus $10. for the first page of printed specification plus $2. for each sheet of drawing. Any balance of the issue fee due, in payment for any additional pages of printed specification, is billed by attachment to the patent grant, and must be paid within three months of the date of the patent to avoid lapse of the patent. (860 OG 2)

taxe minimale de délivrance—la somme dûe du demandeur, son concessionnaire, son avocat, ou une partie d'intérêt enregistrée, payable dans le délai de trois mois après la date de la notification d'acceptation, consistante de $100. plus $10 pou la première page de spécification imprimée plus $2. pour chaque feuille de dessin. Tout solde de la taxe de délivrance dûe, comme paiement pour des pages additionnelles de spécification imprimée, est attachée à l'octroi du brevet, et on doit le payer dans le délai de trois mois de la date du brevet pour éviter la déchéance du brevet. (860 OG 2)

Missbrauch eines Patents—Verwendung eines Patents durch einen Patentinhaber um dinge ausserhalb des Bereichs der Rechte in dem Patent zu lenken und eine Verteidigung gegen einen Patentverletzungs-Anspruch zu schaffen

misuse of patent—employment of a patent by a patent owner to control matters outside the scope of the rights in the patent, providing a defense against a claim of infringement of the patent

abus de brevet—l'utilisation d'un brevet par un titulaire de brevet pour contrôler des matières hors de l'étendue des droits dans le brevet, rendant une défense contre une revendication de contrefaçon du brevet

Mitanmelder—Erfindergemeinschaft, die ein Patent anmeldet

joint applicants—joint inventors who apply for a patent

co-demandeurs—des co-inventeurs qui demandent un brevet

Miterfinder—einer von zwei oder mehr Erfindern, die zusammen eine Erfindung machen

joint inventor—one of two or more inventors who, together, make an invention

co-inventeur—un de plusieurs inventeurs qui, ensemble, créent une invention

Miterfinder—zwei oder mehr Personen, die gemeinsam eine Erfindung gemacht haben

co-inventors—two or more persons who jointly made an invention

co-inventeurs—plusieurs qui ont créé ensemble une invention

Mittel—angewandte Kraft; eine Art der Betriebsmethode; besondere Behandlung besonderer Objekte; ein Teil, der ein mechanisches Ergebnis erzielt

means—a force applied; a mode of operation; a specific treatment of specific objects; a part accomplishing a mechanical result

moyen—une force appliquée; une façon d'opérer; un traitement spécifique des objets spécifiques; une partie qui accomplit un résultat mécanique

Modell—eine strukturelle Darstellung, die dem Patentamt—wenn vom Commissioner nicht besonders angefordert—nicht uebergeben wird (R. 91)

model—a structural embodiment of the invention; not received by the Patent Office unless specifically called for by the Commissioner (R. 91)

modèle—une incarnation structurale de l'invention; pas recu de l'Office des Brevets à moins que le Commissaire le demande spécifiquement (R. 91)

muendliche Verhandlung—Vorbringung muendlicher Beweisgruende vor dem Board of Appeals durch den Beschwerde-Fuehrenden (Berufungsklaeger); es steht dem Pruefer frei auch seinerseits muendliche Beweisgrunde vorzubringen (R. 194)

hearing—presentation by appellant of oral argument before the Board of Appeals; the examiner has the option of also presenting oral argument (R. 194)

audience—la présentation d'un argument, oral par le demandeur devant la Commission d'Appel; l'examinateur peut aussi choisir de présenter un argument oral (R. 194)

mutmassliche Gueltigkeit—die wiederlegbare Annahme, dass ein erteiltes Patent gueltig ist

presumption of validity—the rebuttable assumption that an issued patent is valid

présomption de validité—la supposition refutable qu'un brevet délivré soit valide

N

negative Begrenzung—ein Wort oder Satz in einem Anspruch, der verschwommen und unbestimmt ist, da etwas ausgesagt wird, was in dem Anspruch nicht vorhanden ist

negative limitation—a word or phrase in a claim that is vague and indefinite because it recites what is not present in the claim

limitation négative—un mot ou une phrase, dans une revendication, qui est vague et indéfinie parce qu'elle récite quelque chose qui n'est pas présent dans la revendication

neuartig—in dem Fachgebiet nicht vorhanden

novel—not present in the art

nouveau—pas présent dans la technique

neue Anwendung—eine Klasse patentfaehiger Gegenstaende, die ein auf dem erfinderischen Gebrauch eines bekannten Verfahrens, einer Vorrichtung, Herstellungsweise, Zusammensetzung von Gegenstaenden oder eines Stoffes, beruhendes Verfahren hervorbringen (Sec. 100)

new use—a class of patentable subject matter providing a process based on an inventive use of a known process, machine, manufacture, composition of matter or material (Sec. 100)

application nouvelle—une classe de matière brevetable fournissant un procédé basé sur une utilisation inventive d'un procédé, sur une machine, sur une fabrication, et sur la composition connus de matière ou de matériel (Sec. 100)

neue Materie—eine Offenbarung, die in der Beschreibung (specification) oder den Zeichnungen oder Anspruechen der urspruenglichen Anmeldung nicht gemacht wurde. Eine Hinzufuegung zu der urspruenglichen Offenbarung und daher durch Berichtigung oder Antrag auf erneute Erteilung nicht zulaessig. (R. 118, Sec. 132, 251)

new matter—a disclosure not set forth in the specification, or drawings or claims of the original application. An addition to the original disclosure, and therefore not admissible by amendment or by reissue application. (R. 118, Sec. 132, 251)

nouvelle matière—une divulgation qui n'est pas présentée dans la spécification, ou dans les dessins, ou dans les revendications de la demande originale. Une addition à la divulgation originale, et ainsi pas admissible par amendement ou par "reissue" demande. (R. 118, Sec. 132, 251)

nicht-ausschliessliche Lizenz—Lizenz unter einem Patent, das in seiner Laufzeit in geographischem oder anderm Umfang begrenzt ist und daher die Erteilung von Rechten an andere unter dem Patent nicht verbietet

non-exclusive license—a license under a patent that is limited as to duration or geographical or other scope, and thus does not prohibit the granting of rights to others under the patent

licence non-exclusive—une licence d'un brevet qui est limitée de la durée ou de l'étendue géographique ou autre, et ainsi ne défend pas la cession des droits à autrui sous le brevet

nicht-formgerechte Zeichnung—eine Zeichnung, die mit den Anforderungen von R. 81–84 nicht uebereinstimmt, die zum Zweck der Pruefung zugelassen werden darf, aber korrigiert werden muss, oder—nach jeweiligem Verlangen—durch eine neue Zeichnung ersetzt werden muss

informal drawing—a drawing that fails to comply with the requirements of R. 81-84, which may be admitted for purpose of examination but must be corrected or a new drawing furnished, as required

dessin casuel—un dessin qui ne conforme par aux exigences de R. 81–84, qu'on peut admettre pour l'examen mais on doit le corriger ou en présenter un nouveau dessin, comme exigé

nicht-rechtsverbindliche Gegenstaende—Erfindungen oder Entdeckungen, die unter Sec. 101 nicht patentfaehig sind, wie zum Beispiel, die blosse Anordnung von Gedrucktem, etwas in der Natur Vorkommendes und im Wesentlichen unveraendert Bleibendes, eine Methode der Geschaefts-fuehrung, oder ein von jeder greifbaren Struktur entfernter wissenschaftlicher Grundbegriff (MPEP 706.03(a))

non-statutory subject matter—inventions or discoveries that are not patentable under Sec. 101, such as the mere arrangement of printed matter, a thing occurring in nature that is substantially unaltered, a method of doing business, or a scientific principle divorced from any tangible structure (MPEP 706.03(a))

matière non statutaire—des inventions ou des découvertes qui ne sont pas brevetables sous Sec. 101, tel que le simple arrangement de matière imprimée, une chose qui arrive dans la nature qui est vraiment sans changement, une méthode de faire les affaires, ou une principe scientifique qui est séparée d'aucune structure tangible (MPEP 706.03(a))

Nicht-Selbstverstaendlichkeit–Unterschiede zwischen dem zu patentierended Erfindungsgegenstand und dem Stand der Technik, die solcher Art sind, dass der Erfindungsgegenstand als Ganzes zu der Zeit, als die Erfindung gemacht wurde, einem auf dem Gebiet des Erfindungsgegenstandes Sachverstaendigen nicht selbstverstaendlich gewesen waere (Sec. 103)

unobviousness–differences between the subject matter sought to be patented and the prior art of such a nature that the subject matter as a whole would not have been obvious at the time the invention was made to a person having ordinary skill in the art involved (Sec. 103)

"unobviousness"–les différences entres la matière qu'on veut rendre brevetée et la technique antérieure, d'une telle nature que la matière entière n'aurait pas été évidente à une personne qui a une habileté moyenne dans la technique à l'heure où on a créé l'invention (Sec. 103)

nicht-wesentliches Material–vgl. Eingliederung durch Hinweis

non-essential material–see incorporation by reference

matière non-essentielle–voir incorporation par renvoi

Nuetzlichkeit–wirksam und nicht frivol, betreugerisch oder gegen das Wohl der Oeffentlichkeit (MPEP 706.03(p))

utility–operative and not frivolous, fraudulent or against public policy (MPEP 706.3(p))

utilité–opératif et pas frivole, frauduleux ou contre la politique publique (MPEP 706.3(p))

O

oder—vgl. alternative Ausdrucksweise; Markush Anspruch

or—see alternative expression; Markush claim

ou—voir expression alternative; revendication "Markush"

oeffentlicher Nachschlag-Saal—ein der Oeffentlichkeit zugaenglicher Raum im Patentamt, wo Kopien aller Patente der Vereinigten Staaten nach ihrer patentamtlichen Klassifizierung eingeordnet sind. Eine zusaetzliche auch der Allgemeinheit zugaengliche wissenschaftliche Bibliothek enthaelt wissenschaftliche und technische Buecher und Zeitschriften in verschiedenen Sprachen, die officiellen Veroeffentlichungen auslaendischer Patentamter und Kopien auslaendischer Patente in zahlenmaessiger Anordnung und gemaess den Klassifizierungen des Ursprungslandes des Patents. Ein zusaetzliches, ebenfalls der Oeffentlichkeit zugaengliches Aktenzimmer enthaelt die Protokolle und Akten von erteilten Patenten, mit den Patenten der Vereinigten Staaten in zahlenmaessiger Ordnung und eine Ausgabe des Amtsblatts.

Public Search Room—a room in the Patent Office, open to the public, in which copies of all United States patents are filed according to the Patent Office classification. An adjunct Scientific Library, open to the public, contains scientific and technical books and periodicals in various languages, the official journals of foreign patent offices, and copies of foreign patents arranged in numerical order and according to the classification of the country of origin of the patent. An adjunct record room, open to the public, contains the records and files of issued patents, United States patents arranged in numerical order, and a set of the Official Gazette.

Salle Publique de Recherche—une salle à l'Office des Brevets, ouverte au public, où sont déposées selon la classification de l'Office des Brevets, des copies de tous les brevets des Etats-Unis. Une Bibliothèque Scientifique adjointe, ouverte au public, contient des livres et des périodiques scientifiques et techniques en langues diverses, les journaux officiels des offices étrangers des brevets, et des copies des brevets étrangers, organisées en ordre numérique et selon la classiffication du pays d'origine du brevet. Une salle d'archives adjointe, ouverte au public, contient les archives et les dossiers des brevets délivrés, les brevets des Etats-Unis organisés en ordre numérique, et un ensemble de la Gazette Officielle.

Offenbarung—Darlegung der Erfindung durch jede Art von Beweismaterial, wie durch Beschreibung (specification), Zeischnungen oder Anspruech

disclosure—statement of the invention as set forth in any evidence, i.e. as set forth in the specification, drawings or claims

divulgation—la déclaration d'une invention présentée, i.e. présentée dans la spécification, les dessin ou les revendications

Offenbarungs–Urkunde—eine Erfindungs–Offenbarung, vom Erfinder unterzeichnet und vom Erfinder oder seinem Rechtnachsfolger dem Patentamt mit der Gebuehr von $10. zugesandt, einem an den Absender zurueckadressierten Freiumschlag—und getrennt davon—das unterzeichnete Ersuchen des Erfinders die Erfindungs–Offenbarung anzunehmen und sie zwei Jahre unter dem Patentamt Offenbarungs–Urkunden–Programm als Beweis fuer die geistige Erfassung aufzubewahren

disclosure document—an invention disclosure signed by the inventor and forwarded to the Patent Office by the inventor or his assignee, with the $10. fee, a stamped self-addressed envelope and the inventor's separate signed request that the invention disclosure be accepted and preserved for two years under the Patent Office Disclosure Document Program as proof of conception

divulgation document—la déclaration d'une invention avec signature de l'inventeur, dépôt dans l'Office des Brevets par l'inventeur ou son cessionnaire avec la taxe de $10., une enveloppe timbrée addressé à l'inventeur, et une lettre signé par l'inventeur demandant dépôt et maintenance de la déclaration pendant deux ans dans l'Office de Brevets Programme de Divulgation des Documents en evidence de conception

(offizielles) Einreichungsdatum—das Datum, an dem die vollstaendige Anmeldung oder der letzte Teil derselben, in zur Pruefung annehmbarer Form, im Patentamt empfangen wird (R. 55)

filing date—the date on which the complete or the last part of an application, in form acceptable for examination, is received in the Patent Office (R. 55)

date de dépôt—la date où la demande entière ou la dernière partie d'une demande, dans une forme acceptable pour l'examen, est reçue dans l'Office des Brevets (R. 55)

P

Papier-Patent—ein Patent, dessen "lehren" nicht handelsmaessig ausgefuehrt worden sind

paper patent—a patent whose teaching has not been practised commercially

"paper" brevet—un brevet dont on n'a pas pratiqué commercialement l'enseignement

Pariser Verbandsuebereinkunft—die internationale Verbandsuebereinkunft zum Schutz gewerblichen Eigentums

Paris Convention—the International Convention for Protection of Industrial Property

Convention de Paris—la Convention Internationale pour la Protection de la Propriété Industrielle

Patent—ein von der Regierung erteiltes Recht andere zu verhindern die in den Patentanspruechen definierte Erfindung herzustellen, zu benutzen oder zu verkaufen

patent—a grant by the Government of the right to prevent others from making, using or selling the invention defined in the claims of the patent

brevet—octroi par le Gouvernement du droit d'empêcher à autrui de fabriquer, d'employer ou de vendre l'invention définie dans les revendications du brevet

Patent angemeldet—Mitteilung eines Anmelders, dass eine Patentanmeldung an einer Erfindung beim Patentamt eingereicht worden ist

patent applied for—notice by an applicant that an application for patent on an invention has been filed in the Patent Office

brevet demandé—notification par un demandeur qu'une demande de brevet pour une invention a été déposée à l'Office des Brevets

Patent anhaengig—vgl. Patent angemeldet

patent pending—see patent applied for

brevet pendant—voir brevet demandé

Patentanmeldung—ein Antrag oder Gesuch um Erteilung eines Patents (R. 61), Beschreibung (specification) und Ansprueche (R. 71-77), Eid oder eidesstattliche Erklaerung (R. 65), notwendige Zeichnungen (R. 81-88) und die vorgeschriebene Anmeldegebuehr (R. 21)

application for patent—a petition or request for a patent (R. 61), specification and claims (R. 71-77), oath or declaration (R. 65), necessary drawings (R. 81-88) and prescribed filing fee R. 21)

demande d'un brevet—un pétition ou une requête pour un brevet (R. 61), la spécification et les revendications (R. 71-77), le serment ou la déclaration (R. 65), les dessins nécessaires (R. 81-88) et la taxe de dépôt nécessaire (R. 21)

Patent-Anwalt—Mitglied einer Bundes- oder Landesanwaltskammer, der den Bedingungen entspricht und beim Patentamt zugelassen ist (R. 341). Dies schliesst Personen ein, die nicht Mitglieder einer Anwaltskammer sind, die vor 1931 als "eingetragene Patent-Anwaelte" zugelassen wurden.

patent attorney—a member of a Federal or State bar who has the qualifications required for and who has been admitted to practice before the Patent Office (R. 341). Includes persons not a member of any bar who were admitted as "registered patent attorneys" before 1931.

avocat de brevets—un membre d'un barreau Fédéral ou d'état qui a les qualifications exigées pour la pratique et qu'on a admis à la pratique auprès de l'Office des Brevets (R. 341). Cela comprend des personnes qui n'appartiennent à aucun barreau, qui etaient admises comme "avocats enregistrés de brevets" avant 1931.

patentfaehige Erfindung—ein neues, nuetzliches und nichtselbstverstaendliches Verfahren, Vorrichtung, Herstellungsweise oder Zusammensetzung von Gegenstaenden, oder eine Verbesserung davon

patentable invention—a new, useful and unobvious process, machine, manufacture or composition of matter, or improvement thereof

invention brevetable—un procédé, une machine, la fabrication ou la composition de matière, ou le perfectionnement de cela, qui est nouveau, utile et non évident

Patentfaehigkeits-Untersuchung—vgl. Untersuchung

patentability search—see search

recherche de brevetabilité—voir recherche

Patent-Gesetz—die Statuten, die auf Patente Bezug nehmen (hauptsaechlich im Titel 35 des US Code) und die Auslegungen dieser Statuten durch Gerichte und Verwaltungsbehoerden

patent law—the statutes covering patents (found principally in Title 35 of the US Code) and court and administrative agency interpretations of such statutes

loi de brevets—les statuts au sujet des brevets (trouvés principalement dans Titre 35 du Code des Etats-Unis) et les interprétations juridiques et administratives de tels statuts

Patent-Prozess—eine zivilrechtliche Klage, die von einem Patentinhaber gegen einen angeblichen Verletzer bei einem Bundesgericht erhoben wird, um von weiterer Patentverletzung abzuhalten und/oder auf Entschaedigung fuer die angebliche Verletzung; eine Klage, die erhoben wird um ein Patent fuer ungueltig und/oder als durch den Klaeger nicht verletzt erklaeren zu lassen

patent litigation—a civil legal action brought in a Federal court by a patent owner against an alleged infringer to enjoin further infringement of the patent and/or for compensation for the alleged infringement; an action brought to have a patent declared invalid and/or not infringed by the claimant

litigie de brevet—une action civile et légale, présentée dans un tribunal Fédéral par un titulaire de brevet contre un contrefacteur allégué pour enjoindre la contrefaçon continuée du brevet et/ou pour la restitution dûe à cause de la contrefaçon alléguée; une action présentée par le demandeur pour faire déclarer invalide et/ou pas contrefait un brevet

Patentpruefverfahren-Handbuch—ein ausfuehrliches Nachschlagewerk ueber die Praxis und das Verfahren bei Patentpruefungen, hauptsaechlich zum Gebrauch des Prueferstabs des Patentamts

Manual of Patent Examining Procedure—a detailed reference work on patent examining practice and procedure, primarily for use by the Examining Corps of the Patent Office

Manuel de la Procédure d'Examiner les Brevets—un ouvrage à consulter détaillé, au sujet de la pratique et du procédé d'examiner les brevets, principalement employé par le Corps d'Examinateurs de l'Office des Brevets

Patenturkunde—einem Erfinder das Recht erteilen andere auf begrenzte Zeit vom Gebrauch seiner Erfindung auszuschliessen. Weist auch auf den Patenterteilungs-Schein (Patentverleihungs-Schein) hin.

letters patent—the grant to an inventor of the right to exclude others, for a limited time, from using his invention. Also refers to the certificate of the patent grant.

"letters patent"—accorder à un inventeur le droit d'exclure autrui, pendant un terme limité, d'utiliser son invention. Cela fait aussi référence au certificat de la délivrance du brevet.

Patent-Vertreter—eine Person—kein Rechtsanwalt—die die Bedingungen erfuellt und die zugelassen ist vor dem Patentamt zu praktizieren (R. 341)

patent agent—a person, not an attorney at law, who has the qualifications required for and who has been admitted to practice before the Patent Office (R. 341)

agent de brevets—une personne, pas un avoué, qui a les qualifications exigées pour la pratique et qu'on a admise à la pratique aupres de l'Office des Brevets (R. 341)

Pflanzen-Patent—Patent fuer die Erfindung oder Entdeckung und Vermehrung ohne Befruchtung einer bestimmten und neuen Pflanzensorte (einschliesslich von Kulturabarten, Mutationen, Hybriden und neugefundenen Saemlingen, ausser einem Knollengewaechs oder einer in einem unkultivierten Stadium gefundenen Pflanze) (Sec. 161–164, R. 161–167)

plant patent—patent for the invention or discovery and asexual reproduction of a distinct and new variety of plant (including cultivated sports, mutants, hybrids and newly found seedlings, other than a tuber propagated plant or a plant found in an uncultivated state) (Sec. 161–164, R. 161–167)

brevet de plantes—un brevet pour l'invention ou la découverte et pour la réproduction asexuelle d'une espèce de plante nouvelle et distincte (y inclus les variations des burgeons, les mutations, les hybrides cultivés, et les semis nouvellement trouvés, pas une plante tuberculeuse propagée ou une plante trouvée dans un état incultivé) (Sec. 161–164, R. 161–167)

Pflanzen-Patentserie—die besondere Serie von Nummern fuer Pflanzen-Patente, der die Buchstaben "P.P." voranstehen (MPEP 901.04)

plant patent series—the separate series of numbers for plant patents preceded by the letters "P.P." (MPEP 901.04)

série de brevets de plantes—la serie distincte de numéros pour les brevets de plantes précédée des lettres "P.P." (MPEP 901.04)

Pionier-Patent—das erste Patent auf einem Gebiet, das niemals vorher offenbarte Mittel oder eine Funktion mit Anspruch belegt. Es wird grosszuegig ausgelegt und ist zu einem weiten Bereich von Aequivalenzen berechtigt.

pioneer patent—the first patent in a field, claiming means or a function never before disclosed. It is interpreted liberally and is entitled to a broad range of equivalents.

brevet pionnier—le premier brevet d'un domaine, revendiquant les moyensou une fonction qu'on n'a jamais encore divulgée. On l'interprète libéralement et a droit à une large étendue d'équivalents.

Postanschrift—die Adresse, unter welcher der Anmelder ueblicherweise seine Post empfaengt (MPEP 605.03)

post office address—the address at which the applicant customarily receives his mail (MPEP 605.03)

adresse—l'adresse où le demandeur reçoit d'ordinaire son courrier (MPEP 605.03)

Prioritaetsdatum—vgl. Prioritaetsrecht

priority date—see priority right

date d'antériorité—voir droit de priorité

Prioritaetsrecht—das Recht den Termin des Inkrafttretens fuer das Einreichen einer Anmeldung auf das Einreichungsdatum der ersten entsprechenden auslaendischen Anmeldung vorzuverlegen, vorausgesetzt der auslaendische Staat ist ein "Vertragsland" und das Einreichungsdatum in diesem Land liegt nicht mehr als ein Jahr vor dem Einreichungsdatum in den Vereinigten Staaten

priority right—the right to promote the effective date of filing an application to the filing date of the first corresponding foreign application, provided the foreign country is a "treaty" country and the filing date in that country is not more than one year prior to the date of filing in the United States

droit de priorité—le droit d'avancer la date d'effet de dépôt d'une demande à la date de dépôt de la première demande correspondante et étrangère, pourvu que le pays étrangèr soit un pays "unioniste" et que la date de dépôt dans ce pays—la ne soit plus qu'un an antérieur à la date de dépôt aux Etats-Unis

Protest—Widerspruch gegen die Erteilung eines Patents aus der Oeffentlichkeit. Nachdem die Pruefer zu seiner Information darauf hingewiesen wurde, bestaetigt das Patentamt nur den Eingang eines solchen Schriftstuecks und laesst es zu den Akten legen. (R. 291)

protest—opposition to the grant of a patent, submitted by a member of the public. The Patent Office merely acknowledges and files such papers after referral to the examiner for his information. (R.291)

protestation—l'opposition à la délivrance d'un brevet, soumise par un membre du public. L'Office des Brevets reconnaît simplement et dépose de tels documents après les avoir révélés à l'examinateur pour sa propre référence. (R. 291)

Prozess—vgl. Patentprozess

litigation—see patent litigation

litigie—voir litigie des brevets

Pruefer—ein Beamter der Patentamts, der Patentanmeldungen nachprueft um die Patentfaehigkeit und den Umfang von Erfindungen zu bestimmen und, mit andern Pruefern, die Frage der Prioritaet zwischen konkurrierenden Anmeldern, die den gleichen Gegenstand beanspruchen, zu entscheiden

examiner—a Patent Office employee who reviews patent applications to determine the patentability and the scope of inventions and, with other examiners, the question of priority between rival applicants claiming the same subject matter

examinateur—un employé de l'Office des Brevets qui revoit les demandes de brevets pour déterminer la brevetabilité et l'étendue d'une invention et, avec des autres examinateurs, la question de la priorité entre des demandeurs rivaux revendiquant la même matière

Pruefers Antwort—Erwiderung des Vorpruefers auf den Schriftsatz des Berufungsklaegers beim Board of Appeals, mit einem Bescheid, der alle notwendigen Erklaerungen fuer die beanspruchte Erfindung und die Belege und Gruende der Ablehnung enthaelt (R. 193)

examiner's answer—response by primary examiner to brief of appellant to Board of Appeals, such answer including any necessary explanation of the invention claimed and of the references and grounds of rejection (R. 193)

réponse de l'examinateur—réponse d'un examinateur primaire au dossier du demandeur à la Commission d'Appel, une telle réponse comprenante aucune explication nécessaire de l'invention revendiquée et des raisons de rejet (R. 193)

Pruefers Berichtigung—eine Berichtigung zu einer Anmeldung die von einem Pruefer unter Benachrichtigung des Anmelders gemacht wird, um "augenfaellige Irrtuemer und Auslassungen" zu korrigieren (MPEP 1302.04)

examiner's amendment—an amendment to an application made by the examiner, with notice to applicant, to correct "obvious errors and omissions" (MPEP 1302.04)

amendement de l'examinateur—un amendement à une demande, fait par l'examinateur, avec une notification au demandeur, pour corriger des "erreurs évidentes et des omissions" (MPEP 1302.04)

Pruefung—vgl. Pruefer

examination—see examiner

examen—voir examinateur

R

Rechtnachsfolge—das gesetzliche Instrument zur Uebertragung der Eigentumsrechte an einer Erfindung (auch Zession genannt)

assignment—instrument transferring property rights in an invention

cession—le document qui transfère les droits de propriété dans une invention

Rechtseinwand—das Argument, dass eine Klage nicht korrekt war

traverse—argument that an action was not proper

"traverse"—argument qu'une action n'était pas juste

Rechtsnachfolger(Gesamt)—die Person, auf die alle Eigentumsrechte an einer Erfindung uebertragen wurden (auch Zessionaer genannt)

assignee—the transferee of property rights in an invention

cessionnaire—le cessionnaire des droits de propriété dans une invention

rechtsverbindlich—durch Congress-Beschluss festgesetzt und ordnungsgemaess zum Gesetz erhoben

statutory—established by act of Congress duly enacted into law

statutaire—établi par un acte du Congrès proprement rendu une loi

res adjudicata—der Befund, dass dieselbe Streitfrage gegen die gleiche Partei schon frueher endgueltig entschieden wurde (MPEP 706.03 (w))

res adjudicata—a finding that the identical issue was previously decided finally against the same party (MPEP 706.03(w))

res adjudicata—un verdict que la question identique a été décidée antérieurement finalement contre la même partie (MPEP 706.03 (w))

S

Sachwalter—der Vertreter eines Erfinders, der sich vor dem Gesetz nicht selbst vertreten kann

administrator—the representative of a legally incapacitated inventor

administrateur—le représentant d'un inventeur légalement incapacité

Schadenersatz fuer Patentverletzung—eine Dollarpraemie als Entschaedigung fuer die unbefugte Benutzung von Patentrechten. Die zuerkannte Verguetung umfasst eine Summe, die nicht geringer als eine angemessene Gebuehr fuer die Benutzung inklusive Zinsen und Gerichtskosten ist. (Sec. 284)

damages for infringement—an award in dollars to compensate for unauthorized use of patent rights. Compensatory award includes a sum that is not less than a reasonable royalty for use, with interest and court costs. (Sec. 284)

dommages pour la contrefaçon—de l'argent pour restituer l'emploi sans autorisation des droits de brevet. La décision compensatrice comprend une somme qui n'est pas moins que les redevenances raisonnables pour l'emploi, avec l'intérêt et les frais du tribunal (les frais ne comprennent pas les frais d'un avocat). (Sec. 284)

Schlussgebuehr—die Gebuehr fuer die Erteilung eines Hauptpatents oder die Wiederausgabe eines Patents, $100., plus $10. fuer jede Seite mit gedruckter Beschreibung, plus $2. fuer jeden Bogen mit Zeichnungen; im Falle von Geschmacksmustern ist die Schlussgebuehr $10. fuer eine Frist von dreieinhalb Jahren, $20. fuer sieben Jahre und $30. fuer vierzehn Jahre (Sec. 41)

final fee—the fee for issue of an original or reissue patent, $100. plus $10. for each page of printed specification plus $2. for each sheet of drawing; in design cases, the final fee is $10. for a term of three and one half years, $20. for seven years and $30. for fourteen years (Sec. 41)

taxe finale—la taxe pour la délivrance d'un brevet original ou "reissue", $100. plus $10. pour chaque page de spécification imprimée plus $2. pour chaque feuille de dessin; en cas des dessins, la taxe finale est $10. pour une durée de trois ans et demi, $20. pour une durée de sept ans et $30. pour une durée de quatorze ans (Sec. 41)

Schraffierung—Illustration eines Schnitts in einer Zeichnung durch schraege Parallellinien, die nicht weniger als ungefaehr einen zwanzigstel Zoll (inch) auseinander sind (R. 84 (d))

hatching—illustration of a cut section in a drawing by oblique parallel lines not less than about one-twentieth of an inch apart (R. 84(d))

hachure—illustration d'une section coupée d'un dessin par lignes obliques et parallèles qui ne se séparent pas de moins d'une vingtième d'une pouce (R. 84 (d))

Schriftsatz—Darlegung der Tatsachen, Gruende und Autoritaeten zur Unterstuetzung eines Antrags, Gesuchs, einer Berufung, eines Interferenz-oder Gerichtsverfahrens (R. 181, 192, 243, 244)

brief—statement of the facts, reasons and authorities relied upon to support a motion, petition, appeal, interference action or court proceeding (R. 181, 192, 243, 244)

dossier—une déclaration des faits, des raisons et des sources sur lesquels on a comptés pour soutenir une procédure, un pétition, un appel, une action de "interférence" ou les procédés d'un tribunal (R. 181, 192, 243, 244)

Seric fuer erneut erteilte Patente—die separate Reihenfolge von Nummern fuer erneut erteilte Patente mit dem Vorsatz "Re." (MPEP 901.04)

reissue patent series—the separate series of numbers for reissue patents preceded by "Re". (MPEP 901.04)

"reissue" série de brevets—la distincte série de numéros des brevets "reissue" précédée de "Re." (MPEP 901.04)

selbstverstaendlich—zur Erklaerung vgl. Nicht-Selbstverss-taendlichkeit

obvious—see definition of unobviousness

évident—voir la définition de "unobviousness"

shop right—Recht eines Arbeitgebers, die von einem Arbeitnehmer mit den Einrichtungen oder in der Zeit des Arbeitgebers gemachte Erfindung in seinem Betrieb zu benutzen

shop right—the right of an employer to use in his shop the invention made by an employee with the employer's equipment or time

"shop right"—le droit pour un employeur d'utiliser dans son entreprise l'invention d'un employé, lorsque celui-ci l'a faite avec l'équipement de l'employeur ou durant les heures de travail

Sonderpruefverfahren–beschleunigte Pruefung einer neuen Anmeldung auf einem schriftlichen Gesuch um Sonderbehandlung beruhend, Uebereinkommen die Anmeldung auf zehn oder weniger Ansprueche beschraenkt zu halten, und Vorlage einer Vorpruefungs-Untersuchung und Differenzierung der Ansprueche von dem Hinweisen in dieser Untersuchung. Eine vollstaendige erste Behandlung wird vor allen Anmeldungen unternommen, mit Ausnahme derjenigen, die in der Zulassung begriffen sind oder mit einem festgesetzten Termin dem Pruefer zur Behandlung vorliegen; der Anmelder hat drei Monate Zeit zur Erwiderung; nach einem in Belieben der Beteiligten stehenden Interview muss die Erwiderung auf die gemachten Zurueckweisungen, Einwaende und Forderungen begrenzt sein; der Pruefer trifft innerhalb eines Monats nach der Erwinderung seine endgueltige Anordnung. (R. 102, MPEP 708.01 and 708.02)

special examining procedure–accelerated examination of a new application based upon a written petition to make special, agreement to keep the application limited to ten claims or less, and submission of a pre-examination search and differentiation of the claims from the references of that search. A complete first action will be made prior to all applications except those in condition for allowance or under a fixed time limit for action by the Examiner; applicant will be given three months to respond; after an optional interview, the response must be limited to the rejections, objections and requirements made; final disposition will be made by the Examiner within one month of the response. (R. 102, MPEP 708.01 and 708.02)

procédé spécial d'examiner—l'examen accélére d'une nouvelle demande basé sur une pétition écrit de rendre spéciale la demande, la concession de limiter la demande à dix revendications au moins, et la soumission d'une recherche faite avant l'examen et la différenciation des revendications des renvois de cette recherche. Une première action complète sera faite avant toutes les autres demandes sauf celles qui sont en condition pour action de l'examinateur; on donnera au demandeur trois mois pour y répondre; après une entrevue facultative, on doit limiter la réponse aux rejets, objections et exigences faits; le jugement final sera fait par l'examinateur dans le délai d'un mois de la réponse. (R. 102, MPEP 708.01 et 708.02)

Sorgfalt—in angemessenem Grad andauernde Taetigkeit die Erfindung in die Praxis umzusetzen, oder einen Irrtum in einem schon erteilten Patent zu korrigieren

diligence—continuous activity at a reasonable rate in reducing an invention to practice or in acting to correct an error in an issued patent

diligence—activité continue d'un progrès raisonnable en réduisant à la pratique une invention, ou en agissant pour corriger une erreur dans un brevet octroyé

Stamm-Anmeldung—die urspruengliche Anmeldung eines Patents, worauf eine Fortfuehrungs- oder Teilfortfuehrungs-Anmeldung begruendet ist

parent application—the original application on which a continuation or continuation-in-part application is based

"parent" demande—la demande originale sur laquelle on base une demande de continuation ou de continuation-en-partie

Stand der Technik—die Gegebenheiten auf einem Gebiet technischer Kenntnisse zu einer bestimmten Zeit

state of the art—the data in an area of technical knowledge at a given time

état de la technique—les données dans un domaine de connaissance technique au moment donné

Stand der Technik—Alles aus dem Fachgebiet, das auf die Neuheit einer beanspruchten Erfindung Bezug hat

prior art—all subject matter that is pertinent to the novelty of a claimed invention under Sec. 102

état de la technique—toute matière pertinente à la nouveauté de l'invention revendiquée sous Sec. 102

Stoffverbindung—eine Klase patentfaehiger Gegenstaende, welche die Mischung von zwei oder mehr Bestandteilen umfasst um eine feste Masse, eine Fluessigkeit oder ein Gas zu schaffen, mit Eigenschaften verschieden von, oder zusaetzlich zu den Eigenschaften, welche die individuellen Bestandteile im einzelnen oder gemeinsam aufweisen

composition of matter—a class of patentable subject matter that involves the mixture of two or more ingredients to provide a solid, liquid or gas possessing properties different from or in addition to the properties possessed by the several ingredients, individually or in common

composition—une classe de matière brevetable qui comprend la mixture de plusieurs ingrédients pour produire un solide, un liquide, ou un gaz possédant les qualités différentes des, ou en addition aux qualités possédées par les plusieurs ingrédients, individuellement ou en commun

"streamlined" Fortfuehrungs-Anmeldung—eine Anmeldung in der die Zeichnungen und Beschreibung (specification) mit einer anhaengigen Anmeldung desselben Anmelders identisch sind; die Ansprueche beziehen sich auf dieselbe Erfindung, die in der anhaengigen Anmeldung verfolgt wurden, und die Durchfuehrungsvorschriften zur Uebertragung von Zeichnungen und Beschreibung (specification) von der anhaengigen Anmeldung zur neuen Anmeldung sind befolgt worden (Notice 824 O. G. 1)

streamlined continuation application – an application in which the drawings and specification are identical with those of a pending application of the same applicant, and the claims are directed to the same invention as that prosecuted in the pending application, and procedures for transferring the drawings and specification from the pending application to the new application have been followed (Notice 824 O.G. 1)

"streamlined continuation" demande–une demande où les dessins et la spécification sont identiques avec ceux d'une demande pendante du même demandeur, les revendications concernent la même invention que celles poursuivies dans la demande pendante, et on a suivi les procédés pour céder les dessins et la spécification de la demande pendante à la nouvelle demande (Notification 824 O.G. 1)

Streichung von Anspruechen–Loeschen von Anspruechen einer Patentanmeldung

cancellation of claims–deleting of claims from an application

annulation des revendications–la rayure des revendications d'une demande

"swearing back of reference"–einen Eid leisten, mit dem die Vollendung der in der Anmeldung genannten Erfindung in den Vereinigten Staaten, vor dem Datum des Inkrafttretens des Hinweises beschworen wird (R. 131)

swearing back of reference–making an oath showing completion of the invention of the application in the United States before the effective date of the reference (R. 131)

"swearing back of reference"–exposé sous serment démontrant la complétion aux Etats-Unis d'une invention à une date antérieure à la date d'effet du renvoi (R. 131)

T

tabellarischer Anspruch—ein Anspruch, wobei die verschiedenen Klauseln oder Unterabschnitte vom Rand eingerueckt sind, um die Aufreihung der Elemente und Unterelemente des Anspruchs in Kolonnen anzuordnen

tabular claim—a claim in which the several clauses or subparagraphs are indented from the margin to provide columnar recital of the elements and sub-elements of the claim

revendication synoptique—une revendication dans laquelle les plusieurs clauses ou sous-paragraphes sont mis intérieurement dans la marge pour pourvoir le récit en colonne des éléments et des sous-éléments de la revendication

Tatsaechliche Umsetzung in die Praxis—Konstruktion des Geraetes oder Ausfuehrung des Erfindungsvorgangs

actual reduction to practice—construction of the device or carrying out the process of the invention

réduction actuelle à la pratique—la construction de l'invention ou du mécanisme, ou travaillant de procédé de l'invention

tatsaechliches Fallenlassen der Erfindung—vgl. Fallenlassen der Erfindung

actual abandonment of invention—see abandonment of invention

abandon actuel de l'invention—voir abandon de l'invention

technische Geschicklichkeit—die Geschicklichkeit eines Technikers auf seinem Fachgebiet. Eine negative Probe auf's Exempel—der Erfindung naemlich: die feste Annahme, dass die Fertigkeit eines Durchschnittsfachmanns nicht an das Niveau von Erfindungen heranreicht.

mechanical skill—the skill of a technician in his own field. A negative test for invention, in the holding that the abilities of an ordinary mechanic are not at the level of invention.

habileté mécanique—l'habileté d'un technicien dans son propre domaine. Une épreuve négative d'invention, dans la croyance que les habiletés d'un technicien moyen ne soient pas au niveau d'invention.

Technik—technische Daten aller Art

art—technical data of any form

technique—les données techniques de n'importe quelle forme

Teilfortfuehrungs-Anmeldung—eine Anmeldung, die waehrend der Laufzeit einer frueheren Anmeldung von demselben Anmelder eingereicht wurde, unter Wiederholung eines betraechtlichen Teils der frueheren Anmeldung und unter Hinzufuegung von in dem vorhergehenden Fall nicht offenbartem Material (MPEP 201.8), oder unter Streichung von in dem vorhergehenden Fall offenbartem Material

continuation-in-part application—an application filed during the lifetime of an earlier application by the same applicant, repeating some substantial portion of the earlier application and adding matter not disclosed in the earlier case (MPEP 201.8) or deleting matter disclosed in the earlier case

une demande de continuation—en-partie—une demande déposée pendant la vie d'une demande antérieure par le même demandeur, répétant quelque partie significative de la demande antérieure et ajoutant quelque chose qui n'était pas inclus dans l'affaire antérieure (MPEP 201.8) ou rayant quelque chose divulgé dans l'affaire antérieure

Titel—die Ueberschrift auf der ersten Seite der Beschreibung (specification); eine kurze Darstellung, die allgemein bezeichnend fuer die beanspruchte Verbesserung ist

title—the heading on the first page of the specification; a short description that is representative generally of the claimed improvement

titre—l'en-tête de la première page de la spécification; une courte description qui est généralement représentative du perfectionnement revendiqué

Treuhaender—der Vertreter eines vor dem Gestz unfaehigen Erfinders

executor—the representative of a legally incapacitated inventor

exécuteur—le représentant d'un inventeur légalement incapacité

U

Uebereinkunfts-Frist—Frist eines Jahres (sechs Monate fuer Geschmacksmuster), waehrend welcher Zeit der Stichtag einer Anmeldung unter einem frueheren Abkommen fuer eine Anmeldung, welche unter den Vorrechten der Unionsuebereinkunft eingereicht wurde, beansprucht werden kann

convention period—one year period (six months for designs) during which the date of an earlier convention application can be claimed for an application filed under the benefits of the Union Convention

période conventionnelle ou unioniste—période d'une année (six mois pour les modèles ou dessins) pendant laquelle on peut revendiquer la date d'une demande antérieure conventionnelle pour une demande déposée sous le bénéfice de la "Union Convention"

Uebereinkunfts-Recht—vgl. Uebereinkunfts-Frist

convention rights—see convention period

droit conventionnel ou unioniste—voir période conventionnelle ou unioniste

Ueberfuelltes Fach (gebiet)—ein technisches Gebiet, auf dem in verhaeltnismaessig kurzer Zeit zahlreiche Fortschritte gemacht wurden

crowded art—a technology in which there have been numerous advances over a relatively short period of time

technique serrée—une technologie dans la quelle il y avait des progrès nombreux pendant une période de temps relativement courte

uebliche Fachkenntnis—vgl. technische Geschicklichkeit

ordinary skill in the art—see mechanical skill

habileté moyenne dans la technique—voir habileté mécanique

Umfang des Anspruchs—vgl. Ausmass des Anspruchs

scope of claim—see breadth of claim

portée de la revendication—voir largeur de la revendication

Umfassender als die Erfindung—Anspruch auf einen die Grenzen der Erfindung—wie sie im Patentantrag festgelegt sind—uebersteigenden Umfang

broader than the invention—claim of a scope that exceeds the limits of the invention defined in the application or patent

plus large que l'invention—des revendications d'une portée qui dépasse les bornes de l'invention définies dans la demande ou dans le brevet

Umsetzen in die Praxis—ein Verfahren ist in die Praxis umgesetzt, wenn es erfolgreich ausgefuehrt wird; eine Vorrichtung ist in die Praxis umgesetzt, wenn sie zusammengesetzt und benutzt wird; ein Herstellungsverfahren ist in die Praxis umgesetzt, wenn es vollstaendig hergestellt ist; eine Zusammensetzung ist in die Praxis umgesetzt, wenn sie vollstaendig zusammengesetzt ist

reduction to practice—a process is reduced to practice when it is successfully performed; a machine is reduced to practice when it is assembled and used; a manufacture is reduced to practice when it is completely manufactured; a composition is reduced to practice when it is completely composed

réduction à la pratique—un procédé est réduit à la pratique quand il est exécuté avec succès; une machine, est réduite à la pratique quand elle est assemblée et employée; une fabrication est réduite à la pratique quand elle est complètement fabriquée; une composition est réduite à la pratique quand elle est complètement composée

unbestimmt—vgl. verschwommen und unbestimmt

indefinite—see vague and indefinite

indefini—voir vague et indéfini

ungenuegende Offenbarung—eine Offenbarung, welche versaeumt Daten einzuschliessen, die jemanden, der mit der Technik auf die sich die Erfindung bezieht vertraut ist, in den Stand setzen wuerde die Erfindung herzustellen und zu benutzen (MPEP 608.01 (p))

insufficient disclosure—a disclosure that fails to include data that would enable a person skilled in the art to which the invention relates to make and use the invention (MPEP 608.01(p))

divulgation insuffisante—une divulgation qui manque d'inclure les données qui permettraient à une personne habile dans la technique à laquelle rapporte l'invention, de fabriquer et d'employer l'invention (MPEP 608.01 (p))

unlauterer Wettbewerb—Taeschung oder Betrug im Geschaeftsgebaren, die die gesetzlichen oder billigen Rechte eines Konkurrenten oder der Allgemeinheit verletzen

unfair competition—deception or fraud in business practice that violates the legal or equitable rights of a competitor or the public

concurrence injuste—une déception ou une fraude dans la pratique des affaires qui viole les droits légaux ou équitables d'un concurrent ou du public

Unteranspruch—ein Anspruch, der auf einen einzelnen vorhergegangenen Anspruch zurueckverweist und diesen begrenzt. Mehrere Serien von Unteranspruechen koennen in einer einzigen Anmeldung erscheinen, aber alle Ansprueche in jeded Serie muessen in unmittelbar aufeinanderfolgender Ordnung oder so dicht wie moeglich zusammenstehen. (R. 75)

dependent claim—a claim that refers back to and restricts a single preceding claim. Several series of dependent claims may appear in a single application, but all claims in each series must be in immediate consecutive order or as close to such order as physically possible. (R. 75)

revendication subordonnée—une revendication qui fait allusion à, et limite, une revendication précédante. Plusieurs séries de revendications subordonnées peuvent paraître dans une demande unique, mais toutes les revendications dans chaque série doivent être en ordre exact et consécutif, ou aussi près qu'il soit physiquement possible à un tel ordre. (R. 75)

Unterklasse—die nummerische Bestimmung der Unterteilung der Gegenstaende eines Patents oder einer Veroeffentlichung durch das Patentamt zur weiteren Detailierung der Klassifizierung solcher Gegenstaende

subclass—the Patent Office numerical designation of the subject matter division of a patent or publication, in further particularization of a classification of such subject matter

sous-classe—la designation numérique de l'Office des Brevets de la division de matière d'un brevet ou d'une publication, dans une particularisation plus grande de la classification de telle matière

Untersagung—ein Verbot gegen die Behauptung oder Verneinung einer Tatsache. Das Verbot wurde durch eine vorhergehende Handlung oder Aussage der mit der Untersagung belegten Person hervorgerufen; ein frueheres Handeln, das gewisse folgende Handlungen ausschliesst. Die Veroeffentlichung einer Erfindung seit mehr als einem Jahr stellt, zum Beispiel, einen Hinderungsgrund oder eine Untersagung zur Erlangung eines Patents fuer eine solche Erfindung dar.

estoppel—a prohibition against alleging or denying a fact, the prohibition having been created by some previous action or statement by the person estopped; a prior act that bars certain subsequent actions. For example, publication of an invention for more than one year acts as a bar or estoppel to obtaining a patent for such invention.

estoppel—une interdiction d'alléguer ou de nier un fait, l'interdiction ayant été créée par une déclaration ou une action antérieure de la personne "estopped"; un acte antérieure qui défend certaines actions postérieures. Par exemple, la publication d'une invention pendant plus d'une année agit comme une interdiction ou "estoppel" d'obtenir un brevet pour telle invention.

Untersagung in der Akte—ein Verbot begruendet auf einem Zugestaendnis, das von einem Anmelder im Verlauf der Verfolgung einer Anmeldung gemacht wurde. Wenn, zum Beispiel, der Umfang eines Anspruches in Erwinderung auf die Ablehnung des Pruefers dieses Anspruchs enger gehalten wird, dann befindet sich eine Untersagung in der Akte, welche die Wiedergeltendmachung eines Anspruchs, der umfassender als der verengte Anspruch ist, verbietet.

file wrapper estoppel—the prohibition established by a concession made by an applicant in the course of prosecution of an application. For example, when the scope of a claim is narrowed in response to the examiner's rejection of that claim, there is a file wrapper estoppel prohibiting the reassertion of a claim that is broader than the narrowed claim.

histoire du brevet "estoppel"—l'interdiction établie par une concession faite du demandeur dans le cours de la poursuite d'une demande. Par example, quand l'étendue d'une revendication est limitée en réponse au rejet de la revendication par l'examinateur, il y a un hisoire du brevet "estoppel" (file wrapper estoppel) défendant la nouvelle assertion d'une revendication qui est plus large que la revendication limitée.

Unterschrift—der vollstaendige, unabgekuerzte Vorname, der Anfangsbuchstabe oder volle Mittelname—wenn vorhanden—und der vollstaendige Nachname des Anmelders, der auf der Anmeldung gegengezeichnet sein muss (R. 57)

signature—the full first name without abbreviation, middle initial or name, if any, and full surname of the applicant, which must be endorsed on the application (R. 57)

signature—le complet prénom sans abréviation, l'initiale ou le nom intermédiaire, s'il y en a, et le complet surnom du demandeur, qu'on doit endosser sur la demande (R. 57)

unterstreichen—eine waagrechte Linie unter einem Wort oder Worten in einem Anspruch ist eine Anweisung an den Pruefer solch ein Wort oder Worte dem Anspruch hinzuzufuegen (R. 121)

underlining—a horizontal line placed under a word or words in a claim as a direction to the examiner to add such word or words to the claim (R. 121)

souligner—une ligne horizontale mise sous un mot ou plusieurs mots dans une revendication, comme une directive à l'examinateur d'ajouter tel mot ou tels mots à la revendication (R. 121)

Untersuchung—Nachpruefung von Patenten und andern Veroeffentlichungen um festzustellen, was der Oeffentlichkeit in Bezug auf eine angebliche Erfindung bekannt ist; dadurch wird die Information zur Unterstuetzung eines Gutachtens ueber die Patentfaehigkeit der Erfindung, oder ueber die Gueltigkeit eines Patents an der Erfindung, oder am Stand der Technik gesammelt

search—a review of patents and other publications to determine what is known to the public in relation to an alleged invention, thus collecting the information to support an opinion on the patentability of the invention or on the validity of a patent on the invention, or on the state of the art

recherche—une revue des brevets et d'autres publications pour déterminer ce que sait le public au sujet d'une invention alléguée, ainsi ramassant les renseignements pour soutenir une opinion au sujet de la brevetabilité de l'invention, ou de la validité d'un brevet sur l'invention, ou de l'état de la technique

Untersuchung auf Neuheit—vgl. Untersuchung

novelty search—see search

recherche de la nouveauté—voir recherche

unvollstaendig—ein Anspruch oder eine Offenbarung, welche einen wesentlichen Bestandteil, eine Stufe, oder eine strukturell zusammenwirkende Beziehung von Elementen auslassen

incomplete—a claim or disclosure that omits an essential element, step, or structural cooperative relationship of elements

incomplet—une revendication ou une divulgation qui omet un élément, une démarche, ou une relation structurele coopérative essentielle des éléments

V

Veraenderung des Standpunkts—Aenderung der Einstellung im Hinblick auf das, was die Erfindung in sich fasst oder was die Unterschiede zwischen den Hinweisen und der Erfindung sind

shifting ground—changing position as to what the invention comprises, or as to what the differences are between the references and the invention

"shifting ground"—changer de position quant à ce que comprend l'invention, ou quant à ce que sont les différences entre les renvois et l'invention

Verbandslaender—Mitgliedstaaten der Pariser Union Verbandsuebereinkunft zum Schutze Industriellen Eigentums von 1883

convention countries—member countries of the Union Convention of Paris, 1883, for the protection of industrial property

pays de pacte (unioniste)—les pays appartenant à l'union instituée par la Convention de Paris, 1883, pour la protection de la propriété industrielle

Verbesserung—ein erfinderischer Schritt vorwaerts von geringerem Rang als eine "bahnbrechende Erfindung"

improvement—an inventive advance of a degree less than a "pioneer invention"

perfectionnement—un avancement inventif d'un degré moins d'une "invention pionnière"

Verbindung—zwei oder mehr aufeinander einwirkende Elemente

combination—two or more interacting elements

combinaison—plusieurs éléments dont l'action est réciproque

Verbindung von Hinweisen—Anfuehrung von zwei oder mehr Hinweisen, die zusammen betrachtet, alle kennzeichnenden Eigenschaften der beanspruchten Verbindung tragen und die Assoziation solcher Eigenschaften der beanspruchten Verbindung lehren

combination of references—citation of two or more references that, considered together, show all of the significant features of the claimed combination and teach the association of such features of the claimed combination

combinaison de renvois—la citation de plusieurs renvois qui, considérés ensemble, montrent tous les traits significatifs de la combinaison revendiquée et enseignent l'association de tels traits de la combinaison revendiquée

Verfahren—eine Klasse von patentfaehigen Gegenstaenden, die sich ueber eine zusammenhaengende Reihe von Stufen oder Vorgaengen erstreckt um ein greifbares Ergebnis zu erzielen

process—a class of patentable subject matter covering a connected series of steps or operations for accomplishing a physical result

procédé—une classe de matière brevetable au sujet d'une série cohérente de démarches ou d'opération pour accomplir un résultat physique

Verfahren ueber offenkundige Benutzung—diese Verfahren beruhen auf einem durch beschworene schriftliche Erklaerungen gestuetzten Gesuch; die Verhandlung und das Aufnehmen von Zeugenaussagen ueber die Frage, ob eine Erfindung ein Jahr vor dem Einreichungsdatum der Anmeldung, oder vor dem in einer Vorerklaerung angegebenen Datum, oder vor dem von einer Partei festgesetzten Erfindungsdatum in offenkundigem Gebrauch oder verkaeuflich war (R. 292)

public use proceedings—based upon a petition supported by affidavits, the hearing and the taking of testimony on the question of whether an invention had been in public use or on sale one year before the filing of the application, or before the date alleged in a preliminary statement or before the date of invention established by a party (R. 292)

procédés de l'utilisation publique—basé sur un pétition soutenu d'attestations, l'audience et l'enregistrement d'évidence concernant la question de savoir si l'invention avait été à l'utilisation publique ou en vente un an avant le dépôt de la demande, ou avant la date alléguée, dans une déclaration préliminaire ou avant la date d'invention établie par une partie (R. 292)

Verfallen des Patents—Beendigung der Laufzeit des Patents durch Versaeumnis die Restsumme der Erteilungsgebuehr, die innerhalb von drei Monaten von Datum des Patents faellig ist, zu bezahlen (860 O. G. 2)

lapse of patent—termination of patent term by reason of failure to pay the balance of the issue fee due within three months of the date of the patent (860 OG 2)

déchéance du brevet—la terminaison de la durée du brevet parce qu'on a manqué de payer le solde de la taxe de délivrance dans le délai de trois mois de la date du brevet (860 OG 2)

verfallene Anmeldung—eine Anmeldung, zu der das Patent nicht verliehen wurde, da der Anmelder versaeumte die Schlussgebuehr zu bezahlen (R. 116). Falls die Schlussgebuehr innedhalb eines Jahres and Ablauf der sechs Monatsfrist nicht angenommen wird, gilt die Anmeldung vom Verfallsdatum an als fallengelassen.

forfeited application—an application on which the patent did not issue because applicant failed to pay the final fee (R. 316). If the final fee is not accepted within one year after the six months period for payment has passed, the application stands abandoned as of the date of forfeiture.

forfeited application (demande)—une demande sur laquelle on n'a pas délivré le brevet parce que le demandeur a manqué de payer la taxe finale (R 316). Si la taxe finale n'est pas acceptée dans le delai imparti d'une année après que la periode de paiement de six mois est passée, on considère la demande comme abandonnée de la date de "forfeiture."

Verfolgung—die Massnahmen, die getroffen werden um ein Patent erteilt zu bekommen

prosecution—the procedures followed to obtain the grant of a patent

poursuite—les procédés suivis pour obtenir la délivrance d'un brevet

Verfuegung—eine gerichtliche Verfuegung, die anordnet, dass eine Partei von weiterer Verletzung eines Patents Abstand zu nehmen hat

injunction—a court order directing that a party desist from further infringement of a patent

injonction—une ordonnance d'un tribunal imposant à une partie de cesser de contrefaire un brevet

Verheimlichung—eine Erfindung geheimhalten

concealment—keeping an invention secret

dissimulation—garder secrète une invention

verkettender Anspruch—ein Anspruch, der untrennbar von Anspruechen auf zwei oder mehr richtig teilbare Erfindungen ist, wie zum Beispiel ein Art-(genus) Anspruch, der Gattungs-Anspruech zusammenkettet

linking claim—a claim that is inseparable from claims to two or more properly divisible inventions, such as a genus claim linking species claims

revendication liante—une revendication qui est inséparable des revendications à plusieurs inventions convenablement divisibles, comme une revendication générique qui lie des revendications des variantes

Verletzung—Benutzung oder Verkauf einer patentierten Erfindung ohne Berichtigung oder taetige Veranlassung zu solchem Gebrauch oder Verkauf (Sec. 271)

infringement—use or sale of a patented invention without authority, or active inducement of such use or sale (Sec. 271)

contrefaçon—l'utilisation ou la vente d'une invention brevetée sans autorisation, ou l'encouragement actif d'une telle utilisation ou vente (Sec. 271)

Veroeffentlichung—vgl. gedruckte Veroeffentlichung

publication—see printed publication

publication—voir publication imprimée

verschwommen und bestimmt—einen angemessenen Grad von Genauigkeit und Klarheit vermissen lassend

vague and indefinite—lacking a reasonable degree of particularity and distinctness

vague et indéfini—manquant un degré raisonnable de particularité et de clarité

Vertreter—vgl. Patent-Vertreter

agent—see patent agent

agent—voir agent de brevets

verwarnen—einen Prozessfuehrnden durch Gerichtsbescheid dazu auffordern von der Ausfuehrung bestimmter Handlungen Abstand zu nehmen

enjoin—to require a litigant, by court order, to desist from performing specified acts

enjoindre—imposer à un litigant, par ordonnance d'un tribunal, de cesser d'exécuter des actes détérminés

Verzeichnis von Patenten und Patentinhabern—eine jaehrliche Veroeffentlichung, die vom Superintendent of Documents, U. S. Government Printing Office, Washington, D. C. 20402, verkauft wird; darin sind die Patentinhaber (inklusive Inhaber von Wiedererteilungs-Patenten), Geschmacksmuster-und Pflanzenpatentinhaber, Widerrufe und Verzichte zu Gunsten der Allgemeinheit, und im oeffentlichen Amtsblatt (Official Gazette) veroeffentlichte Entscheidungen aufgezaehlt

index of patents and patentees—an annual publication, sold by the Superintendent of Documents, U. S. Government Printing Office, Washington, D. C. 20402, that lists patentees (including reissue patentees), design patentees, plant patentees, disclaimers and dedications, and decisions published in the Official Gazette

index des brevets et de brevetés—une publication annuelle, vendue par le Directeur des Documents, l'Office d'Imprimerie du Gouvernement des Etats-Unis, Washington, D. C. 20402, qui enregistre les brevetés (y inclus les "reissue" brevetes), les brevetés de dessin, les brevetés de plante, les renonciations et les dédicaces, et les décisions publiées dans la Gazette Officielle

Verzicht auf den Restteil—eine beanspruchte Erfindung fuer den Restteil ihrer Patentlaufzeit dem freien Gebrauch zugaenglich machen (Sec. 253)

terminal disclaimer—making a claimed invention available for free use for a terminal part of the period of the patent (Sec. 253)

renonciation terminale—rendre une invention revendiquée disponible à l'utilisation libre pendant une partie terminale de la période du brevet (Sec. 253)

Verzicht zu Gunsten der Allgemeinheit—eine Erfindung zum freien Gebrauch zur Verfuegung stellen. Ausfuehrbar entweder durch deutliche Erklaerung oder durch Offenbarung und Nicht-Beanspruchung der Erfindung in einer Weise, die einen gesetzlichen oder anderen Hinderungsgrund zur Patentierung in Kraft treten laesst.

dedication—making an invention available for free use. Accomplished by direct statement, or by disclosing and not claiming an invention in such a manner that a statutory or other bar to patenting takes effect.

dédicace—rendant disponible une invention pour l'utilisation libre. Accompli par une déclaration directe, ou en divulguant et ne revendiquant pas une invention d'une telle manière qu'il opère une interdiction statutaire de breveter.

Verzug—Vernachlaessigung, Versaeumnis oder unbillige Verzoegerung in der Durchsetzung eines Rechts; es ist untersagt Durchsetzung des Rechts zur Verhinderung ungerechter Behandlung der Partei, die Verzug geltend macht, anzuwenden

laches—neglect, failure or unreasonable delay in acting to enforce a right; enforcement of the right is barred to prevent inequitable treatment of the party asserting laches

laches—négligence, manque ou délai déraisonnable en agissant pour faire valoir un droit; le droit est défendu pour empêcher le traitement inéquitable de la partie qui présente des "laches"

Vielheit—in einem Anspruch bedeutet "Vielheit" zwei oder mehr Elemente

plurality—in a claim, "plurality" means two or more elements

pluralite—dans une revendication pluralité veut dire deux éléments ou plus que deux éléments

Vielheit von Anspruechen—Ansprueche, deren Anzahl im Hinblick auf die Natur und den Umfang der Erfindung fuer uebermaessig gehalten wird, da die Anzahl der vorgebrachten Ansprueche dazu fuehrt die Erfindung unklar erscheinen zu lassen

multiplicity of claims—claims that are held to be unreasonable in number, in view of the nature and scope of the invention, because the number of claims presented tend to obscure the invention

multiplicité de revendications—des revendications qui sont jugées d'être d'un nombre extravagant, en vue de la nature et de l'étendue de l'invention, parce que le nombre de revendications présentées ont la tendance d'obscurcir l'invention

Vollmacht—das Instrument, das eine Person ermaechtigt fuer eine andere Person zu handeln

power of attorney—the instrument authorizing one person to act for another person

pouvoir d'avocat—l'instrument qui autorise une personne d'agir pour une autre personne

Vorbehalts-Klausel—das Bestreben Eingetumsrechte auf die in einer Anmeldung offenbarten aber nicht mit Anspruch belegten Gegenstaende geltend zu machen; hat keinerlei gesetzliche Wirkung in Anmeldung in den Vereinigten Staaten

reservation clause—an effort to assert ownership of subject matter disclosed but not claimed in an application; has no legal effect in United States applications

clause de réserve—un effort d'affirmer ou de réserver la possession d'une matière divulguée mais pas revendiquée dans une demande; cela n'a pas d'effet légal dans les demandes des Etats-Unis

Vorerklaerung—in Bezug auf jeden Klagepunkt in einer Interferenz bei einer in den Vereinigten Staaten gemachten Erfindung: eine Darstellung des Sachverhalts und Verhaltens, die das Datum an dem die erste Zeichnung fuer die Erfindung gemacht wurde, festlegen (oder eine Erklaerung, dass keine Zeichnung vor dem Einreichen gemacht wurde), das Datum an dem die erste schriftliche Schilderung gemacht wurde (oder eine Erklaerung, dass keine schriftliche Schilderung vor dem Einreichen gemacht wurde), das Datum der ersten Offenbarung der Erfindung einem andern gegenueber (oder eine Erklaerung, dass vor dem Einreichen keine Offenbarung gemacht wurde); das Datum und die Beschaffenheit der ersten beweisfaehigen Handlungen, die die gedankliche Erfassung der Erfindung festlegen (oder eine Erklaerung, dass solche Handlungen nicht stattgefunden haben), das Datum des tatsaechlichen Umsetzens der Erfindung in die Praxis (oder eine Erklaerung, dass ein tatsaechliches Umsetzen in die Praxis vor dem Einreichen nicht stattgefunden hat), und das Datum an dem die taetige Aufwendung angemessener Sorgfalt um die Erfindung in die Praxis umzusetzen, began. Wenn eine Partei sich ausschliesslich auf eine fruehere in- oder auslaendische Anmeldung stuetzt, so kann dies in der Vorerklaerung angegeben und braucht nicht unterzeichnet zu werden (R. 216). Falls die Erfindung im Ausland gemacht wurde, sollte in der Vorerklaerung—unter Angabe der Umstaende und Betaetigungsdaten in den Vereinigten Staaten—angegeben werden wann die Erfindung in die Vereinigten Staaten eingefuehrt wurde (R. 217).

preliminary statement—as to each count of an interference, on an invention made in the United States, a statement of the facts and acts that establish the date on which the first drawing of the invention was made (or a statement that no drawing was made prior to filing), the date on which the first written description of the invention was made (or a statement that no written description was made prior to filing), the date of first disclosure of the invention to another (or a statement that there was no disclosure prior to filing), the date and nature of the first provable acts that would establish conception of the invention (or a statement that there were no such acts), the date of actual reduction to practice of the invention (or a statement that there was no actual reduction to practice prior to filing), and the date when active exercise of reasonable diligence toward reducing the invention to practice began. If a party relies solely on a prior domestic or foreign application, the preliminary statement may so state, and need not be signed. (R. 216)

When the invention was made abroad, the preliminary statement should state when the invention was introduced into the United States, giving the circumstances and dates of activity in the United States. (R. 217)

déclaration préliminaire—pour chaque "count" d'une "interférence", au sujet d'une invention créée aux Etats-Unis, une déclaration des faits et des actes qui établissent la date où on a fait le premier dessin de l'invention (ou une déclaration qu'on n'a fait aucun dessin de l'invention avant de déposer), la date où on a fait la première description écrite de l'invention (ou une déclaration qu'on n'a fait aucune description écrite avant de déposer), la date de la première divulgation de l'invention à autrui (ou une déclaration qu'il n'y avait aucune divulgation faite avant de déposer), la date et la nature des premiers actes prouvables qui établiraient la conception de l'invention (ou une déclaration qu'il n'y avait pas de teks actes), la date de la réduction actuelle à la pratique de l'invention (ou une déclaration qu'il n'y avait pas de réduction à la pratique avant de déposer), et la date où il a commencé l'exercice actif pour réduire à la pratique l'invention. Si une partie dépend uniquement d'une demande antérieure des Etats-Unis, ou étrangère, la déclaration préliminaire peut le proclamer et ne doit pas être signée (R. 216).

Quand on a créé l'invention à l'étranger, la déclaration devrait proclamer l'heure où on a introduit l'invention aux Etats-Unis, énumérant les circonstances et les dates de l'activité aux Etats-Unis. (R. 217)

Vorhergehendes—bestimmte Anfuehrung eines Wortes oder eines Ausdrucks um die abgekuerzte Identifizierung eines solchen Wortes oder Ausdrucks im weiteren Verlauf des Satzes oder Schriftstuecks zu gestatten

antecedent—a positive recital of a word or phrase to permit abbreviated identification of such word or phrase at a later point in the sentence or paper

antécédent—le récit positif d'un mot ou d'une phrase pour permettre l'identification abrégée de tel mot ou telle phrase plus tard dans la phrase ou dans la composition

vorherrschen—einen Anspruchsbereich haben, der eine andere Entwicklung einschliesst

dominate—having a claim scope that includes another development

dominer—avoir une étendue de revendication qui comprend un autre développement

vorherrschendes Patent—vgl. Grundpatent

dominating patent—see basic patent

brevet dominant—voir brevet de base

Vorlage—Antrag des Berufungsklaegers, der Board of Appeals moege die Berufung auf Grund von schriftlichen Unterlagen erwaegen; der Antrag ist durch die Unterlassung des Berufungsklaegers um eine muendliche Verhandlung nachzusuchen veranlasst

submission—request by appellant that the Board of Appeals consider the appeal on the written record, the request being effected by failure of appellant to request oral hearing

soumission—requête de l'appelant que la Commission d'Appel considère l'appel sur le dossier écrit, la requête résulte de la manque de l'appelant de demander une audience orale

Vorrichtung (Maschine)—eine Klasse von patentfaehigen Gegenstaenden, die eine Verbindung von Elementen umfassen, die zur Ausfuehrung einer Funktion zusammenarbeiten

machine—a class of patentable subject matter covering a combination of elements that cooperate to perform a function

machine—une classe de matière brevetable qui couvre une combinaison d'éléments qui coopérent pour accomplir une fonction

Voruntersuchung—eine Ueberpruefung von Patenten, gewoehnlich im Patentamt durch eine Privatperson auf Kosten des Erfinders vorgenommen, um festzustellen, ob die Erfindung durch den Stand der Technik vorweggenommen ist

preliminary search—an examination of patents, usually made in the Patent Office by a private searcher at the expense of the inventor, to determine whether the invention is anticipated by prior art

recherche préliminaire—un examen des brevets, fait d'ordinaire à l'Office des Brevets par un chercheur privé au dépens de l'inventeur, pour déterminer si l'invention est antériorisée par une technique antérieure

Vorwegnahme—vgl· vorwegnehmen

anticipation—see anticipate

antériorité—voir antérioriser

vorwegnehmen—Feststellung, dasse eine angebliche Erfindung nicht neu ist

anticipate—to establish that an alleged invention is not novel

antérioriser—établir qu'une invention alléguée n'est pas nouvelle

vorzugsweise—benutzt um anzuzeigen, dass das Wort, worauf es sich bezieht, beliebig gewaehlt und nicht wesentlich ist oder nicht notwendigerweise das Ergebnis in einem Mass, das einen Unterschied in der Art ausmachen wuerde, verandert

preferably—used to indicate that the word to which it relates is optional and not essential, or not necessarily effective in changing the result to a degree constituting a difference of kind

préférablement—employé pour indiquer que le mot auquel cela rapporte est facultatif et non essentiel, ou n'est pas nécessairement effectif à altérer le résultat à un degré constituant une différence de type

W

Wahl der Gattung—Auswahl der Gattung seiner Erfindung durch den Anmelder in Erwiderung auf eine Klage, dass kein vorgebrachter umfassender Anspruch zulaessig ist. Durch Auswahl der Gattung soll der Anspruch auf diese Gattung beschraenkt bleiben, sofern kein umfassender Anspruch als endgueltig zulaessig anerkannt wird. (R. 146)

election of species—selection by applicant, in response to an action holding that no generic claim presented is allowable, of the species of his invention to which his claims shall be restricted if no generic claim is finally held allowable (R. 146)

choix de variantes—choix d'un demandeur, en réponse à une action avançant qu'aucune revendication générique ne soit acceptable, de la variante de son invention à laquelle seront restreintes ses revendications, si on ne tient finalement aucune revendication générique comme acceptable (R. 146)

"wahrer Fachmann"—die nur in der Vorstellung vorhandene Person, von der angenommen wird, dass sie mit allen Kenntnissen auf ihrem Fachgebiet vertraut ist. Um patentfaehig zu sein, muss der Unterschied zum Stand der Technik derart sein, dass die beanspruchten Gegenstaende als Ganzes, zur Zeit als die Erfindung gemacht wurde, einem auf dem Gebiet des Erfindungsgegenstandes Sachverstaendigen nicht selbstverstaendlich gewesen waeren. (Sec. 103)

skilled in the art—the imaginary person assumed to be familiar with all the teachings in his technical field. To be patentable, the difference from the prior art must be such that the claimed subject matter, as a whole, would not have been obvious, at the time the invention was made, to a person having ordinary skill in the field of the invention. (Sec. 103)

adroite dans la technique—la personne imaginaire qu'on assume est au courant de tous les enseignements de son domaine. Pour être brevetable, la différence de la technique antérieure doit être telle que la matière revendiquée, en tout, n'aurait pas été évidente, à l'heure où on a créé l'invention, à une personne qui a de l'habileté moyenne dans le domaine de l'invention. (Sec. 103)

Warenzeichen—von einem Kaufmann zur Identifizierung und Unterscheidung seines Erzeugnisses von den Erzeugnissen anderer benutztes Wort oder Zeichen; der Gebrauch eines Warenzeichens zur Definition eines Erzeugnisses ist in einer Patentanmeldung normalerweise nicht gestattet

trademark—a word or symbol used by a merchant to identify and distinguish his product from the product of others; use of a trademark in a patent application to define a product is normally not permitted

marque de fabrique—un mot ou un signe employé par un marchand pour identifier et distinguer son produit du produit d'autrui; on ne permet pas d'ordinaire l'emploi d'une marque de fabrique pour définir un produit dans une demande de brevet

wechselseitige Lizenz—gegenseitige Bewilligung von Patentrechten, die zwei oder mehr Eigentuemer solcher Rechte einander zugestehen

cross-license—the reciprocal grant of patent rights to each other by two or more owners of such rights

licences-réciproques—l'accord réciproque des droits de brevet l'un à l'autre par plusieurs proprietaires de tels droits

Weitschweifigkeit—unwichtige Einzelheiten so vortragen, dass dadurch die Erfindung verborgen oder unverstaendlich gemacht wird (MPEP 706.03 (g))

prolixity—reciting unimportant details in such a manner as to hide or obscure the invention (MPEP 706.03(g))

prolixité—réciter des détails insignifiants d'une telle façon qu'on cache ou obscurcit l'invention (MPEP 706.03 (g))

im Wesentlichen—in Anspruechen eine Einschraenkung, deren Bedeutung durch Illustration in der Beschreibung (specification) unterstuetzt werden sollte

substantially—in claims, a qualification having a meaning that should be supported by illustration in the specification

"substantially"—dans les revendications, une qualification qui a une signification qu'on devrait soutenir par illustration ou par example dans la spécification

wesentliches Material—vgl. Eingliederung durch Hinweis

essential material—see incorporation by reference

matière essentielle—voir incorporation par renvoi

"whereby clause"—eine im Belieben des Anmelders stehende Klausel in einem Anspruch—gewoehnlich die allerletzte Klausel—welche die Funktion der beanspruchten Zusammensetzung oder des Verfahrens darlegt

whereby clause—an optional clause in a claim, usually the ultimate clause, setting forth the function of the claimed combination or process

"whereby" clause—une clause facultative dans une revendication, d'ordinaire la clause finale, qui présente la fonction de la combinaison ou du procédé revendiqué

Widerruf—schriftliche Erklaerung, durch die ein ungueltiger Patentanspruch, der ohne Taeuschungsabsicht gemacht war, aufgegeben wird. Der Widerruf muss beim Patentamt aktenmaessig beurkundet sein. (Sec. 253, R. 321)

disclaimer—written statement of abandonment of an invalid claim that had been filed without deceptive intent. The disclaimer must be recorded in the Patent Office. (Sec. 253, R. 321)

renonciation—une déclaration écrite de l'abandon d'une revendication invalide qu'on a déposée sans intention déceptive. La renonciation doit être enregistrée dans l'Office des Brevets. (Sec. 253, R. 231)

Widerrufung—Gerichtsentscheid, der eine Patenterteilung fuer nichtig erklaert

revocation—ruling of a court cancelling the patent grant

révocation—décision d'un tribunal qui annule la délivrance du brevet

Wiederinkraftsetzung—Wiederherstellung der Anhaegigkeit einer fallengelassenen Anmeldung durch Gesuch beim Commissioner mit einem beglaubigten Nachweis unvermeidlichen Verzugs in der Verfolgung der fallengelassenen Anmeldung, zusammen mit der vorgeschlagenen Entgegnung und der Antragsgebuehr von $15. (R. 137)

revival—restoring the pendency of an abandoned application by petition to the Commissioner with a verified showing of unavoidable delay in prosecuting the abandoned application, together with the proposed response and the petition fee of $15.00 (R.137)

renouvellement—rendre la viabilité d'une demande abandonnée par pétition au Commissaire avec une preuve vérifiée d'un délai inévitable en poursuivant la demande abandonnée, accompagné de la réponse offerte et la taxe de pétition de $15. (R. 137)

Wiederverhandlung–nochmalige Erwaegung einer Beschwerde durch den Board of Appeals; nach freiem Ermessen, auf ein Ersuchen innerhalb von dreissig Tagen vom Datum der urspruenglichen Entscheidung bewilligt (R. 197(b))

rehearing–reconsideration of an appeal by the Board of Appeals, granted optionally on a request made within thirty days from the date of the original decision (R. 197(b))

nouvelle audience–la réconsideration d'un appel, accordée facultativement sur une demande faite dans le délai de trente jours de la date de la décision originale (R. 197 (b))

wissenschaftliche Bibliothek–vgl. oeffentlicher Nachschlage-Saal

Scientific Library–see Public Search Room

Bibliothèque Scientifique–voir Salle Publique de Recherche

Wohnort–die Stadt, oder der Staat, oder das Land in dem der Anmelder wohnhaft ist (MPEP 605.02)

residence–the city and state or country in which the applicant lives (MPEP 605.02)

demeure–la ville et l'état ou le pays où demeure le demandeur (MPEP 605.02)

Z

Zedent—die Person, die die Eigentumsrechte an einer Erfindung uebertraegt

assignor—the transferor of property rights in an invention

cédant—celui qui transfère les droits de propriété dans une invention

Zeichnung—das Aufzeigen eines jeden Merkmals der im Patentanspruch beschriebenen Erfindung, angefertigt in Uebereinstimmung mit den Vorschriften 81-88 der Rules of Practice

drawing—a showing of every feature of the invention specified in the claims, prepared in accordance with Rules 81-88 of the Rules of Practice

dessin—une représentation de chaque trait de l'invention spécifiée dans les revendications, préparée en accord avec les R. 81-88 des Règles de la Preatique

Zivilklage—Klage beim Distriktgericht fuer den Distrikt von Columbia (Washington, D. C.) um einen Entscheid des Board of Appeals (Sec. 145) oder des Board of Patent Interferences (Sec· 146) nachzupruefen

civil suit—action in the District Court for the District of Columbia to review a decision of the Board of Appeals (Sec. 145) or to review a decision of the Board of Patent Interferences (Sec. 146)

proces civil—action dans le District Court of the District of Columbia pour revoir une décision de la Commission d'Appel (Sec. 145) ou pour revoir une décision de la Commission des "Interférences" des Brevets (Sec. 146)

zulaessig–vgl. Zulaessigkeits-Benachrichtigung

allowable–see notice of allowability

acceptable–voir la notification de "allowability"

Zulaessigkeit–vgl· Zulaessigkeits-Benach richtigung

allowability–see notice of allowability

"allowability"–voir la notification de "allowability"

Zulaessigkeits-Benachrichtigung–Mitteilung des Patentamts, dass der Anmelder zu einem Patent berechtigt ist, aber die Erteilung des Patents aufgeschoben wird, da die Anmeldung Material enthaelt, das zum Schutz der nationalen Sicherheit nicht veroeffentlicht wird

notice of allowability–advice by the Patent Office that the applicant is entitled to a patent, but grant of a patent will be postponed because the application contains matter that will not be published to protect national security

notification de "allowability"–conseil de l'Office des Brevets que le demandeur a droit à un brevet, mais que l'octroi d'un brevet sera remis parce que la demande contient de la matière qu'on ne publiera pas pour protéger la sécurité nationale

Zulassung–vgl. Zulassungsbenachrichtigung

allowance–see notice of allowance

acceptation–voir la notification d'acceptation

Zulassungs-Benachrichtigung (Annahme-Nachricht) – Benachrichtigung durch das Patentamt, dass der Anmelder zu einem Patent berechtigt und die Erteilungsgebuehr innerhalb von drei Monaten vom Benachrichtigungsdatum zu entrichten ist (R. 311)

notice of allowance—advice by the Patent Office that the applicant is entitled to a patent, calling for the payment of the issue fee within three months from the date of the advice (R. 311)

notification d'acceptation—conseil de l'Office des Brevets que le demandeur a droit à un brevet, demandant le paiement de la taxe de délivrance dans le délai de trois mois de la date du conseil (R. 311)

Zurueckweisung—eine Handlung des Patentamts, welche die Patentfaehigkeit in Abrede stellt, einschliesslich einer Mitteilung ueber die Beweggruende der Handlung, zusammen mit Auskuenften und Hinweisen auf denen die Zurueckweisung begruendet war (Sec. 132)

rejection—action of the Patent Office denying patentability, and including notice of the reasons for the action together with the information and references on which the rejection was based (Sec. 132)

rejet—action de l'office des Brevets niant la brevetabilité et y inclus la notification des causes de l'action accompagnée des renseignements et des renvois sur lesquels a été basés le rejet (Sec. 132)

Zusammenfassung der Erfindung—eine allgemein gehaltene Darstellung des technischen Fortschritts, der Vorteile, welche die Erfindung mit sich bringt und eine kurze, verallgemeinerte, funktionelle Schilderung, wie die erfinderische Idee ueberragende Ergebnisse erzielt; enthalten in der Beschreibung (specification), nach der Darstellung des Hintergrundes der Erfindung

summary of the invention—statement in general terms of the advance in the art, the advantages provided by the invention, and a brief, generalized functional description as to how the inventive concept attains the superior results, included in the specification after the statement of the background of the invention

sommaire de l'invention—une déclaration en termes généraux du progrès de la technique, les avantages fournis et produits par l'invention, et une brève description fonctionnelle et généralisée de comment le concept inventif achève des résultats supérieurs, incluse dans la spécification après la declaration du fond de l'invention

Zustaendiger Anwalt—der Patentvertreter oder Patentanwalt, der vom Anmelder bestellt ist seine Interessen vor dem Patentamt zu vertreten. Die Handlungsvollmacht des Anwalts muss in der eingereichten Anmeldung beurkundet sein.

attorney of record—the patent agent or patent attorney appointed by applicant to transact his business before the Patent Office. The attorney's power to act must be recorded in the filed application.

avocat "of record"—l'agent de brevets ou l'avocat de brevets nommé par le demandeur pour fairs ses affaires avec l'Office des Brevets. Le pouvoir d'agir de l'avocat doit être enregistré dans la demande déposée.

